Rose Terry Cooke

Steadfast: the story of a Saint and a Sinner

Rose Terry Cooke
Steadfast: the story of a Saint and a Sinner
ISBN/EAN: 9783743422940
Manufactured in Europe, USA, Canada, Australia, Japa
Cover: Foto ©Lupo / pixelio.de

Manufactured and distributed by brebook publishing software (www.brebook.com)

Rose Terry Cooke

Steadfast: the story of a Saint and a Sinner

STEADFAST

THE STORY OF

A SAINT AND A SINNER

BY
ROSE TERRY COOKE
AUTHOR OF
"SOMEBODY'S NEIGHBORS," "THE SPHINX'S CHILDREN,"
"HAPPY DODD," ETC.

BOSTON
TICKNOR AND COMPANY
211 Tremont Street
1889

PREFACE.

In sending out this book, I am aware that I shall meet with some sharp criticism about the statements made therein concerning the action of a certain ecclesiastical body. I have only to say that everything I have recorded relating to the acts of the consociation of Congregational churches of "Newport" county is strictly historical fact; that, as far as his experience with that consociation goes, Philemon "Hall" was a living man; though I have changed his surname, as well as the name of the county.

I also desire to express here my obligations to the history of Wallingford, Connecticut, by Dr. Charles H. S. Davis, from which I have drawn the aforesaid facts, and copied the manifestoes of the consociations and Mr. Hall's replies.

Rose Terry Cooke.

CONTENTS.

CHAPTER		PAGE
I.	Death	11
II.	Love	23
III.	Continuance	36
IV.	Circumstance	47
V.	Here	59
VI.	Cloudy	70
VII.	Clear	80
VIII.	At Midnight	88
IX.	After	97
X.	Fraud	107
XI.	Done	117
XII.	L'Imprévu	126
XIII.	A Will	136
XIV.	Despair	146
XV.	A Change	158
XVI.	Again	169
XVII.	Reward	181
XVIII.	Grist	192
XIX.	Delay	202
XX.	Judgment	212
XXI.	Tempy's Turn	223
XXII.	Counsel	234
XXIII.	Finality	246
XXIV.	A Conflict	257
XXV.	Downward	267
XXVI.	The Lay Sister	278

XXVII.	A Climax	289
XXVIII.	The Curse of a Granted Prayer	300
XXIX.	A Compact	309
XXX.	Daily	319
XXXI.	In the Beginning	329
XXXII.	A Surprise	339
XXXIII.	No!	348
XXXIV.	Patience	358
XXXV.	A Confidence	368
XXXVI.	The World	378
XXXVII.	More	389
XXXVIII.	At Last	399
XXXIX.	Not Destroyed	409
XXXX.	Life	418

STEADFAST.

CHAPTER I.

DEATH.

*Whereunto is money good ?
Who has it not wants hardihood.*

"O MOTHER!" said Esther Dennis, looking at the bowed head, clenched hands, and quivering figure that sat crouched in an old flag-bottomed rocker by the dying kitchen fire; a black bombazine bonnet, evidently new, poked over the face in a distracted fashion; a limpsy crape veil, by no means new, dragging on the floor, and a gown and cloak like the bonnet, draping the slight shape of a woman whose heart was not only broken, but just buried with her dead husband. She did not answer Esther; sob after sob burst slowly from her dry lips as if wrenched upward by some pressure no longer endurable, though long resisted.

Mrs. Dennis had preserved unbroken silence through that weary and dreary funeral service in house and church; she sat like a stone through the long sermon in which Priest Beach detailed her loss and bemoaned her sufferings in a way to exasperate any creature not brought up in the reticence and self-control of her place and time; the long wailing minor of the doleful hymns that went shrieking about the cold bare meeting-house like orthodox Banshees, did not move one rigid muscle of her pale, delicate face, or moisten the long eyelashes that drooped on her cheek, and the mitigated tenderness of the almost interminable prayer never caused a quiver on her set white lips. She walked to the graveyard, only a few rods from the meeting-house, clutching Esther's arm as a drowning man clutches a plank; she saw the cold shape, whose arms had upheld her so many years, whose eyes had smiled at her in all her sorrows, whose lips had kissed her at the altar, and on the edge of death, uncovered in its dead unanswering terror for the neighbors and friends to see once more; and then she saw it lowered into its kindred clay, forever hidden from her sight, without one sigh or tear. But now, when all the funeral company were gone, when the decencies and conventions filed away from her door and left her alone with her only child, nature revenged itself on propriety; all its waves and billows went over her; a positive convulsion of grief racked her delicate physical constitution, and despair, black as death, settled on her timid soul.

"Mother!" sobbed Esther in despair, kneeling down by the poor woman and leaning her head against the chair. "Mother! don't! oh, don't; oh, what shall I do? Mother! ain't he happy?"

If she had seen the thought that answered her, she would have recoiled; it was the outcry of bereft love, of breaking life. "What of that ? am *I* not miserable ?" but the poor woman had been trained in rigid obedience to her duty; her lips parted, she gasped out, "Oh yes, yes! I ought to submit, Esther! It's all right; it's all right." Yet the heart within her tolled back, "It's all wrong; all wrong; all wrong!"

Poor enough were the surroundings of this homely, everyday tragedy; nothing more than the old furniture of a kitchen in a New England farmhouse of the last century. A cross-legged table stood against the wall; three or four spindle-backed wooden-bottomed chairs were ranged formally about the room, a high settle and the wainscoting of the wall were painted alike a livid leaden blue; a tall clock stood in one corner and swung its pendulum to and fro with relentless accuracy, passing and repassing its ornamented and glazed hole in the clock door, as if to impress its dutiful life on the sight as well as hearing of its housemates; there was an open fireplace in which swung a crane; pothooks and trammels hung from nails in the chimney corners; a half-burned stick of wood just uncovered from the ashes simmered now on the iron firedogs; the high shelf above held sundry kitchen utensils, flatirons, brass and tin candlesticks, a tinder-box, a horn lantern, a Farmer's Almanac; on one side of the fire stood a bake-kettle and a four-legged pot; by the south window a flax wheel stood at rest; a small cherry table with two leaves, and a corner cupboard, with a smaller one in the wall above the shelf, completed the belongings of the dingy little room used as living-room and kitchen at this season, and dull enough now that no sunshine came through its green-paned windows, but only the gathering gloom of a dark November storm.

Esther Dennis was not demonstrative; she had said all she could; she too loved her father, with the honest, but not inconsolable affection a young girl has for a silent busy father, whom she seldom sees, but she had no sort of idea what this loss was to her mother; she could not fathom or understand a sorrow that shook that ordinarily bright, gentle, and unselfish nature into such a rebellious passion of wild grief. She had not been taught or even allowed to learn the sweet tongue of caresses and coaxing; it never occurred to her to put her arms about her mother, to kiss the agonized face, to smooth the ruffled hair, to take away the heavy insignia of mourning and persuade the shaken woman to lie down, as a girl of this day would have done; she had ventured as far as she could; a certain sense of propriety in her soul, of respect for religion and the eternal fitness of things, had been appeased by her mother's admission that all this sorrow was "right," or as she dared only to faintly guess, not to formulate the thought, God had not done wrong in removing from these two women the centre and support of their lives. There comes a time to most of us, if we ourselves live long enough, when we can see that the death we most resented and wept was the best thing possible to be ordained when and where it was, both for the dead and the living;

but it takes years of grief and pain — why should I not say of life? — to teach us this lesson; it could not be expected to pour its awful consolation into these newly stricken souls.

Esther got up from her position by her mother, feeling that there was nothing more to be said; instinctively she turned and looked at the clock; as if it answered her, it immediately struck five, and in habitual obedience to that summons, she went into the shed for kindling wood, started the fire afresh, filled and hung on the tea-kettle, brought bread and butter from the swinging shelf in the cellar, milk from the pantry, made her tea as soon as the kettle boiled, raked out some roasted potatoes from the ashes in the chimney corner, brushing them clean with a turkey's wing from one of the small closets, and set the frugal supper on one leaf of the round table previously laid with a homespun linen cloth. By the time this was done, her mother had recovered self-control enough to rise from her chair, take off her outer garments, cool her hot eyes at the sink in the shed, where a pipe supplied them with living water from a mountain spring, and make her scanty hair smooth and decent. Mrs. Dennis was swayed by long habit in all she did; she would not have thought, even in her despair, of coming to supper with ruffled locks or weeping eyes; she did not even know, consciously, that she was going through that routine, all she did know was that it was tea time, that food was on the table, and that she must sit down to it. The tea was made of sage leaves, the bread of rye flour, but the mere effort to eat and drink was of service to this disconsolate woman, whose only real wish was to die and go to her husband. However the hot drink warmed her chilly blood, and the homely sweetness of the food rekindled her flickering vitality and set her back into her orbit; she was too honest and unconscious to feel anything but relief at the scanty cheer that food and fire brought to her; the very leap and crackle of the blaze had a sound of comfort in it, and the song of the kettle as it piped away on the shortened hook, where it kept hot for the dish washing, had a customary familiarity about it that soothed her. It was not till everything was restored in spotless cleanliness to its usual order, the one candle lighted, the fire replenished, and the wild November wind rose, yelling in the spout of the shed roof like a lost spirit, that her grief faced her, not now with the chaotic aspect of despair, but in its everyday practical bearings.

Doctor Dennis had been the only physician in Plainfield for years; night and day his shabby gig and rawboned horse had traversed this hilly country to bring relief or healing; his work had been the work of a country doctor, the hardest, most unremitting, worst-paid work in the world, but he had been faithful to his calling. That grave, kindly face had stood beside many a dying man and woman, that steady, cheerful voice had brought words of hope to many an anxious soul, and when a sudden and sharp fever, the result of overwork and constant exposure to the treacherous and exasperating New England weather, carried him out of this life spent in alleviating and restoring the lives of others, he was mourned wherever he was known.

But his books were sadly in arrears; many a poor creature never figured on those red-lined pages, though he had provided medicine as well as counsel for them, sometimes for year after year; others had paid him in produce, apples, potatoes, poultry, hay, all consumed as they came in, when their value in money could and would have been far more useful and more economically disposed of than these supplies. Here and there a bill was paid in cash, but daily necessities had forestalled all such payments always, and they were few and far between, for Plainfield was a farming town, and farming in New England was then but a delusion and a snare; it could be summed up in the epigrammatic sentence of Triptolemus Yellowley, concerning agriculture in the Shetland Isles: "The carles and the cart-avers make it all, and the carles and the cart-avers take it all!"

What scant food the iron-bound and rock-ribbed country yielded to the demands of incessant and severe labor was consumed by the laborer; there was but a living, and a squalid living, to be wrung from the thin dry soil that clothes our beautiful hills, and the tiny, alluvions of the brooks that rush madly from their mountain springs to the one great river; true, the grass was sweet, but the milk was scanty, and if rye grew up to the very edge of sharp granite ledges, it was never luxuriant enough to supply the full demand for it. Wheat was a rare luxury; potatoes indeed grew as they always grow on newly upturned ground, abundantly, and of good quality, and orchards were lavish of their spicy fruit, but all these things did not mean or make money; these hills raised men, not crops, and when Doctor Dennis died, there was left for his wife and child one hundred and fifty dollars in a pigeon-hole of his desk, two or three medical books, a few poor old implements of surgery, and the small brown farmhouse with its garden and orchard under the ledge of Pine Hill; that was all. He had no debts, and funeral expenses were light enough in Plainfield. Through the doctor's illness the neighbors had sent in good store of food, to express sympathy and save the two women from any trouble of cookery, so that they might devote themselves to the sick man. There was at least two weeks' provision in the house; three barrels of potatoes and four of apples in the cellar, a bushel of white beans, a keg of pork, a half barrel of flour also in the pantry, and the neighbor who supplied them with milk and butter had by no means paid up her bill to Doctor Dennis yet, but after this? —

"I don't know, Esther, what upon earth we shall do," said the widow, after a little preliminary talk, and taking of stock with the aforesaid results.

"I don't see where our livin' is to come from. You a'n't old enough nor eddicated enough to teach, and if you was we haven't got but one school in the township, and that's two mile off. I can't do anything but take care of a house, and knit and sew. I shall be able to do that quite a spell, but the outlook's pretty dark, pretty dark."

"A'n't there any bills coming in at all, mother?" asked Esther.

"I presume there may be; I presume likely we can collect as much as ten dollars more'n is down on the books. There's Squire Pettigrew had typhus fever you know, two months back; I don't see as he is paid up yet; and Lawyer Green's wife had a spell of rheumatiz, that ain't charged for, but that is skerce enough to be much help." Esther leaned her head on her hand and looked into the fire. She was sixteen years old, a tall, thin girl, only saved from being angular by her small bones, which, even ill covered as they were, showed no obtrusive joints or coarse outlines. Her noble head and slender throat, her dark pensive eyes, sensitive mouth, and rich abundance of dark hair, brown hair with red lights in it, gave her a certain distinction of aspect that lasts and attracts longer than positive beauty, if it is not so bewildering and gracious. She was yet a child in directness, unworldliness, and the undreaming sleep of passion within her; she loved nobody but her parents, for she knew no one else; there were no young men in Plainville, even in the Centre, as the nucleus of the village was called, except a clerk in the "store," and an hostler at the tavern; such boys as had grown up there had naturally gone out into the world to seek the fortunes their fathers had never found on those barren hills, and as this girl had never read either novels or poetry, she was still only a girl, only a child.

But suddenly an idea came to her as she stared into the red coals.

"Mother!" she said, starting up. "Haven't you got an uncle somewheres down by the shore?"

"Why, yes. Uncle Dyer lives down to Trumbull; he always has lived there since he married Squire Kent's daughter."

"Well; he's your own uncle, ain't he?"

"To be sure; he was mother's brother; all the kith and kin, near to, that she had. I used to see him quite frequent when I was a child, for our folks lived next door; but when I was eight years old, he went to Trumbull to live, and we skercely ever saw him; not once after he married Judge Kent's daughter, for she had means, and he went into the West Indy trade, and what travellin' he did do, was done to York, and sometimes a voyage to Jamaica. Then mother died, and father he didn't live a year after I married, and moved up here to live, so I expect I sort of slipped Uncle Dyer's memory, though I'm all the niece he ever had."

"Well, mother, can't you write to him and ask if he can't find some work for us? I expect there must be more to do where there is more people, and Trumbull is quite a sizeable place I've heard."

"Oh, dear! Esther. I don't know as I darst; poor folks want a welcome everywhere, Grandsir Starks used to say. Seems to me I haven't got a mite of courage left. Father dead, and we comin' to want; why, it seems as though I couldn't anyway have it so. I don't know which way to turn."

"You're awful tired, mother; that's what ails you. You wouldn't be so scary if you wa'nt. Why there's lots of poor folks in the world that live somehow; and why shouldn't we? I guess you had better go to bed; I'll fetch down the cot, and set it right here by your door, so's you won't be lonesome, and I guess by time it's morning, you'll take heart some, and think it's a good plan to write to Uncle Dyer."

This ignorant, girlish courage somewhat reassured the timid woman who had lost heart, and lost all thereby; she went to bed, and at last to sleep; waking at early dawn with that dim frightful sense of lurking trouble, of fatal loss, that the outwearied soul cannot at once grasp with the scarce awakened senses, but that comes fully in sight at last, and, like an armed man, despoils the mourner of the sole good life has left him,—a temporary unconsciousness, a brief forgetting,—and arouses with the pang of its first fresh bitterness the agony we must needs accept anew.

It was with difficulty Esther made her mother try, at least, to take food to-day; she no longer felt the faintness of exhaustion that urged her to eat, but at length that sense of duty in which her life had been moulded came to her aid; she took a cup of rye coffee, a decoction calculated to divert any sort of thought from the unaccustomed taste, but which afforded no diversion of feeling to her, used as she was to its bitterness and flat flavor: and, encouraged by the resolution her mother showed, Esther began again to talk of her idea about Uncle Dyer.

"Well, Esther, if it's best, and I don't know but what *'tis* best, I will write to him. I presume likely there would be more openings for them that want work down there than there is here amongst the mountains; anyway, I should like a change; I can't feel but what father's comin' in to the door every minute; and then it comes home to me that he won't never step in any more, and seems as though I should give up! If it's so to be that you and me can earn a living down to Trumbull, why I shall learn to sense it better that father's gone for good, and it won't stir me up so. I do strive to be real resigned, but seems as though I'd got to have something else to think of but what's always been here and ain't here no more, before I can really feel to say, the will o' the Lord be done. Yes. I'll write to Uncle Dyer to-night."

CHAPTER II.

LOVE

*Smote the chord of Self, that, trembling,
Passed in music out of sight.*

FIVE years before this day of loss to the Dennis family, Rachel Mather, an orphan girl in Deerfield, had married Philemon Hall, a young minister to whom she had been engaged for five years.

There is nothing strange in so long an engagement, when the young man has to wait for his education and settlement, but yet this marriage made an unusual stir and talk in Deerfield. Rachel was poor, as well as an orphan, and had lived from her tenth year in the house of her aunt, the Widow Peek; but her beauty and her sweetness of temper would have excused any man in those primitive days for loving and marrying her, had it been the governor of the State himself. She had more than one lover, but only one love, and that was Philemon Hall. She had been his sweetheart from the days when they trudged up to the Rock Corner schoolhouse hand in hand; and when he made up his mind to become a minister, and asked Rachel if she would wait for him, it seemed to her as if a sudden glory out of heaven had fallen upon her.

She had a hard life in her aunt's house; four little children and but a small amount of money were Mrs.

Peek's portion in this world, and she was a hard-natured, energetic woman, not inclined to indulge herself in laziness, or anybody else. Rachel was up before dawn and kept at her tasks till night. If candles had not been a luxury, even night would not have been spared to her. In winter a roaring fire of pine and hickory gave her light enough to spin by, but when a fire was no longer needed she could sit out on the doorstep, sometimes with Philemon beside her, and find in the fragrant breath of field and forest, the cries of young birds in their nest, the soft whisper of summer winds in the leaves, and the consciousness of a dear presence beside her, such a rest and refreshment as helped her to possess her soul in patience through the days of loveless and exhausting toil that were her lot. Day by day she seemed to grow lovelier; her figure was slight and angular, there was no grace in its movement, no rounded outlines, no dimples; her chest was flat and narrow, her shoulders square, but her head was the head of a Greek statue, the straight features, the calm full lips, the low upright forehead and level brows, all illuminated by great blue eyes with thick golden lashes, and a wealth of pale gold hair waving, coiling, clinging about her beautiful head in classic fashion, as rare as lovely. Her skin was pale, but its colorless glow was the tint of health, and any sudden emotion flushed it with the very pink of a wild rose, as fair and as fleeting as that most delicate blossom.

Aunt Peek was furious when, before Philemon left

Deerfield to study theology with Father Niles in New Haven, he avowed his engagement to Rachel. It seemed as if for the next four years she set herself to work to devise fresh toils for the poor girl daily, toils whose only respite was the brief annual visit of her lover, who after a good old fashion spent his vacations teaching school, in order to help defray the expense of his own education. But Rachel worked in hope, and therefore uncomplainingly, undergoing a discipline she was soon to need. Mrs. Peek did not hesitate to express her feelings openly as the time for Philemon's return drew near.

"It's everlastin' hard," she confided to a neighbor at an apple-bee. "I've fetched her up sence her folks died; I've gin her fair schoolin', board, lodgin', an' clothin', — and jest as she's gettin' real useful, she's got to up and get married. Seems as though she had ought to hev thought some of me."

"Couldn't ha' done no more 'ef she'd been your own daughter," dryly answered Mrs. Allen.

The Widow Peek stared; like many other people, she had looked so intently on her own side of the matter that there seemed no other view possible to take, no other interest concerned in it.

The next day it happened to be Rachel's duty, after baking and ironing, to spread out a whole piece of homespun linen on the grass to bleach, and every hour or two to wet it thoroughly; the heat of the Indian summer day was unusual and intense; the girl was worn out with her work in the hot kitchen, and about four o'clock one of those autumnal thunderstorms set in that are so furious and so sudden. Occupied with her duties, she had not stepped out of doors since last she sprinkled the lengths of cloth lying across the sward of the home lot, but she was startled by a rapid darkness in the air, and looking out at the door she saw the black curtain of the storm coming over the mountain fast and furious, and a heavy rattling peal of thunder told how near its vanguard hung; without stopping even for her sun-bonnet, she ran for the linen; it must be brought in or the heavy rains would beat it into the grass and stain it, the wind tear it up and away, or, possibly, sharp assaults of hail riddle it. But the storm was swifter than her flying steps; before she could fold those lengths of solid linen, it was doubly weighty with water, and she herself drenched to the skin. Holding it up in her slender arms, blinded by the lightning and dazed by the loud thunder, she stumbled and groped slowly back to the house and then set herself, with no consideration for her own condition, to wringing the soaked cloth till it was dry again, or at least fit to hang before the fire, and not drip on the clean floor. Regardless of herself still, and afraid lest her aunt should come back to find the work of the day undone, she finished the last few bits of her ironing, hurried up into the shed loft to turn the heavy cheeses, and by that time the shower had passed over, and she must go to pasture after the cow, milk her, give her water, and then get supper.

Mrs. Peek and all her children had gone nutting in some distant woods that day, and they were sure to come back hungry, and expect Rachel to take back the neighbor's horse and wagon they had borrowed; so it came about that her wet clothes were not changed till, as soon as darkness put an end to labor, she crept upstairs to the "garret-chamber" where she slept, and, aching in every fibre lay down to sleep if she could.

But people on the rack do not sleep: Rachel could not even rise when the dawn came; she was helpless as a man fettered to his dungeon wall.

Her aunt scolded and fretted, but was forced for her own sake to fetch the doctor, and he shook his wise old head; it was rheumatic fever, no one could tell how long it might last, or in what condition leave the patient. It is idle to detail her long and weary sufferings: ill with the most agonizing of diseases; one that demands careful handling, exquisite nursing, warmth, nourishment, cheer; Rachel had not one of these necessities; her room was colder even than the barn, for that at least had a deep lining of hay, but her roof was leaky and old, snows drifted on her bed, and rain beat in at the dormer window, dripping in a pool to the floor beneath; her food was scanty and grudgingly doled out to her; and such nursing as she got was occasional voluntary service from the neighbors; when spring at last came, the old doctor said, sadly and unwillingly enough, that there was no hope for her, not even the hope of dying; she must live a bedridden cripple so long as life remained to her.

Mrs. Peek was furious; she had no pity at all for this young life brought to so terrible a stand in the midst of its bloom and promise; she considered this a personal injury done to herself, and never wearied of assuring Rachel that just as soon as the roads settled she should " cart her off to the town-house " a threat she was only too likely to fulfil. But, in her heavy trouble, Rachel had learned where the one consolation of loss can be found; educated in the Puritan strictness of the time, she had learned chapter after chapter of the Bible, by heart, and almost all the hymn-book; and now that her wandering mind, shaken first by physical and then by mental torture, began to grasp the situation, and try, with that wonderful instinct the mind has, to adapt itself to its surroundings, she betook herself to such prayer as only the despairing can offer; it seemed to her that her strong pleadings laid hold on heaven; for in the very anguish of the flesh the gracious words of the Father, the pitiful and tender promises of the Son fell upon her like dew upon the parched ground and gave her strength to endure; that strength so hard to attain.

While she lay ill in her garret, Philemon had more than once written her; but the epistles had been thrown on the fire by Aunt Peek, who had no time to read them either to herself or Rachel, and neither wish nor ability to answer them.

But those were days of heavy postage, and weekly mails, sometimes lost from the boot of the stage that carried them, swept out in the fording of a swollen river, or dropped by the breakage of a strap on some lonely mountain road. Philemon did not wonder that his epistles were not answered; his character was generous, confiding, unselfish, and just by nature; and his earnest religious faith had but confirmed these traits, reformed his native obstinacy into perseverance, and controlled to an imprisoned and safe motive force that strong, high temper which might otherwise have desolated his life and the lives of those most dear to him. He never had a doubt of Rachel's affection, and the one refreshment of his heart through this, his last winter of theological grubbing, was the prospect of his return to Deerfield and to her, in the coming spring.

To her, the thought of seeing him again was exquisitely painful; she knew that her life was set apart from all the ties that help women to live and be helpful; she knew just how hard it would be for Philemon to give her up; and, in her pure pity and love, wept bitterer tears for him than ever she shed for her own wreck of hope and health; she tried every day, fortified by prayer and the remembered word of Scripture, to look forward and realize in her imagination the long future of poverty, solitude, and pain in store for her; she did not yet know that the daily manna of the wanderers in the desert was but a type of the bread wherewith God feeds our hungry souls, a provision only given with the hour of need; and she wondered sorrowfully why she could not gather courage to accept the life ordained for her, though not yet visited upon her as a fulfilled terror.

At last Philemon came back to Deerfield; it was a sunny April day; the season was early, and Aunt Peek had said to her oldest girl that very morning, —

"The roads is most settled; I must go up to the poorhouse an' tell Simonses folks to fix up one o' them rooms, below stairs for Rachel, for I shall jest git rid of her as soon as ever the turnpike's got so a cart can be driv' over it. I'm most tuckered out with fetchin' an carryin'; its nigh about noonspell now, Mary Ann, you carry up her gruel, it's warm enough; I dono but what it's smoked a mite, but beggars mustn't be choosers."

Hard indeed and rough of speech was Rachel's unwilling hostess; yet would the blade have cut less deep had it been inlaid and polished steel? You can answer, poor and pitiable sisterhood, who live by sufferance in houses where your richer brothers and sisters endure you as a necessary evil; where you wear your lives out in thankless service, scantily rewarded, "traversing another man's stairs" in lifelong humiliation, and abject acceptance of such a fate. Why have you not the courage to go out boldly and earn your bread in some honest calling for a just wage? Why cannot you break these poor fetters of custom, and heartily and contentedly find and fill the places crying aloud, all about you, for the work of just such women as you are? Is your false pride of position agreeable or comfortable enough to compensate you for a life of sufferance, of contempt, of real oppression, and nominal reward? If it is, if you prefer husks to bread, continue then to eat them; but never complain to man or woman of their huskiness, or stretch out your feeble hands for alms of pity.

However, though she did not know it, or expect him, Philemon had come, and he had not been an hour in the village before he heard of Rachel's wretched condition, and her aunt's intention. He, too, was an orphan, with an old uncle in Deerfield, his guardian and only relative; a simple, kindly, good old man, who considered Philemon the "expectancy and rose" of all New England, and would not have thwarted him in his wildest wishes had it been in his power to grant them. There had been times in this young man's life when he thought sadly of his homeless state, and longed for the tender affection of a mother, or steady and wise fatherly guidance; but now he felt a half unwilling thrill of joy that he was entirely his own master, and in full possession of the two thousand dollars that remained of his small property, since his education was finished and paid for. His first step was to visit old Doctor Prime and hold a long consultation with him, from which the doctor emerged winking his eyes very hard, growling under his breath, shaking his head, and generally behaving in an ominous manner. The two repaired at once to the parsonage, where a younger brother of the doctor held sway, and there another hour was spent in triple council; all these movements eagerly observed and commented on by female eyes, wherever the line of vision made it possible. But all that even the most assiduously observant woman heard, was these four words from Philemon's lips, as he shut the parsonage door after him in coming out, — "Remember! half-past four."

It was three already when Philemon Hall arrived at Mrs. Peek's house, and nodding to the astonished Mary Ann, left on guard while her mother had gone up to settle Rachel's affairs with Mr. Simons, went straight up to that dingy garret where his Rachel lay.

She did not faint or cry out when he entered; she had so long dreamed of this hour, waited, watched for, prayed over, feared it, that there was no shock of surprise, no start of unexpected emotion in her soul; she looked up and smiled.

But Philemon stopped short on the threshold, and the love that, in tranquil surety of fulfilment, had so long grown with his growth and strengthened with his strength, seemed suddenly to reveal itself and take possession of his whole nature with a power that shook him to the heart.

It was not the beautiful, innocent, gentle girl he had left, who lay in that squalid bed, with eyes as large and limpid as the rock pools of an ebbing sea, with tangled masses of dull gold hair fringing the blue-veined forehead and wan, sunken cheeks; the Rachel of the past was a child, this was a saint; the very calm of heaven on her emaciated features, and its light in her tranquil eyes just dewed with unshed tears. He knelt down beside her and set a reverent kiss on her forehead, and then looked at her without a word. She was first to break the silence.

"Are you well, Philemon?" she said, gently and primly, as a daisy might speak if it could.

"But you, Rachel!" he answered, careless of any answer to her speech. "Do you suffer? do you ache? cannot you be lifted?"

"I ache some," she said; "sometimes not so much, though," with a piteous little smile. "Nobody has tried to lift me; I can move just a little."

"I'm coming back in one minute," he said, hurriedly.

Rachel thought he had gone out to control himself, that he could not endure the change in her aspect; she did not know that she was lovelier than ever; she sighed, for she was a woman, and she loved him.

But, in the shortest possible time, if it was more than a minute, he returned with Aunt Ruthy Wells, the nurse and friend of all the village; and with her soft, strong hands, her skill of experience, her tenderness, and gentle ways, another hour saw Rachel bathed, clothed afresh, her bed daintily neat, her hair untangled, smoothed, braided loosely about her head and covered with a little linen cap; then she fetched her a cup of hot broth with a spoonful of wine in it, and fed her like a child; rested and refreshed she looked up at Aunt Ruthy with grateful eyes, and had parted her lips to speak, when the door opened, and in walked Parson Prime, the doctor, and Philemon.

It was a stroke of strategy to be so sudden. Philemon did not stop to consider; this was not a matter of duty; he loved Rachel with all his strong, faithful heart; he could not leave her an hour longer in suffering; there was, in his eyes, but one thing to do, and that was to marry her. If he gave her so much as an hour to consider, he knew where her unselfishness and good sense would land his plans and purposes, therefore, he would not give her that hour, but took for granted that her consent, given so long ago, was valid still; and refused to listen to the hurried remonstrances she tried even now to make.

"I guess you'd as good keep still; talking 'll only wear ye out." grimly remarked the doctor. "He's as sot in his way as I ever see a man, and you haven't had dealings with 'em so long as I have. I tell you what! if the man's the head of the woman, as the Scripter says, you'll have a big head, Rachel, and you can't bend it much!"

"Brother!" said Parson Prime, with an official scowl, "this is not a time to laugh."

The doctor took a pinch of snuff, and shut his mouth, but his eyes twinkled wickedly; and overborne by persuasion, by masculine dogmatism, by the suddenness and surprise of the thing; protesting with every power of her mind, assenting with every throb of her heart, looking up at Philemon with the deprecating adoration of a mortal who beholds an angel stooping to earth's helpless, needy level,—Rachel Mather was married to Philemon Hall without a crowd of friends, a wedding feast, a veiled bride, or even the flowers that should have lent the last adornment to such a scene; but no death-bed marriage could have been more solemn or as serene; it was like a translation to the hopeless, earthly life of the woman; an opening of heaven's gates; and it was the rapture of fulfilment to the man, without one tinge of earth or self in its joy; the stainless rapture of a seraph over the soul gathered to the love of eternity, safe in the heavenly rest. Strange, unworldly, unwise, impossible to mortal man as this tale seems, oh! friendly reader, it is true. And while you stare and wonder and almost disbelieve, just as Deerfield people did; yet knowing that it was, and is, a fact of well-attested history, will you not for this man's sake have a grain of faith hereafter in the possibilities of humanity, when God breathes into its shape once more the breath of His life?

CHAPTER III.

CONTINUANCE.

*Here may ye see that 'men can' be
In love meek, kind, and stable.*

WHEN Mrs. Peek came home from her visit to the poorhouse, which had been prolonged beyond her expectance by a sturdy squabble with Simmons, who kept it, concerning certain arrangements for Rachel, she was stunned to find her burden taken off her hands in such a way. She did not dare encounter Philemon's keen gray eye, which looked through her flimsy pretence of kindness, to the cruelty and injustice beneath; and he, with that masculine wisdom which teaches a man to be silent in cases where a woman thinks, or rather feels that she must speak or die, did not offer any accusations or ask any explanations concerning the past.

He merely entered into certain discussions of a business nature, for it was needful that Rachel should have a place where she could be comfortable till he had a home of his own. He could have taken her to his uncle's house, but Doctor Prime would not allow her to be moved twice; her extreme exhaustion and delicacy forbade the attempt. Philemon had been preaching during his last term of study in the little village of Trumbull, a growing town on the seashore, where certain magnates of the West India trade in New Haven had built them goodly homes, and attracted by their daily needs such tradesmen as the scant custom of an ordinary village did not allow. There was little doubt that when the young student was ready to be ordained he would receive a call to this parish, but till he was fairly settled it seemed best to have Rachel remain in her aunt's house.

After much higgling on Widow Peek's side, and a certain thrifty demur and sense of justice on Mr. Hall's, it was at last arranged that Rachel should occupy the spare room, which had a cheerful, sunny outlook, and an open fireplace; and Aunt Ruthy be established as her nurse, providing and cooking both her food and Rachel's; the bargain including the use of Mrs. Peek's kitchen fire for the latter purpose.

This being decided, Philemon set himself to his outside work, visiting his wife daily, bringing refreshment and rest in his very presence; reading to her; praying at her side; soothing her fears, her self-reproach, her doubts, with all the patience of love and the fervor of faith. Rachel grew happier, and, in that way, better, basking in all this sunshine; but even the most profound affection, faithful care, and skilful nursing cannot restore to the distorted muscles and shattered nerves their supple strength and healthy calm. It became more and more unquestionable that she was to be a cripple for life; and when, in the early fall, Philemon received and accepted his call to the church in Trumbull, and by slow and painful stages, in a vehicle fitted up for the purpose, Rachel was carried to her new home, she felt that it was for life and death; that never again her feet would tread the elastic sward, her eyes see the hills and valleys of her native township, or her knotted fingers pluck the spring-born blossoms from their lonely woodland haunts.

Aunt Ruthy had resolved to stay with her charge, whom she had learned to love with almost maternal affection, as general servant, nurse, and friend. She was tired of nursing from house to house, she was well-nigh fifty years old, and begun to hunger for a home; and as her only child was a sailor, wandering from land to land with that craze for adventure that lays hold on some men to the extinction of natural ties, she had no prospect for her old age better than that offered her in the house of the minister. In those days a settlement in any parish meant a lifelong position, except under some peculiar circumstances, and Aunt Ruthy in becoming a member of Philemon Hall's family felt herself secure.

The patriarchal relation of servants to the served in the older times was, in the country, almost universal; and though Aunt Ruthy cooked, washed, ironed, swept, dusted, sewed, and cared for the invalid beside, when her methodic and capable strength had done the day's work up with a calm despatch and neatness modern service knows nothing about, she put on her tamboured collar, changed her stuff skirt and check short gown for a gay chintz gown and petticoat, put a clean mob-cap on her gray hair rolled neatly over a small cushion, and sat down by Rachel to keep her company, helped to entertain her guests, and, with the quiet tact of an intelligent and self-respecting woman, made herself agreeable without being intrusive, and companionable without presumption or impertinence. Dear old Aunt Ruthy! you, whom I remember in your old age, with dark, dovelike eyes in whose depths lurked a great sorrow and a greater love; your benign face and suave features lit with affection and appreciation, with love to God and man. You, who had the royal heart and the lavish hand of the ideal queen, where are your kind gone to? Why have we, instead, a tribe of over-dressed, flaunting, silly, selfish creatures, good only for factory hands? Is it education, is it liberty, is it cheap manufactures, or yellow-covered novels that have wrought this result in our women?

It is not to be supposed that when the first flush of enthusiasm, generosity, pity, and indignation passed by, and Philemon Hall took up his life with a daily increasing consciousness of its incompleteness, that he was a happy, or a contented man; for him, in lieu of the active joyful wife, ready to share in his work, to bear and guide his children, to be his heart's delight, companion as well as comforter, — there was only this sweet, pale saint shrined in her chamber, a creature quite,

>   . . . "Too bright and good
>   For human nature's daily food."

and he was not yet old enough or disciplined enough to like daily manna, though it tasted of heaven.

He might almost as well have been a monk in a cell, with a shrined Madonna for his household goddess; only that the image would not have been sensitive to every sad look, long-drawn breath, or heavy-hearted expression of its votary. It is hard to be a martyr at the stake, no doubt, but there are the exultation of triumphant faith, the wondering eyes of the crowd of witnesses, the rapture of victory, the abstraction of soul and spirit, all enabling the flesh to endure that sharp short agony; but a martyr by pin-pricks, or stung to death by mosquitoes would demand wonderful grace and faith to live to the end of his slow torture.

Yet Philemon Hall was so generous a man, so patient in his strength, so filled with deep affection for this shipwrecked love of his childhood and youth, that never a word of regret, of impatience, or coldness met her ear; and if, in her morbid sense of dereliction from duty and unfitness for her position, she imagined traces of loss or weariness in his eye or voice, he learned at once to detect her thought, to meet the upturned eye with a look of cheerful affection, and soothe the apprehensive ear with words of tenderness and consolation.

If his struggles were sharp in the solitude of his study, or in his long lonely walks through the odorous pine woods, or along the sea-resounding shore; if the life that might have been arose at times and tempted him with its visionary troops of possible delights and broader experiences; he learned from the very temptation he endured, to be tender of his brethren who yielded to the assaults his position and his circumstances, as well as divine aid, enabled him to resist; and, walking side by side with Him, who fought the world, the flesh, and the devil, in their most alluring shapes on a lonely mountain top of Judea, and came off more than conqueror, this humble follower of the Master fought his own good fight, proved his armor thoroughly, and fitted himself to speak as one having authority and also sympathy with his human audience. And Rachel too, unaided by education, or outward nature, shut in upon herself, and conscious of a mistake in her life that to her rigid sense of duty seemed a sin; though at first she fretted silently and long to think she had not had the fortitude and persistence to refuse to marry Philemon, at last she learned that,—

"Where thou art placed, serenely there to stand," is the great virtue of daily life, and demands the most thorough subjection of the soul to its religious faith and immortal necessities. In this she was mightily aided by the vigorous common sense of Aunt Ruthy, who understood perfectly the danger of morbid feeling in a person placed in Rachel's exceptional circumstances.

One day, for the first time since they were settled in Trumbull, as Aunt Ruthy sat in the bedroom knitting, and her charge half dozed in the bed, Rachel turned her head, and unconscious of any hearer sighed out faintly,—

"O why! why, did I let him marry me?"

"Well," said Aunt Ruthy, placidly, as if the question had been addressed to her, "I expect there was several reasons, dear; first and foremost, he was sot that ye should, and he ain't one to stay nor delay with, when he starts out; then you was took sudden; you hadn't no time to think about it, bein' weak and stunned as it might be. 'He knoweth our frame and remembereth that we are dust,' ye know. I've seen too many sick folks not to know how often the sperit is willin', but the flesh is too weak not to block the way, and I don't b'lieve the Lord that made us is goin' to overlook our weak spots any more'n our strong ones. But land! why be I talkin' all abroad this way? The thing's done; its laid away; and you nor me ha'n't no call with what's over; we must forget them things that's behind an' press forrard; do the best we can with what we've got. We've all got to go to school, I expect, and we don't all get the same lesson to l'arn, but the one we do get is our'n, 'taint nobody else's, and if its real hard, why it shows the teacher thinks we're capable."

Rachel drank in this homely wisdom and laid it up in her heart; it had the true ring, and in these weary days and years, her simple conscientious nature strove daily to accept not only patiently, but gratefully, the burden that was laid upon her; she interested herself in all the sick and poor of the parish, and instead of complaining of her own aches learned to be thankful that she had such a home, such care, and such love as surrounded her every hour, when so many others lacked even daily bread in the tortures of disease, and worse than all, had to witness helplessly the poverty and distress of their families. Even, after a long time, she learned to thank God that if she had missed the joys of maternity, she had also missed its awful responsibilities, that she had no living soul to answer for but her own, in that day ever present to her thought, ever near to her expectancy. Her white-draped bed and cheerful room became a sort of chapel to the good, and also to the bad people in Trumbull, where they went for confession, counsel, or to ask prayers in some stress of life or death. She had a welcome hand and look for every one; she knew their joys, their sorrows, and their doubts; to her the family skeletons were unveiled, and the family hopes confided; her table had the first and latest flowers brought to adorn it, and nobody in the village ever made a social celebration of any sort but a bit of its daintiest morsels was set aside for Mrs. Hall.

Madam Stanley, the governor's lady, a shrewish but handsome dignified woman of thirty when Parson Hall came to Trumbull, let no week pass without a visit at the invalid's bedside. Her skilful hands concocted many a delicious dish to tempt Rachel's fastidious appetite, and she herself carried it to the parsonage in some quaint old basket, with a nosegay of lavender, damask roses, smellage, old man, clove pinks, heartsease, or whatever sweet old-fashioned flower her parterres furnished. It was like a picture to see her, stately in her dove-colored paduasoy gown and lilac satin petticoat, her full kerchief and thread-lace ruff, a black lace mantle with a hood across her bosom and on her powdered hair, her pouting lips, deep gentian blue eyes, and rosy countenance full of pride, passion, and yet kindly withal, beside the white bed of this frail gold-haired creature, as evanescent of aspect as a pearly cloud in heaven tinged by the dying sun. Hither too came Sybil Saltonstall, the governor's niece, a girl in the blush and bloom of seventeen. Shy, reticent, alive to every shade or shine of life, a strange compound of dreams and realities, so proud that she would not show even her kindest and truest feelings, so true that she paraded her faults and hid her virtues lest she should gain credit she did not deserve; she was a delight and a puzzle to Rachel, whose nature was limpid as a mountain tarn, and could no more understand Sybil's flights and notions than a blossom can understand a bird, yet she could not help loving the girl, feeling, though she did not see, the depth and devotion dormant in her heart, and refreshed with delight by her noble aspect, the breadth of her white forehead, her clear, sea-gray eyes, pellucid as a spring, yet holding deep the spark of a star under the long veiling lashes, her peach-bloom cheeks and crimson lips, her frank, proud glance.

Even the little children made Mrs. Hall's room a place of resort; hushed their noisy laughter, calmed their rosy faces, and stole in smilingly and gently with their small offerings; sometimes a red apple or two, sometimes a handful of nuts, an early wild blossom half crushed in the eager hand that had plucked it, or a new-laid egg from the pet pullet.

"It beats all!" said Isaac Bunnel, the man who came daily to do the minister's "chores" about the barn. "She's the most of a sick woman I ever see. When my woman-folks is ailin' they let me know on't, now, I tell ye! It's 'Isik! fetch me some sage; Isik! *do* get that are brick; oh land! I shall die, Isik, ef ye don't make haste;' but she's as mum as a clam. Don't fret none, Aunt Ruthy says, nor don't scold; jest lies there an' looks like a ship's figger-head a-smilin', as though the world run on greased wheels. I know there's a lot o' grace to work, as they tell about; but seems as ef grace could work in some naters better 'n others; jest, you may say, as the same sort o' corn grows a sight higher in good land. She must ha' been medder soil to begin with, I expect."

And beside her in this quiet village, hidden from the sight of the world lying in wickedness, not shaped by the agencies of life's central seething fires, such as shake it with war, and persecution, and strife; but moulded by the daily forces of the tranquil hour, growing from within by virtue of the deep root, the dropping dew, the sudden shower and stressful winds, the sunshine and the night; — grew up to the full stature of a man in Christ Jesus, the saint who left behind him a real saint's record, Philemon Hall. If his wife could have known how much her influence had done to refine and sweeten his firm and powerful character;

how much he owed of his strong enduring purpose, and patient faith to the working of the very position he had so rashly assumed, and she so deeply regretted, she would have been satisfied; but these things work like the forces of nature upon us, and we know them not till we see the results; and it is herein we walk by faith, not by sight. And now, when Parson Hall and his wife had, after four years' hard service and patience, become at home in every sense in Trumbull; found their place in the hearts of its people and grown into their lives; far away in the mountain town of Plainfield, Doctor Dennis dies, and his stricken, homeless wife writes a letter to Uncle Dyer, a retired merchant living also in Trumbull, a letter about to bring together Esther Dennis and her fate.

CHAPTER IV.

CIRCUMSTANCE.

We consider not sufficiently the good of evils.

WHEN Mr. Dyer received his niece's letter, he found it difficult to answer. His wife was lying ill of a lingering consumption. It was impossible for him to ask his relations to come and visit him, as he would gladly have done. He could not but perceive that in the event of his wife's death he should himself be glad of Mrs. Dennis's care and companionship, but this was a prospect he could not decently offer as an inducement. Nothing occurred to him as a probable or possible occupation for two lonely women, and at last after much thought he sent them the following letter. If it is not orthographically correct, let us have the charity to remember that spelling was not a test of education in those days; even George Washington was incorrect in that particular. Can I offer greater excuse?

TRUMBULL, Novr ye 27, 1748.

MY DEAR NEICE, — I Rec'd your favor of ye' 19th inst Per Male duly. I regret to hear of y'r Mellancholly Afliction; death spares no Man; Wee must all dye Sooner or Later. I hope you are Resign'd to the Will of god; having Comfortabel Asurance that ye' Deceas'd is depparted to a Better Condishion of Things.

In Respect of ye' Matter of w'ch you Writ, I see nothing at Present open to your Intention: but I think when Spring arives their may Bee something found. I Forward in this a Bill ov Draft w'ch you can have Cash'd in the Town by Mr. Seers, he Being a Customer in time past of Mine. It will help you in the Winter time to wait more Comfortable, and I will keap you in Mind, if, as I now Think there may be Need of you Herafter.

Yours to Command
JOSHUA DYER.

Mrs. Dennis handed the letter to Esther without a word; she was disappointed. Her hope and thought had been to escape at once from this house haunted by the idea and shape of her husband; for it seemed to her bereft soul that he stood beside the fireplace when she entered the room, but eluded her sight when the door opened; or, that he still leaned over the office table and vanished when she looked in; every step startled her, every sound struck sharp upon her ear with a possibility never realized, and she wanted to get away to some place where no association tortured her. But this letter put an end to the thought; a woman has so little resource in such a position, she is so helpless, so cramped. A man can go and come as he will; find some place in life out of and beyond the dwelling of his dead; but a woman must sit down and endure. She took the bill for two hundred dollars as simply as if it were her right; Uncle Dyer had enough and to spare, it was kind in him; but she was not humiliated or angered by the gift, she had that rare generosity which can take as cordially as it can give.

Esther was not as surprised or as grieved as her mother; she had not built much on the help Uncle

Dyer would give them, and it was a sort of respite to her not to leave the home where she had always lived. She was a true New England girl, shy, sturdy in resolve, quick in action, reticent, and perhaps proud, having under all a character that circumstances alone could develop, that was even yet a mystery to herself. So they endured in their little house the long Vermont winter. Esther cleared the snow from doorsteps and paths herself, went for the milk, kept the fires going, cooked their slight meals, and helped the heavier work along, while her mother spun yarn on the big wheel to supply the knitting that occupied their evenings, and once a week the butcher, whose cart stopped every Saturday at the door, carried such socks and mittens as were finished to "the store" in Plainfield and exchanged them for groceries which he carried back the next week. The winter was long and lonely, but it wore away; the last week in February came a brief note from Uncle Dyer, telling them of his wife's death, and three weeks after, a longer letter asking them to come at once to Trumbull, and live with him, as he needed care and company as much as they needed a home. It did not take many days to dispose of their few goods; fortunately, the butcher, who had been so friendly to them through the winter, wanted to rent a farm, and would take their scanty furniture and other household goods at a fair valuation; two old hair-trunks with initials in brass nails on the top, and trimmings of pinked leather nailed on all around, held their clothes, and a great bandbox carried precariously their best bonnets. The drive was long and tedious, travel by stage coach has become a faint memory to-day to the few who recall it at all, yet there are a few who cannot forget the swaying and bouncing motion of those great stiff springs, a motion as disturbing to the reeling head and sympathizing stomach, as if the luckless traveller were given over to be bandied about between the centrifugal and centripetal forces of nature, yielding now to one and now to the other, neither getting the victory in the end, but tossing the victim to and fro at their seething point of contact till he wished either of the tormentors might conquer, though it were his own death. Then there were the slippery cushions, the unsavory straw under foot, the windows never open but that some one else wanted them shut, or shut but that some one insisted on their opening; the evil smell of damp leather, the enforced companionship, the cramped position, all these exchanged now for the ease, the swiftness, the comparative privacy of a railway car, where at least there is some attempt at ventilation, and only your very nearest neighbor dare growl at your window. It was with an extreme sense of exhaustion and relief that Esther and her mother at last clambered down the rattling steps of the "stage," at Uncle Dyer's door, and received his warm and earnest welcome.

Joshua Dyer was a kindly, just, and honest man. If he had made money in trade, it was done in the most conscientious way; gifted with that talent for business that is in its way as much a separate gift as genius, he had been able to seize the moment of propitious circumstance in all his long mercantile life, just when there was a demand which he could supply, and he had retired to private life carrying with him the respect of all his compeers and those whom he had employed. His wife was a dull, uninteresting woman, whom he had married in one of those youthful passions inspired by a vivid complexion, shining hair, and capacity for giggling, and whom he had discovered, when the passion burned out as rapidly as light wood will, to have nothing companionable, inspiring, helpful, or even amusing about her, yet to have a capacity for jealousy, for hoarding, and for meddling, that showed how narrow was the nature, how uneducated the mind beneath her roseate cheeks and sparkling eyes.

If she had been jealous of him alone, perhaps Joshua Dyer might have looked on her more kindly, considering it a proof of her love for him, as indeed in some ardent and direct natures it is. That cannot be necessarily a low emotion whose earthly name God himself condescends to apply to his own will that his children should love him supremely, and there is a human love which has, from its own utter and entire forgetfulness of self and its eager devotion, an inalienable right to demand that the love given to it in return shall be equally pure, single, monopolizing, and faithful; but Mrs. Dyer had no such noble hunger or divine right within her narrow nature; she was jealous of her position, her precedence, her social privileges, her due honor, and the respect she imagined she deserved. Her life was one long accusation of those about her, and consequently their alienation; and it was a relief to her husband, though he dared not acknowledge it even to himself, when death, the inexorable leveller, put an end to Mrs. Dyer's claims, and calmed with his tyrannic silencing her perturbed soul. It was a real home that the Widow Dennis found in Trumbull. She stepped into the right place quietly and thankfully. Nothing was required of her but to order and superintend the house, the kitchen was out of her province and had its own ruler and governor. "The constant service of the antique world," had its representative there in the person of a ten years' occupant, who was glad enough to relinquish the sweeping and sewing into other hands. Uncle Dyer was easy to provide for, since he had little company to entertain, and was of the simplest tastes and habits himself.

Esther, too, was happier than she had expected to be. Mr. Dyer had read a great deal in his later years, and read judiciously; he saw at once that Esther's education had been necessarily slight and superficial, and it was a real pleasure to him to direct her choice of books; she spent her mornings in his quiet library, and, in the evening, told him what she had read, and talked her books over with him, adding to her own intelligent comprehension the wider ideas of a man who had not only read, but seen, observed, and indeed lived in a world whose motives, passions, influences, and results were all unknown as yet to her.

In the afternoons of the slow-coming spring, she rode abroad with her uncle in the yellow chaise, or took long and lonely walks; nature had been her friend and companion through all these years at home, and the new faces of the old friend that this sea-softened air and sandy soil showed her, had an added charm of novelty to her observant eye. She had, too, for the first time in her life, a girl friend; for Sybil Saltonstall and she met on certain social occasions, and were at once attracted to each other from the very difference of their natures. Esther's childlike direct simplicity, her credulous acceptance of things for their outward seeming, her yet unsullied faith in life and man, were all interesting and amusing to Sybil. She had herself lived too long in society, been too conversant with the political machinery that penetrated with its subtle atmosphere even the upright family life at Governor Stanley's, to trust any one with that infantile confidence and ignorance of character Esther showed; but she loved the fresh soul and unspotted nature of this country girl just as a lover of hot-house splendors delights to see the shy grace and dew-born purity of a woodland blossom lighting the green forest solitude.

So a year passed by. Esther learned much in its tranquil progress; to her already fine face, awakening intellect added now its subtle charm, and the warm love she had given to Uncle Dyer and Sybil gave her beautiful sad eyes a tender depth they had never worn before; if there lay within them any deeper radiance it still slept; no dream of love had yet disturbed their depths, wearing the too facile wings, the too keen-pointed arrow of the Annoyer. She saw but few young men, only one who interested her at all; and if she gave curious and strenuous thought to young Colonel Stonebridge, it was because he came to Trumbull as Sybil's declared admirer, though not yet her accepted lover.

Yet all this time Uncle Dyer, who had his own match-making instincts, as most old people have, careless and fearless about laying their hands on the Ark of the Lord, had planned a future for this girl, becoming so dear to him daily; though he wisely refrained from speaking of it to any one. But whenever the chance came in naturally, he would talk to and before Esther of his nephew Philip, the only child of his wife's dead brother, a boy who had come to him in his lonely orphanhood, and been taken at once into his heart, and as far into his home as Mrs. Dyer's jealousy and thrift would permit.

Philip Kent was now in the West Indies, settling some business for his uncle; he had gone there just after his aunt's death, and was still absent; another year might bring him back, and it seemed to this old man that his last years would be his best if he could see Philip and Esther sharing his home, ministering to his comfort, and going down with him in his loneliness to the edge of the grave. Day after day he dropped some word or two about Philip; his character, his business capacity, his early youth, his aspect, till gradually Mrs. Dennis and Esther felt as if he had always been one of the family with them, and was gone but a little while.

But only one person, with that keen insight that nothing gives but an entire withdrawal of personal interest in outer things, perceived the thought of Mr. Dyer's heart.

Rachel Hall, lying quietly in her bed, had welcomed the new-comers to Trumbull, and so fascinated Esther that scarcely a day passed without finding the girl a visitor to the minister's wife; in her girlish unreserve she poured out all her thought into Rachel's ear, and often spoke of this unknown Philip, not with a marked interest, but as a factor in the life of the Dyer household as truly as if he were always counted among its constant inmates.

Uncle Dyer, too, made it his duty to go and see Mrs. Hall once a week, and in the delight and pride in Esther which he expressed freely there, Rachel observed that he always linked, quite unconsciously, a thought or a word for Philip with his mention of his grand-niece, as if they were so inseparably linked in his mind, or his intention, that he could not think of them apart.

One day as the minister was sitting beside her with his book, now and then reading, but more often looking up to say a tender or cheerful word to his wife, Rachel said in her gentle voice, —

"Husband, my mind misgives me that our good old friend, Joshua Dyer, has a thing borne in upon his mind that may be troublous to him; has he spoken aught of his plans or hopes about Philip to you?"

"No, Rachel," answered the minister; "he is not a man who is free to speak. But why should he vex his soul about Philip, who is beyond his influencing now, and, if I know the lad, ever will be?"

"I think he has it in mind to have Esther and Philip more than friendly when the youth returns. He holds them both very dear. Philip has ever been the apple of his eye, as you know, and Esther is, I think, almost as precious in his sight. It would be pleasing indeed if he could have them both to comfort his later days, and share his worldly goods, but I fear a disappointment for him; those things do not fall out like seedtime and harvest; and men are wilful in their youth, they love not interference."

"Nor much better in their age, Rachel," said the minister, smiling.

"I have ever thought that even as no man can help the bird of the air to build her curious nest or choose her mate, but rather terrifies the pairing and casts down that wonderful architecture with touch or taint of mortal finger, so it is more vain to put forth the hand to aid those solemn conditions of humanity which are the fountain of life, both earthly and heavenly. "Guide not the hand of God," saith the learned and wise Sir Thomas Browne, and indeed it is but vanity and presumption to try such irreverent guidance. I, too, should be sorry to see our good old friend's purposes broken off; but what can we do, Rachel?"

"Nothing but pray," she said, softly.

"Yes, prayer is left, and it is mighty to save; but who shall say in what path the salvation cometh? Its delivering steps perchance tread the very path of our fears, the way of our disappointment. 'If it be Thy will, O Father!' Think on these words, beloved, for He who spake them found no escape from the cross or the agony; shall the disciple be above his master, or the servant above his lord?"

Rachel sighed; for her own sorrows she had not a complaint when Philemon was with her, but she had thrown her whole heart out in sympathy with the little world around her till it truly seemed as if, in a finite sense, she bare their griefs and carried their sorrows.

She knew Philip Kent, though she had seen him less than almost any other transient member of her husband's parish; but her perception of character was keen, and she did not thoroughly trust him; she would not willingly have seen him married to Esther. Her sweet soul, too, was in anxious dread just now about Sybil's future; for she knew by report that Colonel Stonebridge was hovering about the governor's mansion with intent apparent to carry away its brightest jewel, and well she knew what record the Stonebridge race held in colonial history, what wild blood ran in their veins; they were a reckless, godless tribe; wearing all the polish and glitter that attracts; courtly, debonair, handsome, and quick-witted; here and there a woman had sprung from this black soil pure as a lily from the slimy substratum of a shallow pool, but the legend ran that Stonebridge men were granite and their women wax; such a race was no garden whereupon to set the rose of the Saltonstalls.

While Rachel Hall lay pondering these things in her heart, her husband having betaken himself to his study, her door opened and in came Sybil and Esther. Their bloom and freshness, their smiling beauty, and dainty attire, were like a fresh breath of life to the invalid; Esther had developed a taste in dress hitherto latent for want of means and observation, but Mr. Dyer's ample allowance and Sybil's friendly hints enabled her to carry out her ideas; and to-day in her rose-pink chintz gown, and little white cloak; the tiny rose-wreathed chip hat, set aslant on her high-heaped dark hair, yet unpowdered; her face, warm with the rich glow of health and feeling; she was as fair a contrast to Sybil in her sea-green satin petticoat and pearl-colored gown, with a satin hood to match the petticoat, drawn about her head and shoulders, and ruffs of rich lace at her throat and elbows, as a painter ever dreamed. It seemed almost an answer to Rachel's tearful, prayerful thought so suddenly banished, almost a warning, when Esther said, with a ring of delight in her voice, —

"Dear Aunt Hall! Philip is coming home to-morrow, and we are all so pleased!"

CHAPTER V.

HERE.

*Well I know
Thou strikest, like Olympian Jove, but once.*

UNCLE DYER had gone into the garden to inspect his currant bushes, just now set thick with branches of fruit which the sun was turning here and there a dusky pink, the first shade of their ripe crimson, and Mrs. Dennis was packing away blankets in the camphor chest upstairs when Philip came; he did not come by the coach, but rode over from New Haven where he had landed the night before, on a strong dapple-grey horse he had bought at his uncle's request to replace the old roan; a purchase that had, as he wrote, delayed his arrival in Trumbull a day or two, so that he was not expected definitely. So Esther was alone in the summer parlor when he came in; filling the great china punch bowl with those exquisite old-fashioned white roses almost unknown to florists now, but like Eve in Milton's involved description

"Loveliest of her daughters."

One half-blown bud, holding in its milky cup the mellow saffron tinge of dawn, and set in its own blue-green leaves, Esther had put into the dark rolls of her hair, which it illumined and perfumed, and just as Philip entered she was leaning with her chin in the hollow of her hand over the mass of roses before her, delighting her eyes with their perfect dewy loveliness, unconscious that she herself was as striking as the flowers. Philip stopped on the threshold, and Esther looked up at him; a gleam of recognition banished the dreamy expression of her eyes, but the long deep look he gave her arrested her in a moment; there was some strange thrill borne on that cool ray into her very soul; the quick color rushed across her face, she made an instinctive effort at self-possession and said slowly, "You are Philip?"

A keen smile twisted his lips oddly; it was partly amusement, partly sarcasm, but she was too unsuspecting to analyze it.

"Yes," he said, "I am Philip."

"I will go and call Uncle Dyer," and with that she went out of the other door filled with a strange feeling, a new blind consciousness she did not observe, or therefore, stop to interpret.

Philip Kent was not a man to attract men; he was not particularly brilliant, well bred, or well educated, nor was he handsome; his features were coarse, his stature below the average height of men; nothing about him was remarkable but a pair of almost femininely beautiful deep-set gray eyes, those blue-gray eyes that have in them the deceit of blue and the perception of gray, thoroughly different from the sea-gray that in their lucent greenish clarity have the deep sparkle of the sea still shining, and mean genius, passion, purity, and strength.

Still, to women, there was something curiously attractive about the man, something so intangible that the phrase of charlatanism, "magnetic," comes nearest to its description. He was thoroughly selfish, exacting, and self-conscious, capable of a certain sort of lasting affection for anything that belonged to him, an outgrowth of his selfishness; and a man who amused himself in studying and drawing out character, pulling the strings of feeling and action, experimenting on the sacredest emotions and passions of his kind, as if the world were his puppet-show, and when his *marionettes* had played their parts to his satisfaction, throwing them aside with an easy manner of idleness and custom, as if indeed they were painted wood and cloth, and had not hearts and souls far more capable of suffering than his own.

He added to these evil traits a sort of careless generosity in money matters, underlaid by the minutest thrift in trifles; it gave him such a comfortable sense of superiority to lend his friends money, and receive their gratitude; it was so agreeable to be admired, lauded, spoken of as the best friend in the world, that his vanity drank and was satisfied, though of costly draughts.

But to women perhaps his chief charm was the romantic confidences always given in charge to the reigning favorite; his misanthropy, his doubts, his sufferings — always *his* — were poured into the tender and sympathizing soul that ached with and wept for him. If a woman is a true woman, nothing is so bewitching, so absorbing to her, as the office of consoler. I once heard a man say of a certain acquaintance, "If I had a friend who wanted Miss Blank to fall in love with him, I should advise him to break his leg at her door," and what he thought true of one woman is in reality true of almost all. None of them paused to observe that Philip never stirred hand or foot to aid their troubles, or found any interest in their griefs. He had learned in his intimate friendships many a small art to interest the young girls who one after another played at friendship with him; he could tie up flowers like an artist; he played the flute with as dulcet strains as Apollo; he danced a minuet with consummate grace, and was learned in female frippery such as laces, gloves, and ribbons, while no saint or hero could evolve in language, as if from his inner experience, more lofty theories or nobler sentiments than this man who knew not at all how to be noble, high-minded, or really generous.

It seemed however to Esther Dennis, when she had brought Uncle Dyer and her mother in to welcome this son of the house, and set herself in the corner to look and listen, that this man was the one man on earth. There are those doubters who say that love at first sight is a myth, the nonsense of a school girl, the dream of a rhymester; but nevertheless it is true that this is first love, and this only. This full-born passion that strikes the heart like lightning, and makes it captive with one blow, is the Eros of classic anthology, king and conqueror by divine right. Few indeed there are, who are direct, unworldly, pure enough to receive the heavenly visitation, but to them it is life or death. The Cupid of men and women at large is a lesser god than this awful and beauteous shape of a victorious angel; he is a thwart and mischievous baby who makes confusion, laughter, madness, brief joy, inconstant passion, idle tears, despair, weariness, disgust; the methods of his warfare and the consequences of his reign; annoyer and destroyer; but the rightful monarch has for his crown faith, devotion, trust, truth, reliance, and a passion pure and solemn as the silent planets in a night-blue heaven, and his reign is like the reign of death, once and forever. Whatever wrong, whatever cruelty, neglect, cold acceptance or bitter rejection it meets with, it still lives, like the shrinking bulb that withdraws itself into the humility of the dust, and folds its radiant blossom close in its heart while winter shames and repels it, but is ready to spring and bloom when the sun looks and smiles for it, so long as life shall endure, yet even that life will die of too long hiding, perish for lack of light. To this young girl, in the first dreamy hours of her womanhood, so the king came. All night long from her sleepless pillow her great dark eyes looked at the starry heavens of June, and a voice in her heart sang over and over "Philip! Philip! dear Philip!"

It did not seem to her unmaidenly, strange, dreadful, a thing to be resisted; for she never once was conscious of herself. Another identity filled her heart and permeated her brain; she was in a sort of wonderful happy trance, and when at last the sun shot a long, bright ray athwart the coolness of her chamber, full of the rose-scented air of the night and the freshness of summer dews, she felt like an adorer in the adytum of a temple, unwilling to return from the high converse of his divinity in the vaulted silence of that sacred abode, to the dust, the glare, the common humanities of the usual day.

Philip, with the acuteness, native and experimental both, that belonged to him, saw in the droop and quiver of the long lashes that veiled Esther's eyes from his greeting look when they met that morning, some part of her thought; he certainly understood that his usual power of interesting women had not failed here; but the real depth and strength of feeling he had awakened he did not at all appreciate. He only set himself to be pleasant to the companions of his coming life, and succeeded; he liked to have some people like him, not the crowd, but those necessarily about him, for so his life was made more comfortable, more exciting, amusing, and less wearisome. His own traits, wants, ideas, occupied him it is true, most of the time; but he had not yet arrived at the age when all other things fall into insignificance, and the voracious "I" of the egotist becomes his own tyrant, and the despot of all around him.

Philip Kent soon discovered how interesting a

character was here brought into contact with his own; he had seen women before, but they were the average sort of women; silly, sensible, or only commonplace and pretty. He had flirted in his own quiet forcible way with many another girl, but Esther's simple nature, her quick intellect, her utter girlishness untouched by folly or affectation, her devotion to her mother and Uncle Dyer, were all new traits to him.

He had before gathered his flowers from the garden; cultivated, conventional, well-bred posies, proper for nosegays, to make life bright or sweet, — while they lasted; here was a spray from a wild grapevine, perfumed with the very breath of pure nature, full of promise for the future; and he devoted himself to the new exploration.

It is so easy to destroy promise and performance, so easy to gather the clusters that no time can ever recall to fruitage, or even restore to fragrance, but who thinks of it in the eager desire to make that bloom his own? Certainly Philip Kent was not one of those rare natures that

"Loved the wild rose and left it on its stalk."

He had time and opportunity enough now to study Esther at his leisure; the dapple-gray horse was a good roadster and Uncle Dyer had two outlying farms; one six miles further on the shore, where he still bred a few horses for home trade; another three miles inland, a sheep-farm, where his flocks whitened the Connecticut hills, and yielded stores of heavy fleeces, both for sale and for use in his own family; for in those days the plague of dogs did not infest the country, and sheep could live and die in peace when every laboring man did not add to his labor and expenses the keep of a ravening cur, like unto their spiritual congener who "goeth about seeking what he may devour" continuously.

Many an errand Uncle Dyer found for Philip to do at the Long Beach farm, or at Hillside; and almost every day Esther was offered a place in the old chaise, and rolled along the silent green-bowered roads talking with Philip; or, in that silence more eloquent than words for which the air has an echo, and the stillness of the woods an answer.

Then there were so many pleasant walks about the village; there were paths through the stunted cedars and scrub oaks that led down through tall, glittering beach grasses to the clean sand and abrupt rocks of the shore.

Was Paradise sweeter than those long moonlit evenings on a buttress of granite, with the quiet sea breaking and recoiling at their feet, the distant plash and rattle of a row-boat's oars, the long celestial ray upon the waters, across which now and then flitted the ghostly sail of a coasting vessel, like a dream of another life? Esther was as one who walked in her sleep; the daily duties of life began to jar upon her, she went less often to see Mrs. Hall, she had little time to walk or talk with Sybil Saltonstall, and was really almost glad when Sybil went to

Albany, — a long and awful journey in those days, to visit her aunt there.

Poor Esther! her world was fast narrowing to the measure of one man! As Philip and she grew more intimate, and he poured into her pitying ear the sorrows of his soul — sorrows compounded, be it said, of selfishness and dyspepsia, — she felt for him that exquisite, that almost supernatural sympathy, that is the child of pure passion and utterly selfless affection. She lay awake at night in terror lest Philip should commit suicide from sheer despair of happiness; a hint he had darkly thrown out for the express purpose of seeing how it would affect Esther; for he would not have cut his own little finger on any consideration!

She felt for him that divine pity that is only possible for utter love to feel; in her eyes he was something so far above her, even in his sorrow, that she would have laid down her life to serve or to save him, and gloried in the thought that she, a simple, commonplace little country girl could be the friend of one so lofty, so good, so proudly sad. For Philip had imbued her with those stale ideas of friendship, a tie stainless, enduring, rapturous, with no tinge of earth about it, that were all new to Esther, though they were the staple of Philip's conversation with women, and their use had enabled him for years to make passionate love under the *pose* of a "friend." Subtle disguise! illusion that has betrayed and broken the heart of many a girl, before the abounding novel had portrayed its futility, and scoffed at its method; we "have changed all that" in our modern wisdom; one good that should be scored for the luckless novelist, so scorned and denounced by the "unco guid." It was Rachel Hall whose observant eyes first discovered Esther's condition. Lying there on her pallet, freed from the personal experiences of life wherein the soul is driven to and fro, confused and perturbed by its own emotions, it seemed to Aunt Ruthy who had also lived her life, but in the usual fashion, that Rachel was like a guardian spirit, who sees through the veiling mists of earth the vagaries of its wayward children, and inspires them with discretion when they need guidance, or hope when they would else despair.

Rachel watched Esther with a yearning of that maternal affection denied its natural channels; she grieved silently over the distant look of the great dark eyes that quickened into vivid light and ardor if she heard Philip's step or voice; the rapid glow of color that illuminated her pale face, the brooding, languid sweetness of her voice; but she dared not speak to her with any questioning, she knew too well how dangerous it is to force open a delaying bud, and so blast it with premature light. Yet in her wise heart, she distrusted Philip Kent, and dreaded Esther's future.

Aunt Ruthy saw and understood the sad, thoughtful face she wore after Esther's visit.

"It does seem hard sometimes, now don't it?" said the good woman, "to think we can't fix other folkses ways just as we would have 'em to be. But I think likely we should make some amazin' blunders, if we could, and did. The Lord made 'em, and he certinly knows best how to manage 'em; and it's good to think He doos."

CHAPTER VI.

CLOUDY.

*Oh, how this Spring of love resembleth
The uncertain glory of an April day.*

WHEN winter fairly began in the nominally autumn month of November, Philip was obliged to leave Trumbull for New York, to manage some business for Uncle Dyer; Esther parted from him with outward tranquillity; no one knew that the night before he had said his farewell to her on the way from "evening lecture," with all the tender words — of friendship! — that her hungry heart could ask. Not by one incautious syllable had he ever intimated any deeper feeling, any desire for a dearer tie; he had pressed Esther's hand long and fervently, he had paid her all the small and thoughtful attentions a lover could show, he anticipated her little wants, cultivated a knowledge of her tastes, brought her nosegays from field and wood, dainty leaf-baskets of fruit, stores of nuts; he helped her gather blossoms for her bowpot, and perfumed leaves for her pot-pourri that sent out its quaint musty odor on the air of the unfrequented parlor, and made an atmosphere of its own about the sea-green satin furniture, with its odd gimp borders, the Indian matting on the floor, the "hundred-legged" ebony tables, the wheezy spinnet, the Chinese dragons, and the alabaster vases on that high, carved mantel. Yet Philip had never said, "Esther, I love you! do you love me?" and the dreaming, innocent, ignorant girl had never noticed the omission, never even acknowledged to herself that she loved Philip, any more than she had said to herself, "I breathe."

But now, in the awful blank that his absence made, the stillness and tastelessness of her life, she began to recognize that her heart had gone away from her possession — that Philip had won it utterly and entirely.

She was neither introverted, proper, or proud; she was a girl of that direct and simple nature which is now traditional only; she was glad to love Philip, to feel that she had given him her whole soul; she neither looked forward to consequences, or considered if he returned her devotion; it was enough that she loved him, and the sweet absorbing consciousness beguiled her grief at his absence, filled her dreams with joy, woke with her in the morning like the scent of the roses that June had breathed into her window at dawn, filled her eyes with tender light, colored her fair face with roseate bloom, and made her gracious and sweet to all about her.

If her mother had been a woman of suspicious or penetrative nature she would have witnessed this change in Esther with dread; but ever since her husband's death, Mrs. Dennis had seemed wrapped in the past; she was perfect in all her duties; Uncle Dyer's house was kept in the extremest order; flies dare not invade any room therein, and spiders found their occupation gone; dust was eliminated from the premises as fast as the inconsiderate air deposited it there; every crack in linen, every rent or hole in wearing apparel, was exquisitely darned, and when these daily tasks were over she sat down in the back porch in summer or by the "keeping-room" fire in winter and perused "Boston's Fourfold State," "Jenks' Devotion," Jeremy Taylor's "Holy Living and Dying," and her well-worn Bible by turns; an Irishwoman would have said she was "makin' her sowl," and it was neither more nor less than the Protestant shape of that occupation. She was naturally a timid woman, and her husband's death was her first experience not only of loss but of death itself, for she was too young to remember the death of her parents; so this had crushed her to earth, filled her with desolation, and absorbed her in the contemplation of that nearing fate for herself, and that awful veiled eternity to follow, that she must face, and for which she must prepare herself. So long as Esther made no complaint and obeyed her without remonstrance, when she set her to certain household tasks, Mrs. Dennis saw no further; as long as Uncle Dyer's long stockings were evenly knitted and well shaped it did not occur to her that those flying needles kept time to a fast beating heart all ready to leave every other tie and cleave utterly and solely to the new love.

Uncle Dyer, grave, reserved, but kindly and shrewd, perceived the matter but said nothing, for it was his hope that Esther and Philip should marry; he had already learned to love this girl with a warmth he supposed his old heart incapable of feeling, and when through this bitter winter he watched the lovely dreaming face at the fireside, or beside him in the sleigh, for she always accompanied him on those drives of inspection Philip used to take, he thanked God that these two young people, both so dear to him, would inherit his home and his fortune and take the place therein of the children never granted to him.

And there was another inmate of the household also in possession of Esther's open secret: Delia Pratt was "hired girl" in Mr. Dyer's family, and had ruled over the kitchen for the last ten years; she was one of those- old-fashioned servants well called "help" a capable, brisk woman of thirty, her crisp black hair knotted tightly on the top of her head, and secured by a horn comb. Her black eyes, high cheek bones, firm chin, well-colored cheeks, all expressing energy and strength; while the sparkle of her eye, and the dimple of her cheek, betrayed an underlying fund of humor that softened the otherwise harsh traits of her nature. Her reign in the kitchen was despotic, even Mrs. Dennis never interfered there. Delia knew just what Mr. Dyer liked, and it was the business of her life to see that he had it. Nobody in Trumbull could make such pot-pie, such baked beans, such Indian pudding, such rye bread, or such shortcakes, 'lection cake, or pound cake as Delia Pratt, and she knew it; a "b'iled dinner" was her glory; everybody wanted some of her "empt'ins" to set their own, and her fresh apple pies were an unattainable delicacy anywhere else.

Her own especial captive and slave was Hiram Perkins, the hired man, a shock-headed, slow, honest creature, who "did chores" all the year round for Mr. Dyer, slept in the "shed charmber," and worshipped Delia with all his faithful slow-moulded heart. It was the hope of his life that some day Delia would marry him, but there was a fatal obstacle in the way; he was not a professor of religion, and Delia was fixed in her resolution not to marry a child of the devil, as she was pleased to style all outside her own church.

"Well!" said the remonstrant Hiram, "I can't go an j'ine meetin' ef I ain't converted, Delye, now can I?"

"I dono as anybody asked ye to!" retorted Delia; "tain't real necessary 't I should marry ye, as I know of. I'm reasonable well off where I be; and as for havin' to do with a hypocrite why 'twould be worse'n Ananias an' Sapphiry, in the Bible. I wish you'd stop tewin around, and gettin' in a swivet about a small matter like that!"

"Tain't real small to me, I'd hev ye to know, Delye, and I don't see what harm it would do ye anyway. I go to meetin' real reg'lar, the tithing man never pokes me neither; you would't lose no means of grace through me. I ain't no ways sot aginst religion in the main; I like the talk, but I don't like the way folks perfess an' don't perform. I'd be ashamed to say I was convarted an' act like half the folks in your meetin' that do perfess."

"I don't calculate to marry nobody 't ain't a professor, any way," sharply answered Delia. "It's clear forbid in the Bible, and I'd be dealt with if I done it, so you no need to talk. Land's sakes! ain't you well off where you be? And I hope I don't set by no man livin, enough to rile me a mite, if I can't marry of him."

"I know ye don't! I know ye don't! If ye did"—

The possibility was too much for Hiram. He walked off dejectedly to the barn, and Delia's great wheel flew round faster than ever; certainly if she did not care for Hiram she cared for no other.

It was those same sharp eyes that pierced the hired man's heart that had watched the progress of Esther's innocent passion, and been aware of it even before Esther herself.

Delia did not like Philip Kent. She had known him from a boy, and arrived at a juster appreciation of his character than the uncle he had tried to please, for the sake of that uncle's possessions; or the various girls he had made love to for his own amusement.

He had no special reason for ingratiating himself with Delia; he was not given to dainties like most boys; the generous and savory food always served on his uncle's table satisfied his appetite, and he was always careful of his clothes. Neither did any innate generosity prompt him to give Delia anything, since he asked, and needed nothing from her; and she weighed him in her balance without compunction or hesitancy.

"I don't take no stock in that feller!" she confided to Hiram. "I've summered him an' wintered him, and he ain't one to tie to, now I tell ye; the' ain't but one God an' Lord to his notion, and that one's name is Philip Kent. Land! I hope he won't go to makin' eyes at our Esther! She's jest the one to swaller him whole without pepper; and she'd jest as good swaller p'ison."

"He's a perfessor, though," dryly remarked Hiram.

"Well, what ef he is! Judas was, wa'n't he? I dono as I ever said 't all perfessors was Christians, but I don't b'lieve the's any Christians thet ain't perfessors."

Hiram was tossed on the horns of this dilemma effectually.

"Got it now, hain't ye?" chuckled old Isaac Bunnell, who had come in to the shed door unperceived of Delia, after a dole of poke-berry rum for his rheumatism, promised by Mr. Dyer. Delia turned on him sharply.

"Is it a concern of your'n ef he has?" she asked, with a wrathful spark in her eyes.

"Well, now! the old sayin' is, 'don't ye never put in betwixt the bark and the tree;' but I didn't know as Hi was so clus to ye, really now I didn't!"

The angry color flooded Delia's face; but she had the wisdom to hold her tongue even when Isaac chuckled. Hiram, smiling to himself, had also been wise, and stepped out of the back door; he was slow, but he was not a fool, and instinct warned him not to let Delia see his enjoyment of her tell-tale wrath.

In her silent fashion Delia too, loved Esther; she even admitted to Hiram that she "sot by that girl consider'ble," which meant a great deal from Delia; and it grieved her proportionately to see how Esther had thrown herself away on Philip Kent.

"I can't noways help it!" she soliloquized, as she sat by her kitchen fire at night. "If I could help it 'twouldn't fret me, not nigh so much. When you can do somethin', either to help or hinder, it's a comfort; but I've jest got to set and see it a goin' on, an' I know what it 'll come to! Dear sus! the ways of Providence are dreadful mysterious, as Priest Hall was a sayin' last Sabba' day; and the wust of it is you can't neither change 'em nor see into 'em." And with a sigh over the inevitable, Delia raked up her fire and went to bed.

Meanwhile, Philip was enjoying himself after his own fashion in New York. He was well known there, and being a personable, well-to-do youth, made an important item in the society of the small city; he found many a pretty girl ready and willing to dance a minuet with him at the assemblies, drive with him on sleighing parties up the river, or play spadille and loo in the formal stuffy parlors of the comfortable

Dutch houses, afterward refreshing him with hot flip, oly koeks, or Indian preserves and arrack punch, supplemented perhaps by a hot supper.

If Esther on her sleepless pillow, thinking of him as solitary and hard working, could have looked in on these feasts and revels, have seen his cheek flushed, his eye sparkling, heard the low, tender whisper in Annetje Schuyler's ear as he turned her respectfully in the dance, or seen the embracing arm wherewith he helped Mina Van Alen into the sleigh, drawing her closer at every fresh drift, as if he dreaded an overturn, and Mina was precious, would she have closed those deep eyes so tranquilly, and slept so calmly, even in the repose of soul that came of her ardent evening prayer?

Who can tell! We resent once and again the barriers of time and space; we long madly and rebelliously to see and hear what space and time conceal from us, but if we could overleap these screens of God, would it not always draw down on us that "curse of a granted prayer" that is the worst of maledictions, since it is of our own procuring? No, Esther was far happier in her own love, voiceless as it was, in the dull round of duties which gave her time to dream, in the rare letters Philip sent to Uncle Dyer, stiff and businesslike as they were. He would not write to her; he would not commit himself so far; he knew, so he told her, that of course her mother and perhaps her uncle would not allow her to receive any letters that they did not expect to see, and could he write to his dear little friend such epistles as might be read by every one? She must wait, some better day would come.

Vague promise! but full and definite to Esther; she was content to do Philip's will; confident in his wisdom; certain of his truth and goodness. Philip was not surprised; he expected it; so his winter in New York was one of unsullied enjoyment, and Esther said to herself as the slow days dropped away one by one, "It is almost spring!"

CHAPTER VII.

CLEAR.

Which now shows all the glory of the sun.

At last spring came; not in the sudden splendor of the South, but shy, delaying, tender; bursts of cold rain; a slow greening of mosses in the woods; then a chilly south wind; a day of sleet; here and there hours of pale sunshine; a season of doubt, of feeble hope, of reluctant promise, but still spring. The woods began to look misty with gray buds; the cowslips in the swampy meadows opened here and there a yellow star; Esther found pink buds of arbutus hidden away in and under the dead grass and dry leaves on the north side of Pine Ridge, and inhaled their delicate woodland fragrance as if it were a message from Philip. Had he not fetched them to her the year before, tied up with graceful brown catkins and whorled stems of the upright ground pine? A gift so delicately lovely that a princess might have accepted it, and in Esther's sight an expression of a love she unconsciously believed in.' With the spring came Sybil, more beautiful than ever to Esther's eyes, yet more reticent than ever. She said little about her winter in Albany; once, sitting by Mrs. Hall's bedside, she said slowly, —

"It was a gay winter, Aunt Rachel; there are good

store of youths and maidens in Albany; there were balls, and sleigh parties, and revels enough. I have had enough. I am glad to be beside thee again."

"Dear child," murmured Rachel, "And was there none of these gallants to make Albany more pleasant to my Sybil than this small village?" A soft color stole into Sybil's cheek, a distant look into her eyes.

"Nay. I do not concern myself about marriage; I do not consider it as a state desirable for me. I have had my lesson, Aunt Rachel."

Rachel Hall held her peace; the unshed tears in those clear eyes told their own story; had John Stonebridge proved faithless? or unworthy? Rachel never knew; yet Sybil was but repeating Delia Pratt's experience. So strong was the influence of religion in those days, so stringent its demands on its professors, that to marry an unbeliever was to give sure proof to the church and the world that the professed Christian so transgressing, had no part nor lot in the church, and must either be dealt with and brought to open confession and repentance, or cut off from communion and fellowship with the elect. It was in fact a contempt of the spiritual courts. But Sybil, daughter of the reverend and godly Parson Staltonstall, of Long Neck, and niece of Governor Stanley, a man as pious as he was profound in learning, at once a pillar of Church and State, was trained up from very infancy in the straitest fashion of her time, and sect. The Westminster Catechism had been ground into her brain and soul from early childhood; she knew whole chapters in the Bible by heart; she had experienced religion in a marked and wonderful manner at the age of fourteen, and her walk and conversation were those of the very elect.

Who could discern in this beautiful saint that burning enthusiasm of nature, that lofty pride, that stifled ambition, that strength of passion overborne by greater strength of will, that might have made her a canonized saint and martyr of the Romish church; or, undisciplined and unguided, the empress of a great nation, herself great in sin and tyrannous in power as Messalina, or Cleopatra, or Elizabeth of England?

Perhaps John Stonebridge instinctively recognized in this girl the elements he could best understand, suppressed as they were by education and principle; certain it is that he made himself inexpressibly interesting to Sybil by appealing to springs of thought and action that she had scarcely known in herself. But when he sank from the theoretic talk of politics, travel, and such literature as was fit to talk of to a damsel of that day, and implored her with stormy bursts of passion to "make him happy," with her heart and hand, Sybil recoiled. His oaths of love and constancy, his beaming eyes, his ardent countenance, appalled her, for they shook the citadel within, and thrilled her with the consciousness that she could love him even as he swore he loved her, — madly, blindly, better than heaven itself. But her heart was resolute as fervid, and her faith like the rocks of her birthplace; she held no parley with this besieger; she gave his troop no entrance; all her lifelong principles swarmed to the rescue.

"No," she said, rising from the tall chair where she sat, as if it had been a throne, and she dismissing a traitor; "I cannot answer you, Colonel Stonebridge, in the way you desire. I can marry no man who is not a godly man, and one who walketh in righteousness."

John Stonebridge muttered a sharp oath as he looked at her pale, resolute countenance.

"So you would turn me out to pasture among the goats forever, because I bleat not like a sheep?" he said, with haughty scorn. "Seemeth to me, beautiful Sybil, you godly ones mete out hard measure to us who are astray in the wilderness."

"It is the measure of God," answered Sybil, gravely. "Doth not Scripture say, 'How can two walk together, except they be agreed?' and is it not so according to the wisdom of this world?"

"But how know you that I might not learn of you to walk in that straight way?" he said; for that face before him grew more and more beautiful as contending emotions swept across it as cloud shadows across a limpid lake, and his whole nature longed with almost uncontrollable passion to make this stately beauty return his devotion. Sybil looked away from him; over the outer fields of spotless snow, the sky arched blue and clear; she looked up into heaven for help against herself; had John Stonebridge known it, that moment had for him one frail hope of victory; her heart pleaded for his specious argument, her soul refused it; old, well-known words, repeated over and over so often with so little knowledge of their awful need and meaning flashed across her doubtful thought: "Lead us not into temptation, deliver us from evil." A spasm of agony, a look of stern strength, in turn passed across her expressive face.

"I may not do evil that good may come; else were my damnation just, according to the word of the Lord."

"So I am to take *my* damnation at your hands! Well, beautiful saint; save your own soul, and send me to the devil if you will; but, hark ye! you throw aside a bliss you know not of, a rapture you will taste not again: for, Sybil, had you listened to your woman's heart instead of your Puritan conscience, I would — for I could — have made you more blessed than the angels you dream of, or the heaven you strive so hardly to earn."

Sybil shuddered; she could endure those blazing eyes, those bitter, godless words no longer; she turned away and left him without a word. Swearing savagely, John Stonebridge left the house, his sword clattering on the high stone steps, as he ran down to the river-edge, flung himself into his waiting boat, and was rowed out to the British sloop riding at anchor in the river, just ready to sail for New York with her load of peltry.

Sybil went up to her chamber, and, locking the door, flung herself on the floor in a tempest of agony;

what words shall ever tell the strife of passion and principle that can rack such a woman's heart with all but mortal torture? She knew John Stonebridge had spoken true in that last scoff. Every fibre of her nature cried out for him as the crown and complement of her natural life; all the waves and billows of pain, doubt, loss, of thwarted love, and denied passion, tossed her as if by torrid hurricanes on a raging ocean; but her will held firm, a mighty cable; and her anchor was caught in the clefts of a rock. "It was right! it was right," sung the howling storm, and that one echo kept her soul alive. Was it strange that she should tell Rachel Hall that she had " had her lesson?"

Martyrdom is grand, but the martyr suffers; his flesh and blood are even as ours, my brethren; fire can burn them and steel wound, just as we are burned and wounded; and the exaltation of soul that supports unto death, would not, does not, always last through a lifetime; it is the slow martyrdoms of living that earn the surest psalms, and vindicate most effectively the faith of those who endure to the end.

Esther Dennis could not have done this; she had not the moral stamina or the spiritual training of Sybil Saltonstall; with her, love would still be "lord of all" in whatever guise it came. She was a typical woman, full of tender, unhesitating devotion, of absorbing love; of selfless sacrifice; if in her nature there was that touch of earth called passion it was so slight, so pure, so unconscious, that its reign would be brief and bright, never tempestuous; but her devoted affection could never be chilled or alienated so long as it was cherished or returned.

When Philip came back to Trumbull shortly after Sybil's return, he could not but be touched by the undisguised delight Esther innocently showed in her welcome. No man could have looked coldly on those lovely glowing dark eyes, that speaking face lit with tender joy, or refrained from holding in warm clasp those trembling little hands, so soft, so clinging, so exquisitely feminine in touch and tint. Philip was flattered and therefore moved; it was a tribute to his own good qualities, his charms, his character, all this devoted feeling, and it amused and pleased him; how could he help enjoying it? He even so far forgot his ordinary policy that coming upon Esther that soft May evening, as she sat alone with her happiness on the porch, gazing at the stars through the screen of honeysuckle, and thinking only of Philip, he sat down beside her on the bench, put his arm around her, lifted the drooping head and pressed on those sweet, pure lips a long, loving kiss; the first that had ever touched their cool crimson from the lips of man.

There was silence after that; Esther's dreams had culminated; rapture laid its spell upon speech; she could not speak; Philip would not.

To her that kiss was a solemn betrothal; innocent as a baby in its cradle, she thought no man would kiss a woman he did not mean to marry, and in accepting that caress she felt that Philip had asked her to be his wife and she had consented; her soul was hushed with bliss, her heart at rest forever. Poor child! she had yet to learn that earth has no forever.

As for Philip he was pleased too; such an easy triumph was quite to his taste; no fuss, no resistance, no coyness; evidently, she liked it and so did he. "*On n' arrête pas dans un si beau chemin,*" and after that, Esther's moonlight walks with Philip were marked with long pauses in the shadows of the great pines on the point, or beside the rocks of the cliff, where, with her head on her shoulder, and his kisses on her face, she seemed to drink her fill of that cup which all mortals pine for with the thirst of desperation, but only a few taste, and still fewer drain to its bitter dregs. That Philip said nothing of a future together, made no plans of life, called her no tenderer name than "dear Esther," counted for nothing to Esther's simplicity; she had read no novels, even Clarissa Harlow and Sir Charles Grandison being "conspicuous by their absence" from her uncle's library; and ignorant as innocent, she took it for granted that Philip meant to marry her.

And perhaps he would have done so had her trust in him been less implicit, her love less easy to win, more difficult of expression; but just now he took the sweetness of the present moment with a sense of irresponsibility delightful to his selfish soul; and she basked in that "glory of the sun" that does now and then illuminate even "the uncertain glory of an April day," and asked of life nothing more.

CHAPTER VIII.

AT MIDNIGHT.

> Evening never wore
> To morning, but some heart did break!

AFTER Sybil had come back to her old quiet life in the governor's mansion, she began to long for her dead mother. Beautiful Sybilla Stanley had become the mother of three children during her marriage with Priest Saltonstall, but her two boys died in early infancy, and all her motherly heart had been lavished on Sybil. It is true she tried her best to conceal this affection from its object; stern counsellors warned her that she would love her child too much; her creed bade her beware of making earthly idols, lest they should be broken in the shrine by a jealous God, who would be first in the hearts of his creatures, and demanded a sacrifice of natural affection as the only propitiation of his favor; but mother-love is too powerful, too possessing, to be hid or stifled. Sybil knew, as well as if she had been fed with caresses and fond words, how her mother loved her; that is, as well as a child can know; for who that has not felt it can ever know the abundant patience, the selfless devotion, the all-forgiving, all-enduring, fervent love of a mother? He who made it the symbol of his own affection in the pathetic words, "As one whom his mother comforteth, so will I comfort you," alone can fathom it. But when her daughter was twelve years old, a sharp fever, bred of the sun-smitten swamps about Long Neck, assailed Mrs. Saltonstall so suddenly and fiercely, with such delirium and exhaustion, that the physician, called in as soon as he could be found, had no hope of her life from the first look. She died, unconscious and speechless, with no farewell for husband or child, and broken-hearted Sybil was taken home to Connecticut by her Uncle Stanley; for her father could not look upon that fair face, the very likeness of his lost wife, or bear to hear the passionate sobs that pierced even the solemn gloom of the study, where he sat with his head on his hands, striving by prayer and fasting to conquer the rebellious grief that cried out to God and against Him, "Why hast thou done this?"

There, in the stillness of that lonely house, he lived for years, while Sybil found a home at her Uncle Stanley's; there, he died suddenly and alone, one hand clasping a miniature of his wife, the other resting on his open Bible, when Sybil was seventeen; not much to her loss, for he had been absorbed in his duties before her mother's death, and, though he never acknowledged it, he had also resented all those years the fact that this girl had lived and his boys both died. And when his wife left him, he lost all; neither prayer, nor fasting, nor hard work, nor devotion to his duties, availed to reconcile him to that loss. When his faithful servant found him sitting cold and dead at his study table, his hand on that open Bible, she bent with superstitious curiosity to see where that stiffened and bony index finger pointed on the sacred page. It had stopped its slow progress at these words of Job, —

"Know now that God hath overthrown me, and compassed me with his net.

"Behold I cry out of wrong, but I am not heard; I cry aloud, but there is no judgment.

"He hath fenced up my way that I cannot pass, and he hath set darkness in my paths.

"He hath stripped me of my glory, and taken the crown from my head."

Words that Sybil in her present stress of soul might also have made her own, for she inherited from her father that combatant strength of spirit, that stern judgment, and that reserve, which were his chief characteristics; somewhat modified in his daughter by her feminine organization, and that mental difference of the sexes as certain and ineradicable as their physical variation.

So, all alone in this small world of Trumbull, quite unable to tell her trouble to any one, Sybil set herself to fight out her battle with life. Perhaps, in time, she might have shown so much of her heart to Rachel Hall as to receive from her counsel and consolation, but Rachel after years of patient suffering began to fail, and was obliged to see fewer people than ever, and to talk but very little; the subtle and remorseless disease that had cramped and distorted her limbs and joints, now attacked her slow-beating heart, and she became subject to shortness of breath, faintness, and a dreadful exhaustion at times, from which it was hard to rally.

Still, she gave one short utterance of help and strength to Sybil, for her eyes were clearer than ever now to perceive the need of those she loved, and her heart clave to Sybil more strongly than ever as she saw the darkness of sorrow in her lucent eyes, its rigidity on that fair young face that had been so played upon by every fancy and feeling

"That you might almost say her body thought."

The last time that Sybil stood beside her, looking at the pure outline of that pain-worn countenance with a peace past all understanding on its wan lineaments, and a glow of unearthly love shining in the great sapphire eyes, Rachel took the girl's hand in her slender fingers and whispered, —

"Bear ye one another's burdens, and so fulfil the law of Christ."

The words entered Sybil's ear only, but afterward they found a place in her heart and life; she discovered that her sole escape from the cruel hunger that consumed her, was in sharing and alleviating the woe about her; for her own sorrow there was no relief, for her no solace in all time; she too had yet to learn that earth has no forever. That same day, to that same bed of death, came Esther; her hands filled with late roses, her face shining with the great joy of her heart, a creature full of life, love, and the glory of youth's vast beatitude. As she stood by Rachel Hall, the two showed like a rich red rose in the garden that glows and blooms in splendid pride beside a smitten lily drooping to its grave. To her Rachel had also a whispered message; though it were the word of the Lord, it smote almost cruelly on Esther's ear, as she stooped to gather its broken accents, —

"The world passeth away and the lusts thereof, but he that doeth the will of God abideth forever."

Solemn words, like the knell and echo of a passing bell; words that would return to her like the long, melancholy, vibrating thrill of that bell, when she too should have "had her lesson" as well as Sybil. Only two nights after, Aunt Ruthy woke Parson Hall and called him to Rachel, for at midnight there was a cry made : "Behold the bridegroom cometh, go ye out to meet him."

And when Philemon looked at his wife he recognized the Presence, and his heart sank within him.

But Rachel was tranquil as a summer's dawn; the lines of pain were gone, her face was lit with a celestial smile. Deeper still would Philemon's heart have sunk had he known how Rachel welcomed this hour. Lying there, helpless and useless, as she thought, all these years (for, few in number, they had seemed a lifetime to her), she had learned slowly what she had not been to her husband; how utterly useless as a wife; how great a burden on his position, his means, his affection; and while she admired, respected, and loved him better every day for his patience and tenderness, for the wonderful delicacy that never by word or look showed weariness or regret, for the devout and heartfelt religion that had taught and comforted her own dismayed and doubting soul; she knew that her death would release him from an unnatural bondage, a heavy weight of care, and leave him free to live the full life of a happy man, the husband of some sweet, capable, woman, the head of a Christian household. Had there been any hope of recovery held out to her, she might never have arrived at this saintly attainment, but no physician had ever enlarged her prospect this side the grave, and with unspeakable pangs, continual prayers, tears that moistened her pillow, and that strong crying of the soul that has "no speech nor language," whose "voice is not heard," she had wrestled with the longings of the natural heart for life and love, the terror of death and the grave, the doubts and fears of a noble spirit hampered by suffering flesh, and at last prevailed. Now her reward was at hand! Never in this world would she know that her life had been a spiritual training to Philemon Hall of invaluable service; the stringent circumstances that enforced on him self-denial, self-restraint, that led him up into a mountain-top, even if it brought to him temptation, had so strengthened his soul, so inured it to the strait and narrow way, so caused him to endure hardness, that he had grown to be a good soldier in the Lord's army, and gathered to himself a power and persistence of character that an ordinary experience of life could never have given him. It was to her unconscious ministry that he owed also a diviner patience than commonly falls to man: her unfailing sweetness, her gentleness that was not the result of a feeble nature, but that strong gentleness that comes of seeing things from the standpoint of absolute faith and long-tried love of God, her simple, sublime endurance of pain that might have daunted a martyr, all these had wrought within him a pity and an awed admiration that made him ashamed at his own impulses of perversity or petulance.

"If this weak, tortured woman can smile and be calm, shall not I, a man, think shame of myself if I am quick of spirit with any who sin or suffer?" was the voice of his thought, and she who considered herself the clog and cross of this man's life was truly his greatest blessing, his guide and helper. Would the first breath of that other life reveal to her this reality? Would it be the earliest rapture of heaven to know that she had been a real ministering spirit to her husband?

Certainly she knew it not now, as Philemon knelt beside her, and took her burning, transparent hand in his; her only thought was of and for him; her strength and joy a union of her pure delight in his unfettered future, and a longing to be free herself and forever with the Lord.

Yet, as she looked at that head bowed down beside her, one last pang of human affection rent her spirit;

the actual, the visible, the long-accustomed life and love sent a mighty wave of regret, and a terror of separation over her; Aunt Ruthy saw the tears well up and dim the solemn brightness of her great, pathetic eyes; but then Philemon's troubled, broken voice arose in prayer.

"Oh, Lord, Thou hast been our dwelling-place in all generations. Before the mountains were brought forth, . . . from everlasting to everlasting, Thou art God!"

He broke down then; to him, as to his race and time, the tenderness and strength of Christ were yet to be revealed; a sort of Theism was their positive faith, while they were theoretically Trinitarian; God the Father, the Judge, the Lord of Hosts was their God; the Friend, the Brother, touched with human infirmities; knowing by His human experience every agony of humanity, every infirmity of the flesh, every woe of the spirit, was yet a dead letter; but Rachel, in the long silences of her sequestered suffering, had been taught of that comforting Spirit who takes of the things of Christ and interprets them to the soul; now, on the stillness her voice arose, clear and sweet, as it had not been heard for many a long month.

"Let not your heart be troubled! Ye believe in God, believe also in Me."

Philemon raised his head, and looked at her; a divine light, a look of glory, a smile that reconciled earth to heaven and said at once farewell and welcome, flashed radiantly across her face; the feeble fingers closed tightly on his, then those wan, white eyelids quivered and drooped, her grasp relaxed, a little fluttering sigh escaped her parted lips, and an awful quietness descended on the delicate, weary lineaments. Rachel Hall had gone home.

CHAPTER IX.

AFTER.

> That voice which I did more esteem,
> Than music in its sweetest key:
> Those eyes which unto me did seem,
> More comfortable than the day;
> Those now by me as they have been,
> Shall never more be heard or seen!

WITH all the strength of soul that he possessed, Philemon Hall nerved himself to preach his wife's funeral sermon. It was not unusual in those days for a minister to do so, though it was not always expected; but he felt that since a sermon was customary, he could not endure the handling of Rachel's character and memory, sacred as they were, by any one who had not known her; and who could know her as he did?

This same delicate instinct made him forbid that any hand but Aunt Ruthy's should prepare that wasted body for the grave, or fold it in its last habiliments; and he himself carried the inanimate shape from the couch that had been her earthly habitation, in his arms, like a sleeping child, and laid it tenderly in the coffin. As he looked at the wan chrysalis, from which the bright, informing spirit had fled, and felt that those loving and lovely eyes would never meet his again with their look of life and sweetness that had always welcomed him; that never again would those set lips smile at his coming, or return his tender words; that this yellow pallor of death could not change to the white transparence of a lily's petal, or that dull gold hair fall in its rich beauty about her face; or the delicate fingers clasp his hand with clinging and faithful affection; the full consciousness that this cold, unanswering shape was not his Rachel smote his inmost soul: but with the blow came healing; the word of the Lord sung a triumphant anthem within his brain: "Awake and sing, ye that dwell in dust; for thy dew is as the dew of herbs, and the earth shall cast out her dead!" And from these words he spoke to those who had gathered in the church to do honor once more to Rachel.

It seemed wonderful to all hearers that Parson Hall could preach with such lofty tranquillity a discourse that was full of appreciation, of tenderness, and of gratitude to his wife; that it should be almost triumphant in its recognition of the fact that she had but arisen from earth to heaven was not so wonderful; it was orthodox and proper that he should so speak; but they had expected that he would weep in a decent manner, that his voice would tremble and his words choke him; the calm deep sadness that stilled both face and voice was not understood. To Sybil it seemed like the renewed tolling of that passing bell which had beaten out on the morning air the news of Rachel's death, so mournful, so unimpassioned, yet so thrilling was his sermon; to Esther, throbbing with youth, love, and incipient passion, it was like the chill of a slow-falling, silent, snowstorm: she asked herself if she were to die if Philip would be so calm, so self-possessed? and felt indignant that even of herself she could ask such a question.

But neither she nor Sybil could fathom the real state of mind in which Mr. Hall preached. It was not a wife whom he had lost, but a suffering saint whose shrine had been in his house; the elusive shadow of his earliest love; the disappointment and the blessing of his life. No pang of thwarted mortal passion rent his soul; no loss of that entire intimacy known to no other relation of life, disturbed him; he mourned as one might who had entertained an angel not unawares, but conscious that its flight upward was a certainty, however it might be delayed. Perhaps Aunt Ruthy felt her loss most deeply; her constant care of the delicate, gentle creature; the motherly love that had grown toward her daily more and more; the continual watch and ward lest even the air should visit her too roughly, or the sun smite her with too fierce heat; all these had lost their occupation, their end and aim; her heart cried out for her charge as a mother's for its baby; and her eyes kept her heart company, as she sat in the front pew and beheld that fair waxen shape lying in its formal shroud below the pulpit, that the congregation might by and by take their last farewell of the minister's wife, whom all spoke well of by report, and whom the few that knew her admired and loved. After the wail and woe of funeral psalm and hymn were over, and the parish had said farewell to that impassive shape for all time, the bearers took up the coffin and bore it to the near graveyard. Even there, beside the yawning earth that was to receive this new dust, Philemon Hall preserved his quiet self-possession, he saw the sods piled above that forsaken body, he implored the usual blessing upon the few spectators, and turned away to his empty home without a sigh, a tear, a quiver of feeling, on his composed countenance.

"Takes it real cool, don't he?" remarked Hiram to old Isaac Bunnell, who shook his grizzled head in dissent.

"You can't allers tell: not allers. There's some water runs dreadful still because its deep; an' some because the' ain't no stun's into it. I mistrust the parson is kinder stunned, as ye may say; same as a hen is when ye ketch it by the legs and swing it round sudden', so's to cut its head off. 'Fliction is kind of curus; it don't hurt nothing, at the fust go off, to what it does come to set down and chaw on't. His hard time is a comin'; he's uplifted now to heaven on the p'int of a privilege, as Domine Witter used to tell, and he don't see nothin' but t'other world; but he's got to come down to the mill-grindin' an' the wood-choppin' of this here mortal state pretty consider'ble quick, and then he'll sense his 'fliction. I've seen 'em before. I saw old Priest Saltonstall when his wife up an' died; I went over there with the coffin; why he was as straight up an down as a rake-tail, an' as hard as a nether mill-stone. Well, come to think on 't, he ain't to the p'int nuther, for he never got over it; I *have* heerd that he couldn't never forgive the Lord for afflictin' of him. I dono as that made any difference to the Lord; but 'twas kind of unpleasant for the parson to feel so, I expect. But there's all sorts of folks in the world, and its no great use to be a studyin' of 'em, an' gabbin' about 'em; I'd ruther hoe corn."

With which brief sentiment Isaac turned on his heel and left Hiram a little confounded; his slow mind had not grasped the train of Isaac's rather desultory remarks.

"What be you a-gawpin' at?" asked Delia, sharply, as she came by him in her usual brisk fashion.

"Well, I was just considerin'."

"Hurry up then, do. I want a lot of oven-wood for to-morrer mornin', and the corn had ought to be hoed right off. Folks have got to go to funerals, I s'pose, and I gener'lly expect to go, but they do take up time!"

Hiram obeyed orders and trotted off; while Delia poured out her soul to a crony, Sophronia Smith by name, ruler and governor in the Stanley kitchen, a mild, stout, easy creature, as different from Delia as a pincushion is from a pin, and just as intimate as those two opposing articles are.

"He's so biddable, Hiram is, that it kinder riles me Sophrony; I hate to see menfolks run an' ride whenever you tell 'em, without a peep or a mutter."

"Mabbe, you'd hate it wuss if they didn't," chuckled Sophronia.

"I dono, I dono. Seems as if I'd ruther be like that blessed cretur we've ben a buryin' of, than to be a bossin' round some man or another! She jest lay there and kep' a prayin' and a smilin', and he done for her; he was the master. I think its natteral for womenfolks to be kind of coddled an' took care of; not to stan' for head of the fam'ly; now Hiram won't never be no head to nobody."

"Don't ye be too sartin, Delye, I ain't real spry myself, but I can see out o' my eyes; men is quite different while they're on the anxious seat, as you may say, from what they be when they've got into the saddle; Hiram is waitin' on you, now, he'll show out what's in him when you get to waitin' on him."

"Hm!" said Delia, "it'll be long days first."

They had reached the Dyer house, and further confidences ceased; for Uncle Dyer called out to Delia to ask where Hiram was, and to give her a message for him, and Sophronia waddled away to the governor's mansion.

These verdicts, unrestrained in their expression by the ties of friendship or the sense of reverence that sealed other lips, were nevertheless the judgment of many another who listened to that sermon; but as time wore on, and Parson Hall's grave face settled into sadder and deeper gravity, his friends began to see that his great loss was greater to him than they had supposed.

He felt more and more how much the presence of a saint like Rachel had been to him; he longed for her wise and tender counsel, for the never-failing comfort of her smile and voice, for the strength wherewith her patience and courage girded up his own soul, and armed him for his daily duties. Yet even in death she blessed him; he could enter into the sorrows of his flock with an actual sympathy that he or they had never before known; his prayers with the sick had a deeper fervor, a more consoling faith than ever; and the pathos, the trust, the tenderness of his funeral services were known beyond his parish, and required by many a mourner as a consolation. Sybil deeply felt her loss in this ever-ready friend; her aunt, the governor's lady was an imperious, strong-willed, proud woman, though she had a large, generous nature, and a heart capable of passionate affection; but she was not sympathetic, and Sybil was not of her blood; she did not try to understand her, and did not enjoy her reserve and pride, so different from her own.

Madam Stanley had a fine lively temper of her own; if things went awry with her she would fling the spoons from the table to the floor, stamp her small foot, tear off her lace cap and fling it into the fire, and indulge in the like vagaries; for which Sybil, with the relentless judgment of a girl, despised her aunt's want of self-control, and made known, by look and manner, her profound contempt for such ill-breeding and vulgar fury. This was not altogether soothing, as may be imagined, to Mrs. Stanley's self-love, and though the strict outward respect for their elders in which young women were educated in that day, prevented any open rupture between Sybil and her aunt, there was no love there, and not the least sympathy. Sybil had spent many an hour by Rachel Hall's bedside, soothed by her tender affection, quieted by her words of counsel and love, and never had she needed that rest and strength more than now, when it failed her; she recoiled into herself, fought her battle alone and silently, with an aching heart and a resolved soul, and became a woman before her real girlhood had passed.

Esther, too, missed Rachel; something as we all regret a beautiful creature, who recalls to us the fact that there is a sphere of loftier intellect and purer souls, than that in which we move, but her strongest feeling was for Mr. Hall; in the fulness of her own life and love she could measure what his loss might be; she had forgiven him the manful self-restraint of his sermon, now that his sad visage demonstrated that he did really feel that loss, and she showed in the softened look of her dark eye, and the delicate consideration of her voice and manner toward him, that she sorrowed for him.

Now, too, she was beginning to have her own troubles; Philip was called away oftener on business than ever before, and when alone with her he was too often moody, abstracted, perhaps petulant. If she asked him in the gentlest manner what ailed him, he made a sharp or evasive answer. The thorns of this rose-wreath began to fret poor Esther, who was so dazzled with the garland she had not reckoned with the nature of roses. Nor did he, though lavish of secret caresses and soft words, make any open or positive avowal of a desire to marry her; she lived in a real fool's paradise, conscious of the paradisaic part, but not of the folly; and he played with her as with a toy, that having been somewhat enjoyed has ceased to have the charm of freshness, and is a matter of course, but only a toy at that.

Besides this, Uncle Dyer was not well; he had, in the midst of that summer's brightness and bloom, a slight shock of paralysis; it was only a few days of confusion and trembling, a few weeks of one languid hand and arm, one drooping eye, and he was himself again; but he knew that he had received his first warning, and with quiet, Christian courage he accepted it.

More than ever was he tender to Esther, but he rarely spoke of Philip, who had gone to New York to attend to the business there.

Some anxiety, unexpressed, yet painful, seemed to occupy his mind; and after a week or two he sent for Squire Peters, the village lawyer, and had a long interview with him. Two days after, the squire came again, and his son was with him. Parson Hall was with Mr. Dyer, and remained during the interview. All the family but Esther knew very well what this meant, but she was always and ever dreaming of Philip, longing and waiting for his return; the present condition of things about her was vague, and did not interest her; so they all waited, and held their peace.

CHAPTER X.

FRAUD.

How many things which for our own sake we should never do, do we perform for the sake of our friends.

AT last the blow fell. One cool August day, Uncle Dyer was found on the library floor, speechless, motionless, and unconscious. The doctor was called in haste, Delia and Hiram lifted Mr. Dyer on to his bed in the next room, and Mrs. Dennis took charge of him.

Hitherto a silent, sad, reticent woman, devoted to her simple duties in the household, and undemonstrative to a painful degree, the widow now stepped into the place she could best fill. With a sudden development of faculties long kept in abeyance, she proved that her one talent was that of nursing. She took possession of this patient, and ruled over him and his room with a steady judgment and strict care of detail that seemed incredible to the rest of the family.

"It beats all!" said Delia, confidentially to Hiram. "I'd always giv' her credit for bein' as near nobody as the Lord allows human creturs *to* be, and lo, you! she's got the skercest kind.o' faculty. I've always considered that I could do a'most anything I turned my hand to, but I couldn't no more fix up that bed-charmber the way she doos it, nor keep things there so still, an' cool, an' handy, than I could fly."

"Well, now, I bet you could, Delye. *I* never see nothin' yet but what was nateral to you to do, ef you undertook it; and to do it up real well."

"Oh, sho! you go long!"

But the smile that curled Delia's decided lips, and the quick color on her cheek, denied the repellent words.

Poor feminine nature! a little shining chaff deludes it better than any dull handful of solid grain!

Aunt Ruthy, too, gave in her adhesion to Delia's opinion, when at Mr. Hall's request she had been up to the Dyer house to offer any help she could give.

"I found I couldn't do a thing, Mr. Hall. Mis' Dennis has got everything just right; after all these years I've been out a nursing, I couldn't find a fault. Its wonderful! wonderful! If the poor man could take notice, he would like it. Clean as a pantry, an' tidy as a parlor, that room is; and no more noise in 't than a spider makes spinnin' her web. But I don't like his looks; he lies like a log, and his face has got a kind of purplish shade to it that isn't what it had ought to have, not by no means! I don't believe he'll ever get up."

"I think so myself, Miss Ruthy. I fear not; he has already over-lived the allotment of man, — three-score years and ten. We have no reason to expect recovery at that age; it is but borrowed time, at best, that lies before him."

Aunt Ruthy looked up at the minister as he said this; stalwart, erect, with health shining in his dark eyes, and vigor expressed in every motion and attitude; not yet beyond the half of those years he was pleased to call man's "allotted" time, because David spoke of it as the average length of life. She, who was old enough to be his mother, thought how easy it was for youth to point out the limitations of age; and while her busy fingers knit away at a pair of blue yarn stockings, her mind, like a veritable woman's, went over all the possibilities included in Uncle Dyer's probable death. What would become of Mrs. Dennis and Esther? She knew that Mr. Dyer had made a will quite lately, for Mr. Hall had been called in to witness it, and mentioned the fact to Aunt Ruthy as a reason for being late that day to dinner. He had done the same service for Mr. Dyer once before, soon after Mrs. Dyer's death, before Esther and her mother came to Trumbull; so it was a fair inference in Aunt Ruthy's opinion, that the later will had been made in order to provide for these relatives; for she had read in Uncle Dyer's face the strong affection he had learned to feel for Esther; though, like his race and his time, he never expressed it in words. But what would Philip say, thought this wise old woman, to any division of the inheritance with these new-found relatives.

She did not even consider the idea that his interests and Esther's might be one, for she had no faith in him either as friend or lover; in the course of her long and observant life she had seen too many of his type, the sort that "loves and rides away," not to recognize it easily; indeed it was one of this kind who had shipwrecked her life, in her early youth, when she, like Esther, had loved, with a devotion that knew no limits, and a passion that rejoiced in self-sacrifice, a man who had lied to and deserted her. She had spent an ordinary lifetime in remorse, humility, service, and regret; yet to-day she shuddered as, recalling the past, she foreboded Esther's future.

Esther herself was as unhappy as a dreamer in a vision of bliss could be made by exterior things; she loved her uncle, and she was grieved to lose the comfort of his kind face and steady, friendly voice, but she was so little experienced in sickness that she did not feel his danger, or consider his death as possible, and old Doctor Parker did not even tell Mrs. Dennis his real opinion of the case.

"I trust he'll rally, ma'am! yes, oh yes. The vital forces are, as you may say, in — ah, — yes, in retirement, ma'am. The mass of his mortality is not really affected ser'ously; no ma'am. We must look for a rally; yes, yes, a rally. Let me know when there is a change. Good-day, good-day."

And this oracular utterance was all he vouchsafed to the women of the family. To Parson Hall he was more confiding. Esther had forgotten in Philip's absence, as she always did forget when he was not with her, the little troubles of his recent conduct; and she was full of joy when she heard from Mr. Hall that he was expected home at once, for he had now been absent six weeks. She did not know that Dr. Parker had ordered his return. Nor was she perfectly happy when he came; beyond his natural grief and consternation, there was a hurried apprehension in his manner, an excitement, an evident distress, that disturbed her; he was perhaps more affectionate than ever when they were alone, but that subtle and defensive instinct which is a solitary woman's only aid in matters of the heart, warned her dumbly that he was thinking of something beside her and her love, even amid his caresses. After a day or two had passed, during which Uncle Dyer's condition had not changed at all, Philip said it was needful that he should go out to Long Beach farm to see about some sheep he had sent there from New York, and asked Esther to ride with him. It was a lovely day; warm, tranquil; the sky pure in its lofty azure, only flecked here and there by a soft, white cloud, floating, like the thistledown that imitated it below, in a silvery silence; the lanes were full of the perfume a hot day in August beguiles from odorous pine boughs, spiked clethra blossoms, aromatic bushes of sweetbriar and bayberry, the tips of red cedar, and the last water lilies that linger in shady pools among the swamps of the shore country. Yet soothing as the air, the quiet landscape, the distant murmur of the sea all were, Esther felt an indefinite uneasiness; for Philip was silent, his face gloomy, his eyes fixed on some distant point that yet he seemed not to perceive, and his brows knitted and scowling. After a speechless drive of two or three miles, Esther could not bear the stillness between them any longer; she laid her hand gently on her lover's arm.

"Philip," she said, with the most timid sweetness "What is it? can I help?"

Philip turned round and throwing his arm about her pressed her to his side with sudden violence.

"Esther! I am out of myself with apprehension, You know that I have always been brought up as Uncle Dyer's heir. After my aunt's death he re-made the will that had left his property to her, and made it in my favor; but of late he has been somewhat disaffected towards me; I have not made money so fast as he would have me; there have been certain liabilities overdue by men whom I have trusted, that he was displeased about; and this Parson Hall hath gotten his ear, and set his mind earnestly toward building a new meeting-house here, as I am well informed, a matter that will deprive me of more than half the property, and cripple me for years.

"Do not think, my girl, that I care so much for the money alone, but it will mar my future fatally; how can I bear to put off for years the home I desire? How can I ask any woman's hand, when I must bring her to poverty?"

Esther could have answered this question with all her heart: Philip in poverty would be even dearer to her than with such riches that she could not help or serve him; but maidenly reserve sealed her lips; she only blushed to her temples, and said, —

"Are you sure, Philip, that Uncle Dyer has made a will?"

"Yes; Abner Peters, the squire's son, was an old crony of mine, and for some reason owes me a grudge. I met him in the street t'other day, and he flung it at me that the squire had made a will for my uncle that cut me off with a shilling. And was not the squire closeted with my uncle but a short time before this sickness."

"Yes," said Esther.

"And was not Parson Hall there, and Ab Peters fetched in as well?"

"Yes, yes; I remember it well. Delia spoke of it when I was sealing up plum conserve in the kitchen. I thought no more of it, but now I do remember that she said Squire Peters was with Uncle Dyer, and she mistrusted 'twas about his last will, and she liked it not, for it foreboded death."

"But too well! and here is death at hand; the old meeting-house is still strong, it needeth but small repair, I would take that in hand myself; but, Esther, can you wonder that I am a desperate man so to be cut off from my life's best hope by the devices of a man like Priest Hall, who hath as much of a man's life as a fence-post in his saintly body and cramped soul!"

It never occurred to Esther, as her lover stooped and

kissed her under the shadow of her broad-leafed hat, that it was odd he should know the contents of Uncle Dyer's will so well, when it was made so short a time before the paralytic stroke which set its seal on heart and lips alike; she knew nothing, thought of nothing but Philip and his loss; she was in that condition of existence when a girl's heart and soul are so merged in the lover she worships, that reason is in abeyance, and common sense drugged to sleep; whatever Philip chose to tell her she believed, and he, used to this stage of passion in his various experiments, perfectly comprehended the situation.

He went on, with a voice full of eager longing and pain. "Oh! if I could but know that unjust will were destroyed! If I could but feel it were cancelled by fire and scattered to the winds of heaven, I could once more be happy! And well I know it would be Uncle Dyer's wish, if he could listen to what I have to tell him. I had just arrived at the end of my endeavor, just gotten ready to come up and explain to him the difficulties I had at last surmounted, and absolve myself from any shadow of blame, when I was summoned, and behold he is practically dead, and I can never, never, be righted!"

Esther's eyes filled with tears; she clasped his hand more closely: "Oh Philip!" she said, "it is a shame! it is too, too hard. Could I but help you!"

"You! little mouse!" said Philip, with a sad smile, Esther caught the allusion.

"But a mouse did gnaw the lion's net, you know!"

she said, softly. Philip was silent; he had planted the thought he meant to, in her mind; now, how should he quicken its germination ?

But Esther thought only of him and the injustice he suffered. She was so lost to all things but Philip; so ready to sacrifice all she held dearest to his pleasure, that it was well for her his selfish soul was too considerate of his future, his position, and his purposes, to allow him to be swept away by passion as better men have sometimes been in like circumstances, and so shipwreck Esther's life for his own transient gratification. It is true that religion teaches us that sin is sin, whatever be its name or manifestation, but there are gradations of sin in the world's eyes, and some that in a woman are unpardonable. But Esther was an innocent girl, just now carried beyond the domain of ethics or religion; to her soul one sin ranked with another, and she forgot all other considerations in her absorbing desire to do what would serve or save her lover, whatever it might be.

She said no word to him of her thought or intention, but from that hour her soul was set on the one purpose of getting at that latest will, and destroying it before Uncle Dyer's death.

She was more silent than Philip all the rest of their drive, and he very well understood the reason. When those dark, passionate eyes sought his now and then, with a look of utter devotion and sympathy that touched even his worldly and scheming heart, or her cool, soft lips quivered under the long pressure of his as he bent his head to her's in the fragrant shadow of the forest road, Philip Kent knew as well as if he read it in fiery letters on that twilight sky above them, that Esther would risk her very soul to save him the wealth he so coveted, and it cost even him a slight struggle to cast aside the intrusive idea of releasing her from the unspoken vow he felt she had made. Yet it was but a momentary idea; he clasped her in his arms as they entered the loveliest part of their homeward way, kissed her passionately again and again, and as she lifted her languid eyes and burning face from his bosom, he felt he had fully rewarded her; and she felt ready to die — or live — for him.

CHAPTER XI.

DONE.

> What plea, so tainted and corrupt,
> But, being seasoned with a gracious voice,
> Obscures the show of evil?

FROM that day on, Esther spent her time in devising how to get that obnoxious will and destroy it; she was so new to deception or scheming, so innocent of evil design, yet so impressed with the need of secresy for Philip's sake, for he had over and again insinuated into her mind that not for the world would *he* possess himself of the document, since to do so would in itself (if found out) be fatal to his character and his future; that she lay awake at night and pondered by day on this purpose, until she was utterly absorbed in ways and means.

Still Uncle Dyer lay senseless; Dr. Parker had said that the case was hopeless; that life might flicker up for a moment at the end, and consciousness return, but it would still be the end of life, and probably come about the tenth day; and time had crept on for a whole week, yet Esther had not got the will.

But on the eighth day came that opportunity that evil always fetches to those who traffic with its forces; Mrs. Dennis was seized with a sudden attack of illness, prostrating but not dangerous, and Esther was called to her place at Uncle Dyer's bedside for the day.

It was Delia's washing-day, but she left her tubs to see that Mrs. Dennis was bestowed safely in her bed, and her present needs provided for; then she looked in on Esther with an admonition, whispered but peremptory: "She's all right upstairs; don't you get in a swivet about her; I've giv' her some ros'-berry leaf tea, an' put a hot flat to her feet. You just set still alongside of him, and keep a wettin' his lips with that slipp'ry ellum tea in the mug; that's all the poor cretur needs; he dono nothin', an' he can't say nothin'. I do dread a shockanum palsy myself, dreadfully; seems as though it made folks just like them cherubs on the tombstones in the yard, all outside as you may say; neither live nor dead, *they're* dead I s'pose, but they look kind of lively, an' he don't.

"Well, you keep the lib'ry fire up, Esther; it's kind of damp on this floor after the rain; and jest lock the door so's nobody won't come in suddin. I ain't real certin sure but what he's a mite nervy, if he don't show it, and anyway sick folks had ought to be kept as quiet as the law allows."

So Delia, unconscious *aide-de-camp* of the evil one who stood at Esther's side, shut the door gently and creaked back down the stair to her washing.

Now was Esther's time! she felt it with a thrill of mingled satisfaction and terror; she carefully wet Uncle Dyer's parched lips, half closed the door into the library, locked that through which Delia had passed, and softly opening the door of a little cupboard above the mantel, took from a nail under the shelf, Uncle Dyer's keys.

Well she knew where he kept them, for many and many a time she had mounted in that same red moreen-cushioned chair and opened that very same cupboard over the fireplace to get him the keys, which he never carried in his pocket for fear of losing them, as the locks were intricate and he had no duplicates.

Esther shut the cupboard, and clasping the keys tightly lest they should rattle, stepped down from the chair; she selected first the key of the secretary, a tall piece of old cherry-wood furniture on four slender claw-footed legs, with a desk front, and a book closet above that, surmounted by an odd and clumsy cornice with a curving ornament in the middle; the upper doors were locked, there stood Mr. Dyer's ledgers, and on the shelves above were bundles of bills, filed and receipted; with these Esther had nothing to do; she only unlocked the desk, and let the front down on to two supports which she drew out from the sides of the secretary for that purpose; just then a sudden noise startled her; her hands trembled, and a quick throb at her heart sent the blood all over her face; she held her breath and listened; the noise was outside, Philip had closed the barn door hastily; she stepped to the window and saw him mount his iron-gray horse, and ride off; his face was dark and gloomy as the gathering northeast storm that filled the sky above him, and howled with doleful presage about the old house.

That woful face gave Esther fresh courage; she hastened back to the desk, applied the little key on the ring to a keyhole hidden under a brass ornament which she had pushed aside, and a secret drawer flew open. There lay two folded sheets of parchment side by side.

On each was written in Uncle Dyer's flowing hand, "My Laste Wille & Testament"; but one bore a date of several years before, the other of a fortnight since; there was no doubt of the matter, this last was the will her poor Philip so dreaded.

An older, wiser, or less pre-occupied person than Esther would naturally have asked herself why the older will was preserved; in fact the answer to that question lay folded in the new one, in the shape of a sealed letter to Philip: a letter never to be seen or read, whatever might be its contents. But she was too full of joy at her success to think of anything but that she had achieved her end; she locked the secret drawer carefully, and closed and locked the desk, pushing in its supports with needless caution, for the only ear to hear them creak was sealed with a pressure close as the numbness of death; then she mounted into the chair again, hung up the keys in their place, turned the button on the closet door, stepped down, and carefully shook up the red cushion that bore the mark of feet upon it, moved the chair away, and then thrust that obnoxious will right under the great hickory log that smouldered above a bed of coals in the library fireplace. A cloud of bitter smoke, a sudden crackling, a burst of bright flame, and Philip was righted!

Uncle Dyer's calm face looked down from the wall, where he was depicted sitting at that very desk in his Sunday suit, a pen in one hand, the other resting on a parchment scroll, his dark eyes emphasized by the powdered hair above them, and his firm lips and broad brow as nearly like life as oil and canvas can reproduce humanity when a skilful artist uses them.

Did those grave eyes really glow with indignation and reproach? or was it but the reflection of that sharp flame that flickered on the portrait?

Esther returned to the bedside, and again from the long-necked silver dish that held a little liquid, and was made and used only for this office, she dropped a few drops of the odorous potion on the invalid's hot and dry lips; was there any expression in those half-shut eyes that she trembled so as she bent above them?

What if all this time he were conscious, had heard her and suspected her?

She shuddered, and instinctively went back to the library to make sure her work was done; there was a rank and breathless smell in the room, a smell she knew came from that burnt parchment; there was sure betrayal in the odor; what could she do to prevent it?

On the mantelpiece stood two large blue vases; only a little while before, she had filled them with branches of cedar from a bluff above the shore where she and Philip had often sat together, listening to the crushed whisper of the sea below, as it threw its waves of crested beryl sharply up the beach, and then hissed backward, dragging with it shells and pebbles that clashed together and rasped the sand beneath them into smoothness.

The branches were misty blue with their fragrant berries, and well dried by the heated air of the room; she seized them from the vases and flung them on the fire; a quick flash followed, then a dull but heavy roar; Esther knew well what it meant, she had set the soot that had accumulated in the chimney on fire.

Really there was no danger, but she was excited and unstrung; the nervous tension that had upheld her gave way, she threw up the window and shrieked to Delia, whose tubs stood in the shed between the kitchen and woodhouse, by an open door.

"O Delia! Delia! come quick! the chimney's burning!"

"Well, what if 'tis?" calmly answered Delia, lifting her hands from the suds and wiping them on her apron. "Don't get so scared Esther. I'll come right along up," and in another moment she had run upstairs.

"Sure enough! how come it to blaze up so?"

"Oh I put those cedar branches on; there wasn't much fire; I didn't think; I"—

"Why, child, tisn't nothing; you're as nervy as a settin' hen. I *should* ha' thought you'd known better than to fling red cedar on top of a fire. Land! how it smells! That chimbley had ought to have been burnt out last spring by rights; my! how the sut does come down!"

Esther shivered with excitement, she knew now there was no danger, the northeaster had thickened, first into a driving mist, now into a solid rain that fell in sharp gusts against the house and prevented all danger from burning soot or sparks on the roof; she turned away toward the bedroom, mindful of her office for her uncle; but as she faced the door a stifled cry burst from her lips and startled Delia in her turn.

Uncle Dyer sat bolt upright in the bed, his face darkly flushed and working fearfully in an effort to speak, his eyes full of horror and despair, every vein swollen, and a cold sweat bursting out on his forehead; what had aroused him so, it was idle to inquire; struggle as he might, the palsied tongue refused to obey the yearning desire of the agonized mind; it was the awful and futile revolt of a spirit in prison, and lasted but for a moment, the dark flush, the convulsion of the muscles, the look of anguish passed away like the lurid cloud of a tempest before the south wind, that sweeps those heaped black fleeces from the sky with gentle but forceful breath, and leaves the sunset to its awful peace.

One look of deep affection, a half smile, both for Esther; and then the conquered soul withdrew forever from its battle with the flesh, and Uncle Dyer dropped back, quite dead.

"I never shall think 'twas that burnin' chimbly done it," said Delia, two hours afterward, as she stood by that bed, superintending the offices of two old women who made a business of preparing the dead for burial. "I s'pose his time had come; there's been bigger noises 'n that sence he was took, and he didn't mind 'em no more'n Pharo' King of Egypt; the old apple tree blowed down a week ago in that real severe thunder squall we had, and come bang ag'inst the side o' the house, but he never winked. Esther took on consider'ble; she thought she'd killed him sure, a puttin' on them cedar branches so's to spunk up the fire, and thereby settin' the sut to blazin'; but 'twasn't that!"

"No, no, 'twan't," said the elder crone, shaking her grizzled head, solemnly. "'Twas jest as you say, Miss Pratt, jes' so; his time had come, and when the Lord sees folkses time has come it don't need no airthly cretur's hand to hurry it along; we've all got to be took some time or 'nother, and its good we dono when 'tis."

"Mm," murmured the other, putting her head on one side, like a bird inspecting some doubtful object, "'tis so, certin' sure. Well, Squire Dyer was prepared; he was a good man, and he makes a bewtiful corpse."

A murmur of assent confirmed her remark, and then drawing the sheet up over the sharp, still outlines of the dead, they all withdrew and locked the door upon "the remains." Apt expression! it was indeed only the remainder which the greater part had left; only the worn-out vesture, the frail, broken chrysalis; the cloak that hid even from the nearest and dearest, the integral nature of that vital force it shrouded; why do we honor and adorn it as we do, and speak of the dead as if they slept in the graves we hallow?

Rather, should not it be written above the portals of every graveyard, where Christians leave the dust that must be buried out of sight, the remonstrance of that wiser angel to the wondering disciples, —

"Why seek ye the living among the dead? He is not here, He is risen."

CHAPTER XII.

"L'IMPREVU."

It is always the unexpected that happens.

MRS. DENNIS was worse the next day; she had known that her uncle's state was precarious, but as long as life lasts on earth, the halo of its essential immortality surrounds it; when it really vanishes from the apprehension of sense we are always surprised; for at heart every human being has the infidelity of the Apostle Thomas hidden in some shadowy recess, where it whispers to itself, "I will not believe what I do not see and touch!"

So the widow, already weakened by her illness, received a real shock from the news of her uncle's death; she had arrived at an age when we feel deeply that "blood is thicker than water," and Mr. Dyer was her only surviving relative. It is true, her daughter was left, but Esther had never really understood or intelligently sympathized with her mother; she was too young at her father's death to enter into the full sense of her mother's loss or her own, though she mourned him truly, and with the rebellious passion of early youth; but time and change of scene had really consoled her, and she did not know how the riven heart that had lost its other half, its light, and strength, and joy, still refused to be comforted, still echoed with the sobs she would not utter, and was still overflowed with repressed tears, that her sense of duty and shrinking from demonstration, forbade to fall.

Then Esther had been so absorbed in her mad love for Philip, that she had, with youth's unconscious selfishness, left her mother much to herself, and in this solitude Uncle Dyer had been her companion; beside the crackling fire they had talked together of the past; discussed their losses; recalled those memories that are as fragrant as the dead leaves of an autumnal forest; or, after the fashion of their day, reasoned together concerning theological dogmas, obscure texts in the Scripture; and had insensibly grown nearer to each other thus.

Then like all over-conscientious women, she tormented herself with the idea that she ought not to have left him; forgot the severity of the attack that had forced her to her bed, and felt that a greater effort of will, a little more courage in pain, might have kept her by his side; so her bereft and worried mind preyed on her exhausted body, and she was not able even to give a farewell look at the noble and peaceful face that slept so silently in the darkened room below.

To her Esther's cares were all directed now. She had seen Philip once since her uncle's death, and given him a reassuring look and smile, and a low whisper of "Fear not!" which said much more to his anxious ear; but further communication had been impossible, and he did not seek it; he knew too well that any aspect of unusual confidence or collusion, might be brought up against them both, so he did not even inquire for her before he was obliged to leave; and she spent the three days preceding the funeral in her mother's room.

Mrs. Dennis lay for the most part quite silent; sometimes she watched Esther as she moved about the room, with the sort of dumb yearning one sees in the eyes of a dog; for hers was truly a spirit in prison.

Full of timid, but entire devotion to the very few she loved, she had been taught by her stern religious creed to tremble lest her natural affections should grow into idolatry. She was convinced that for this reason her husband had been taken from her, that she might give to a jealous and angry God the love that had bound itself so utterly to a human being; and when her heart turned to Esther, the living tie that still clasped her to the dead, as a mother's heart naturally would turn, she strictly schooled every thought as well as every utterance of maternal love and longing, lest she too, this lovely and beloved child, should become an "idol." Better that she should die and leave Esther ignorant of her tenderness, than cut short those young days, and jeopard her own hopes of heaven.

Mrs. Dennis was not a reasonable woman, logic was impossible to her sort of mind, or she might and would have asked herself why this God whom she feared had ever implanted within her the power of loving, if it was always to be repressed; or, why he had compared His own tenderness to that of a mother, if her's was blamable.

Now she was forced into close company with Esther; dependent on her for comfort and for society, and her heart yielded itself to that love which has no equal on earth. She dwelt with delight on the noble figure the richly expressive face, the wealth of dark brown hair that in the sun showed its intermingling of deep red threads, and glittered like the shining rind of a new horse-chestnut. She basked in the dream-dimmed affection of the great hazel eyes that were so shy, so beautiful, yet at times so sad; and longed to kiss the exquisite little hands and wrists that fetched her food, lifted her on her pillows, rubbed her tired muscles; or, the taper and rose-tinted fingers that smoothed her gray hair back under the cap border, or fastened the night-dress about her with a gentle deftness, such as a mother might show to a baby. Three days of happiness were hers; even in her grief she could but own their sweetness; then came the funeral. A bountiful table, spread with all the "baked meats" Delia well knew how to furnish for such occasions, was set in the great dining-room for the refection of friends and neighbors. The family and relatives, the minister, and the lawyer, were to sit by the coffin in the bedroom; till such time as one prayer had been made, and then the bearers were to carry the dead to the church for public services there. Esther could not be spared from her mother's side to go so far, but she could not refuse to be present at this prayer; so she tied on a long, black, mourning cloak, and tying its hood above her unpowdered hair, seated herself by the side of a window, and fixing her eyes on the floor, gave herself up to solemn thoughts of death, as was proper.

Her revery was broken by a stir at the door; she knew that Philip had gone to New York on urgent business, directly after her uncle's death; but was expected to be back for the funeral, of course. Secluded in her mother's room, she had not asked if he had returned; but now, as she lifted her head, she saw him come in with a lady on his arm.

Young, beautiful as a statue, with cold blue eyes, and heaped up gold-brown hair; a slight, stiff figure; lips of perfect beauty, but colder in their fixed scarlet curves than even her blue eyes, Esther gazed and wondered at her; saw that she too wore a long, black cloak, and that the little hat poised daintily upon her hair was also black and crape-wreathed; even while she looked at the stranger, Philip's voice, low but distinct, met her incredulous ear as he said to Squire Peters, —

"This lady hath a right of entrance here, sir; she is mine honored wife, the daughter of Peter Stuyvesant, well known to you by reputation, the merchant prince of our goodly city."

Squire Peters bowed low, well he knew the name; but just at that moment Parson Hall entered, and, lifting his hand, solemnly begun the prayer. Afterward, Esther knew why he spared greeting and preamble, and why he pleaded fervently and long for the living who were left alone.

But she heard then no word he uttered; chaos reigned within her; outraged pride; incredulous passion; indignation; despair; all grappled with her soul at once. Hardly was the "Amen" said, when she glided silently from the room by another door than that of the library, where, as well as in the withdrawing room, sat friends from far and near, sorrowing neighbors, and weeping servants; and through Uncle Dyer's tiny dressing-room and a back entryway fled up the kitchen staircase and into her own room.

There, prostrate on the floor, she endured the first onset of an agony that had no outlook, no hope, in its desperate terror; words were vain, prayer idle, palliation impossible, she had the woman's only defence, silent endurance, in itself a horror of great darkness; for to weep, to scream, to beat herself against the stones of the shore and let the fierce water overwhelm her, would have been relief; but as it was she must only endure.

She lay there hour after hour, forgetful of her mother, of her uncle, of all things but one, — that she had lost Philip. Through her window, flung open in an instinctive effort to relieve the breathlessness that her fast-beating heart brought on, she heard from the near meeting-house the wail of the funeral hymns, but only noted them with a sort of relief that they expressed her own desperate, comfortless anguish; when they ceased, her self-control had to be more stringent; but she lay still, silent, solitary, lost in an incredible maze of distress, crushed by an incubus of daylight and reality; powerless to say to herself, "perhaps it is a dream," and loathing with all her soul the perfect, icy face of the woman who had stepped into her place and taken Philip from her arms and her heart. But Esther was still in a world of woes beside her own; she was roused after a time by a light knock on her door; it was a neighbor's child who had been fetched to sit with Mrs. Dennis while Esther attended the prayer.

The exhausted girl slowly rose, and straightened her clothing; she recognized her bitter need of dissimulating courage, and her voice was firm as she said, "What is it, Sally?"

"Oh, come down! do ye now, Esther; I'm all of a tremble. Mis' Dennis she tried for to get up and see out o' the winder, to see the last of him she said, jest as they was goin' to the buryin' ground, and she's fell down, and I can't noway lift her up ag'in."

Esther did not stay to replace her dishevelled hair, but hurried into her mother's room; this new shock did not shake her presence of mind, in fact did not shock her as it would have the day before.

Beside, it brought with it that need for action that

is so wholesome and so quickening under any severe blow; she must get her mother at once back to her bed.

Vainly, however, did she try to lift that rigid, senseless shape, heavy as if already dead; the effort to pay that last respect to her uncle had, from her feeble condition and a certain obscure trouble of the spine that had puzzled her physician by complicating an ordinarily manageable disease, brought on an unconscious condition that was neither a swoon nor paralysis, and only by Sally's help could Esther raise her from the floor and get her back in her bed; then she sent Sally hastily over to the graveyard to hunt up Dr. Parker, and began to chafe her mother's hands and feet, and apply camphor to her temples.

The doctor arrived shortly, but his skill could do no more than Esther had done: he could only read that death-warrant that medical authority has so often to issue, in the usual guarded terms that really conceal nothing of their cruel import, but are a tribute to conventional decencies.

"Your mother is ser'ously ill, Esther; dangerous; yes, dangerous; but we hope she will rally; yes, rally again; while there is life there is hope; the vital fluid is contumacious, and the mass of her mortality is mabbe more tough than some; I dono but what she may get around again after a spell; yes, after a spell; she's had quite a shock to the brain substance, quite; brain is a difficult region to deal with medicinally. I should apprehend that a mess of wilted burdock leaves clapped to the soles of the feet might draw down the evil; and I should put some cold sperrits onto the top of her head; camphire is good, it is revivin', see-*dat*ive, and purifyin' to the blood; let her smell to the camphire quite frequent, and if she doos *not* revive considerable quick, why I'll let blood, I'll let blood. In obstinate defluxions nothing is better. But, Esther, you should have some one with you, yes, it is needful; I will step over to Parson Hall's, and see if he cannot spare Miss Ruthy."

Esther heard him in absolute silence; she sat by her mother after she had bound the dock-leaves on her feet, and wetted her head with rum, like some creature carved of "dureful marble." Once only she flashed out into quick life. Philip's voice was heard on the stairway.

"Lock the door, Sally!" she said, peremptorily. "Let no one in, unless Miss Ruth comes," and Sally answering a rap at the door informed Mr. Kent that, "nobody couldn't see neither of 'em, and the' mustn't be a mite o' noise."

How it was brought about Esther did not know, but that night Mr. Hall and Aunt Ruthy were both installed in the Dyer house as nurse and guardian.

Meanwhile, directly after the funeral, the reading of the will took place; Esther was not there of course; she was shut in with her speechless mother, and the doctor gave an authoritative order that she should not be called down.

It was not proper, Squire Peters insisted, that the

will should be read without her presence, but he was obliged to yield this point, for Philip said he must go to New York that night, and could not return to Trumbull in a long time; the journey was so tedious and the autumnal weather so uncertain; so Dr. Parker, Parson Hall, Squire Peters, Philip Kent, and Philip Kent's wife, a maiden lady who was a cousin of Mrs. Dyer's and had lately come to live in the village, Miss Temperance Tucker, were summoned to the library to listen to Mr. Dyer's last will and testament.

CHAPTER XIII.

A WILL.

> What deadly things we do, that, being done
> We think our wish and will forever won!
> Ah! creatures short of sight. What mortals know
> Whether their will fetch joy or bitter woe?
> They have earth's best, and heaven's most divine
> Who meekly say "Thy will be done! not mine."

It was a small company that assembled about the library table at Mr. Peters's request to hear this will. Nobody looked happy in expectance: Philip was pale as death.

Squire Peters moved a chair to the closet door as Esther had done, and took down the keys; evidently, Mr. Dyer had shown him their place in preparation for this occasion; but when he had unlocked and opened the desk, and the secret drawer, he uttered a quaint ejaculation under his breath, and proceeded to search every drawer and pigeon-hole, to untie bundle after bundle of papers, and at last to rummage the upper closet.

"Amazing! amazing!" he said, as he turned to the waiting company, holding a sealed parchment in his hand.

"It is but a few weeks ago I engrossed a will for Joshua Dyer of a different tenor from that he made succeeding the demise of his late wife; and with my own hands did I deposit it in this drawer whence I have taken this previous will; but there is no trace of it among his papers. I cannot think he hath destroyed it in so brief time," and Squire Peters cast a glance of keen inquiry at the group before him, from under his bushy brows.

Philip had recovered his natural color when he saw the squire begin his search; and looked as surprised as they did.

"Did any one become aware of the tenor of that later will?" asked Parson Hall composedly.

"No, sir!" was the squire's emphatic answer. "I tell no man's secrets to man or woman; lawyer and doctor should be like the grave's mouth, which receiveth all things and returneth nothing."

And the squire spoke truth; Abner Peters's communication to Philip had been an invention of his own to torment the man he never liked.

Philip knew from Mr. Dyer's own lips what the earlier will had been, but even Squire Peters was not aware that Philip had received such a confidence.

"I see then," went on Mr. Hall, "no other explanation of the absence of that document, but that Mr. Dyer changed his mind concerning the provisions thereof, and probably intending so to change it, did away with it, and was too soon smitten with paralysis to frame another."

"Mabbe it is so, mabbe it is so," said Squire Peters, reflectively, "but since none other is to be had, I will now advise you all here assembled, of the contents of this one; if perchance the other should yet be found, these legacies and provisions will be thereby null and void according to the statutes of this colony."

A wild thrill of fear darted through Philip's mind; what if Esther had only secreted that new will, and in her indignation at his betrayal of her affection should restore it? But would she be ready to criminate herself? Racked by doubts and fears that now began their work, he composed himself as best he could to listen to the reading of Squire Peters. There was the usual preamble, with its farcical gift of the soul to God and the body to the ground; a foregone conclusion that one might think better omitted, if they stopped to think at all: and then came small legacies to Hiram and Delia; a gift of valuable books and a gold watch and seals to Parson Hall: a sum of four hundred pounds sterling to Mrs. Dennis; and the rest and residue of all his estate to Philip Kent; "nephew of my late lamented wife."

No mention was made of Esther; indeed when this will was drawn up, Uncle Dyer had never seen the girl; his wife was but just buried, and he had only been reminded very lately of his niece's existence. Unaware of Mrs. Dennis's extreme poverty, for her letter to him only asked for help to find occupation, and did not at all enter into the details of her destitution, he had only left her such a sum in his will as would ensure her from starvation, supposing that she must have some property of her own.

Whatever were the contents of the later will, only

Squire Peters knew now. But there was nothing to be said or done; Squire Peters was executor, with Parson Hall, and Philip drew the latter aside as the small conclave dispersed and said : " Sir, I am indeed grieved that nothing more hath been left to Mrs. Dennis and her daughter; believe me, it is my full purpose to provide for them well, as my uncle past doubt intended. I must betake myself at once to New York on urgent affairs; now that the business hath passed fully into my hands, I must be there directly. But assure the ladies of my good intent; I would fain have seen them, but was denied."

There was something so formal and cold-blooded in Philip's speech, that the parson could hardly control his own words to due frigidity; well he knew how this man had drawn Esther's innocent heart out of her bosom and thrown it away; how broken and desperate it lay now among the ruined hopes so fondly cherished; it had been almost as great a shock to him as to her when Philip entered that death chamber with a wife on his arm, and so far as a man can appreciate a woman's feelings, he understood Esther's, and gave her a sympathy so keen and a pity so overflowing, that he felt toward Philip Kent as Adam might have felt toward Cain when he saw the fair shape of Abel the beloved, streaming with blood, and pallid with death, stretched on the turf by his new built altar, himself the first fruits of the sin which " brought death into the world and all our woe." But he controlled his righteous anger enough to say calmly, —

"Mrs. Dennis is well-nigh at the gate of death; she could see no one save the physician; her daughter is at her side. I think there can be no more removal of the sick woman for some time to come, if indeed she be ever moved except to the grave. I trust you will permit them to find shelter here for a time."

Philip put on a grieved expression, though in his heart he was furious at Parson Hall's manner.

"Indeed, sir, the house is at their service; I must be gone for months, but I trust yet to abide here as a dweller for good part of the year, and I purpose to leave Hiram and Delia in charge. I trust that Madam and her daughter will be at home while they please here, and I shall leave orders that they be cared for duly."

With a cold salutation he turned from the parson, and presenting his hand to his wife led her to the chaise waiting for them at the door, and departed.

Esther neither knew nor cared what was going on downstairs; her mother's fall had been followed by an unconscious condition, from which she now and then roused, complaining of her head in a gentle, piteous way, and then seeming to sleep again; Miss Temperance Tucker had offered to help Aunt Ruthy, but Esther wanted no new face about her, and Miss Tempy went off as Delia described it, "in a fluff."

"She took on dreadful! she scolded 'cause Squire Peters made her stay to the will-readin' for nothin'; she wasn't left so much as a pine-tree shillin' in't, and I dono myself what upon airth he did keep her for.

And Esther didn't want them black eyes of her'n a pryin' an' a peepin' 'round, nor I didn't; but she's madder 'n a settin' hen, and she'll set to and tell more tales! You see if she don't!"

Meantime, Esther, regardless of all other things, sat by her mother's bedside in a silent despair; now that she understood how Philip had deceived her, how she had been a mere tool in his hands, she began to see also that she had committed a great sin in stealing and destroying Uncle Dyer's will. While Philip loved her, and she loved him, nothing seemed wrong to her that he asked her to do; there was no sacrifice of herself she would not gladly have made for him; but when that love was suddenly killed — and in her ignorance of herself she thought it slain forever — the evil she had done for love's sake arose like the genie from his casket, and filled all her atmosphere with its towering shape. She was a thief! branded and disgraced forever in her own eyes; unfit for the company of the good; cast out on earth; hopeless of heaven; and Philip had never loved her.

Absorbed in this crushing and benumbing consciousness, she failed to see how fast her mother was sinking into that last slumber which should leave her orphaned. Once Mrs. Dennis said in a faint whisper, —

"Esther! I am going," but the incredulous girl thought it a dreamy idea of illness, and comforted and reassured her mother as best she could, until the mortal stupor again set in.

Once more, two days after, she whispered, a sort of

dull agony in her voice, a subdued terror: "Esther, pray! pray!" and Esther, shuddering, hid her face in her hands.

She pray! she, a thief! an outcast from all good! she had not lifted heart or voice to God since that hour when she heard Philip present his wife to Squire Peters beside his uncle's coffin. There was no more God for her, the universe was chaos again, and she thrown out into the blackness of darkness forever and ever.

It was but a few days of stupor, broken now and then by a low moan, or the complaining accent of a hurt child, — "Oh, dee! dee! dee!" coming from the weary lips of dying age, and rending the ear that heard, with sharp and cruel pity, and Esther was motherless; the calm of death stilled the restless lips, the wailing cry, the vain appeal of the tortured eyes.

There was another funeral from the Dyer house, and after it was over, Sybil Salstonstall led her friend away to her own home and tried her best to pierce the gloom and silence that had settled on that bright face and eager, generous heart.

For Sybil, wise with her own painful experience, had long seen that Esther loved Philip Kent, and feared as long that her life would be shipwrecked on that affection.

Young as she was, she had a keen appreciation of character, and she knew that a love so lavish, so unconcealed, so utter, as Esther's, would be but a momentary amusement to Philip.

And she had judged him rightly; Annetje Stuyvesant had won him by her very coldness; her appearance of carelessness; her insistant dignity; her apparent self-respect.

No caresses were permitted him, even after their betrothal, except for earnest pleading and humble remonstrance.

Here, too, was the old French saying that in all love affairs there is, "*L'un qui baise, et l'autre qui tend la joue*" carried out; if Annetje held her fair cold cheek even, it was as a royal favor, and duly appreciated.

For in her soul self-love reigned; she wanted to be worshipped, but burned no incense herself; she cared to have an adorer, but she only adored the face in her mirror; and Philip, equally selfish, was stimulated by the difficulty of attaining a creature so beautiful, who must be, he argued, a prize indeed, since she so valued herself. A nature like his could never perceive the fact that the highest characters are the simplest, the most generous; he could hold nothing valuable that was free; nothing worth having that did not imply difficulty of possession; the air that flowed about him, the abundant light of heaven, the stintless bloom of field and forest, were of no value in his eyes; idle adjuncts of common life, neither to be cared for or prized; the slow trickling spring on a mountain-peak, the rare orchid of a hothouse, the odor of a costly blossom might charm him; he wanted to make a queen his thrall; a willing slave filled him with contempt.

He had found it pleasant enough to be worshipped. to see Esther's soul shine in her eyes when he threw her a tender word, or the rich color come and go in her face when he caressed her; it was pleasant for a time to feel her sweet cool lips quiver and tremble under his long kisses; and she had served a convenient purpose in regard to his uncle's will; but what were all these to the charms of Annetje Stuyvesant's coquetry? the uncertainty that tantalized and bewitched him in her manner? the cold beautiful eyes and lips that maddened him with longing to make them burn and thrill?

He hung between heaven and earth till he despaired, and then a coy smile, a *mutine* sparkle in those steely-blue eyes, a tender tone in the somewhat hard voice, would set his heart beating and his blood boiling with hope and passion

Yet, perhaps he never would have won Peter Stuyvesant's proud daughter, had not her father earnestly urged upon her the hand of another man, and the Dutch blood in the maiden's veins rose in obstinate revolt against the mere thought of Garret Heidecker's suit.

But fathers were obstinate too in those days, and Annetje knew her master; she could not rebel, but she could elude, and one fine night she stole out of the stoop door with Philip Kent; her father being well absorbed in drawing out the marriage contract in his library, with Heidecker at his elbow; and embarking in a small sloop that ran up the Hudson, the pair were made one by Dominie Kraut at Spuyten Duyvil, before Peter really discovered that his daughter had not been sound asleep in her bed all night.

Peter, however, was a wise man; he put the marriage contract in the fire, and hearing, after a while, of Philip's inheritance, forgave his daughter and did not alter his will.

So Philip had an abundance of worldly goods, and a conscience too well muzzled to trouble him about sin, so long as it succeeded. He was well rid of Esther, and not having thought it needful to attend his aunt's funeral, he was satisfied to hear that she was at Governor Stanley's, and more amused than disturbed when Parson Hall wrote to him that she refused to accept anything at his hands, even the shelter of his house; now her home no longer, but full of the saddest and bitterest associations of her young life.

CHAPTER XIV.

DESPAIR.

He talks to me that never had a son!

For a time after her removal to Governor Stanley's house, Esther was like one stunned. Dull woe sat on her rigid face; her eyes were dark with an inner darkness that quenched all their glow and sparkle; she ate as little as would sustain life, and seemed to care nothing about what she tasted; had her food been gall and her drink wormwood she could not have been less attracted by them; her voice was the very echo of despair, and her nights the blackness of darkness, for sleepless as she was, yet her waking was full of visions; she walked with Philip again by the shore of that sea that once murmured its summer passion at their feet, and sprinkled them with the diamond dews of its breaking wave; now she heard its melancholy rote through the midnight, and the crushed hiss of the retreating water seemed to scorn her, sinner that she was! But again came the too tender voice, the fond kisses burned on her lips, the eyes of masterful passion beamed above her, and the long powerful fingers stroked her loosened hair; ah! how could he have loved and left her? Poor child!

"That was not love that left!"

but she did not know it.

Then returned upon her the maddening blow that fell at her uncle's funeral; she lived over the shock; the choked breath that stifled her; the chaos that seethed in her brain ; and in natural sequence came her mother's long illness, long to her who counted its moments of misery as if they were years.

She recurred over and over again to that hour when her mother, half consciously struggling with death, whispered "Pray!" and Esther dared not lift her voice to God because of her own sin; the pathetic, childish wail of the dying woman rung again on her ear, and her tortured conscience fixed all its fangs on her spiritual nature like an angry fiend. How could she sleep ?

Even when exhausted nature gave way, her dreams were filled with the voices and the presence of the dead; Uncle Dyer looked at her with grave reproach; her mother was there beside her, but would not speak; her father, too, arose from the grave to rebuke her; it seemed to her when she awoke that all her life had been in the gates of death ; that the loving had all forsaken her for a better country, and the living left her of cruel purpose.

When daylight came and the light cares of arranging her chamber, as became a guest were over, she tied on her bonnet and mantle, and slipping quietly out of the house, began her solitary walk over the dry fields and hills; she went on and on as if pursued by an invisible hunter; rain nor wind deterred her, her whole soul was in an interior tumult that defied the soulless tempests of nature with a sullen disregard, and a fever that averted physical suffering.

What was it to her that showers drenched her, or fierce gales tore off her headgear, and blew her mantle from her grasp? These were matters a broken heart and an indignant spirit neither resented or noticed.

Day after day she traversed the hills and shores for miles about Trumbull; her tall, slight shape drawn against the blue or livid sky, or the white water of the surf; her face pallid, her gloomy eyes fixed, her little cold hands clenched, and her lips set. People wondered that Esther should so mourn her mother, but respected a grief so rare and so genuine; happily for her, but a very few of her best friends understood another part of her loss; not one appreciated its keenest sting, — the sense of her own sin in stealing and destroying her uncle's will.

For Esther was not one of those supernatural young women, sometimes depicted in fiction, who could be comforted for everything by the selfless reflection that Philip had his inheritance secure; she was only a warm-natured, impulsive girl, with an outraged and indignant heart, a lonely girl, orphaned in every sense, for with the dreadful logic of a conscience educated in the stern New England fashion of rigid law, and unsparing self-inspection, she felt that she had no right even to the consolations of religion; that her Father in heaven, hitherto a mighty, unknown, but beneficent parent, had become an angry and an avenging God, and had bereaved her of her nearest friends in swift justice, as punishment for her transgression.

She felt as if his finger had set a mark upon her, that no power could efface, that she was a reprobate in earth and from heaven.

A month passed so, and Mrs. Stanley began to feel in her hard, sensible fashion, that Esther was not the sort of guest she liked; a decent and subdued mourner, who would do her fitting share in the household occupations, and be "company" for Sybil, was one thing; she would not have objected to a few tears, or sobs even, at proper times, if Esther had offered to spin a run or two of thread, or superintend the cider apple-sauce, or help at the tambour frame, where Madame Stanley was sprigging a linen gown with birds, beasts, fruits, and flowers, in all colors that her knowledge of homely dyestuffs allowed; but it was quite another thing to have a silent image of despair about, if only at meals and prayers; a creature so absorbed and crushed as to be a *memento mori* when in sight, and a continual anxiety when out of it; for Madam Stanley held these interminable walks of Esther to be a real indecorum, and felt a certain selfish dread lest she should break down physically under them, and become a burden upon her hands.

She appealed at last to her niece, — "Sybil, I think it is unseemly for Esther to lay her losses to heart as she does. It becomes us all to be resigned to the Lord's will; and to go abroad as she doth, at all times, has an aspect of rebellion. Moreover, I think it is not wholesome for her to tempt all weathers as she doth. Cannot you speak with her?"

Sybil looked up from the tambour-frame with an expression of angelic pity in her great lucid eyes.

"Dear aunt," she said, "I think Esther is sore of heart; I know not how to touch her without giving pain."

"Nevertheless, pain is healing sometimes, Sybil. I wonder that, being a member of the meeting, Parson Hall doth not deal with her."

"But she is only on the half-way covenant, Aunt Stanley."

"That hath its duties nevertheless; she should not hold such controversy with Providence; if you like not to try words with her, niece Sybil, I will do so myself, or send for Parson Hall."

"I will, I will!" answered Sybil, hastily; she dreaded that her aunt should touch Esther's wound with such cautery as her hard spirit would be sure to administer.

Little did Madam Stanley think that the poor girl sheltered under her roof was much further from holding any controversy with Providence than she herself! Esther submitted to her "judgment" as she considered it, with the submission of despair; the words of Scripture echoed through her brain with reiterant force, "I acknowledge my transgression, and my sin is ever before me! Against Thee, Thee only have I sinned, and done this evil in Thy sight!"

If she could have been as indignant with her Maker as she was with Philip, her soul would have been in a more hopeful condition; anger is a healthier passion than despair, and has in it far more re-constructive elements; it was the heaviest and most hopeless of all Esther's burdens, that she had no self-respect to uphold her in this sea of trouble.

One night after prayers, a ceremony duly observed by the governor when he was at home, and by Madam Stanley in his absence, a most dry and formal service, and to Esther's pre-occupied thoughts, a dead letter, Sybil followed her friend upstairs to her chamber.

Esther had put out her candle as soon as she entered the door, and Sybil, following close on her steps, rapped lightly and came in; the hunter's moon at its glorious height filled the low-ceiled chamber with cold radiance. Esther sat in the broad seat of the south window, motionless, her eyes fixed on the glittering waves that plashed gently through the soft autumnal air, her lips as calm and sad as some monumental statue; she did not move when Sybil came up to her and slipping to the floor at her feet coaxed apart the cold hands clasped round her knee, and laying her cheek softly on the palm of the one nearest her said, in the tenderest tones, —

"Dear Esther, cannot I comfort you?"

Esther turned on her a glowing gaze, but answered nothing.

"I grieve so for you, Esther: I know your sorrows my poor girl; I also am an orphan,"

"A-a-ah!" a sharp hissing sigh parted Esther's closed lips; an orphan! was not this that Sybil so pitied the least of her great troubles? Sybil shivered.

"My dear, my dear, cannot I say something to help you? cannot you talk to me?"

"Talk to you!" said Esther, with a little bitter laugh, worse than a cry. "You, Sybil, always good and calm; why should I talk to you about fire, when the smell of it hath never touched your garment?"

"Are you so sure?" Sybil answered, in the lowest voice.

"You! do not I see your still face and your praying eyes, always pure, always sweet? Sybil, were you ever desperate?"

"No, Esther, for the Lord liveth; I can never despair; 'though He slay me, yet will I trust in Him.'"

Esther turned her face and looked down at the sad triumph in the beautiful countenance at her knee; how could she tell Sybil that a great sin came between her and the goodness of God?

"Listen, Esther," Sybil went on; and her voice neither failed or faltered as she told in as few words as she could the story of her temptation and her victory. It was like setting before her an awful, yet beautiful martyrdom, unknown to man; a stake and fagot invisible, a burnt sacrifice of the heart, an offering to God of the first-born. Esther quailed as she heard; there was no comfort in it for her; only a comparison of saint and sinner that plunged her into deeper self-contempt, and stung her into frantic bitterness.

"You call that love?" she said, with hot scorn. "Why had I loved — well, any man; I would have given him my very soul. What would heaven be without him? What should I care for hell if he were there, too?

"Esther!" said Sybil in a tone of horror, rising to her feet, pale and fair in the moonlight as an accusing angel, shocked in every fibre of her nature, "Have you no God?"

Esther laughed again.

"Oh, yes! I have a God, an avenging God; 'infinite, eternal, and unchangeable in his being, wisdom, power, holiness, justice, goodness, and truth.' At least, the catechism says so! But what has that God to do with a sinner but to punish? Do you think I resisted like you? I am not a stone! A-a-ah!" Again the long, bitter sigh that was all but a groan, and spoke more than any words, rasped on Sybil's ear.

What should she say to this wretched girl whose face was stamped with such passion, such despair?

Sybil was unlearned in the tender message of the Gospel; the Law, in all its unflinching sternness, was the customary preaching and teaching of her day; if here and there a soul taught of heaven recounted the old, old story, of One who came to seek and to save the lost, to pity and forgive the chiefest of sinners, there was a stir of trouble, a clamor for doctrines, a murmur of "right-hand defections, and left-hand fallings off," that silenced the gentle spirit, and daunted with Puritan grimness all efforts to set aside the stark routine of duty and decrees.

But the very spirit of heaven filled Sybil's soul; horror gave place to a divine pity; she laid her cool hand on Esther's burning forehead, looked steadily into the eyes that burned with wrath and scorn.

"My poor sister!" she said, lowly and slowly, "the Lord heal thee from thy bitterness even as he healed the fountain of Marah by His rod!"

Esther's head sank into her hands; she could neither speak nor move: Sybil was far, far above her plane, she could not even reach after her, but as she passed out of the chamber door those gloomy eyes followed her with a look of adoration and abject despair, though the lips dropped no word of recall.

"Well," said Aunt Stanley, when Esther closed the parlor door behind her, after breakfast the next day, "have you spoke with Esther, Sybil?"

"Yes, aunt."

"And I trust you took her to do, smartly; these airs are unseemly enough. Hath there been no sorrow in the world before, that she should make such a matter of hers?"

"Aunt Stanley, I believe that Esther is in deep straits of soul; I cannot reach her. I have done my best; she is at variance with God and man it seemeth to me. I wish Parson Hall could be fetched to see her without her knowledge of his purpose. I think it may be he could deal with her as I cannot."

"He shall come!" said the Madam, who was wont to have her word law.

But happily for Esther, she met Mr. Hall that day far out on the sandhills, where she had wandered; he came upon her sitting in the long, glittering grass as yet unseared by frost, that waved around the sheltered hollow into which she had sunk, tired with the length of the way. Before her spread the water, blue as the heavens above it; white gulls played up and down, from sky to sea; a screaming fish-hawk soared, poised, darted down on its prey, and flapped heavily away to his perch in a dead oak-tree, but Esther saw them not; she did not even start when Mr. Hall appeared upon the beach, drew near, and sat down beside her; she bent her head in greeting, but neither smiled or spoke.

"I am glad to have come upon you here, Esther," he said, gravely and gently. "I have wished much to see you; and here in the peace of the shore I can speak with you more freely than when there are others at hand."

Esther was silent.

Mr. Hall looked at her with the deepest compassion; he understood her better far than Sybil did, for he had lived longer, — "My dear young friend," he went on. "I grieve to see you so entirely stricken down by the chastisements that have come upon you. Are you right, Esther, in giving up your young life to such distress? Have you not much left still to be thankful for?"

"Have I?" she answered, looking back on her loveless youth; her broken hopes and purposes; her sin. "I do not think I have, sir. I do not think God wishes me to lie to Him. He knows I am not thankful for my life, and I will not pretend to be!"

"My child!" he said, sadly. "Think of what you deserve, rather than of what you have desired."

Esther's eye kindled, and the dark blood flushed her cheek; her voice was harsh with pain and defiance.

"Why do I deserve it? Did I ask to be born? Was I ever inquired of if I was willing to have life with all its sufferings and responsibilities thrust upon me? And yet you say He expects me to be thankful for it. I will not lie to God! I have had enough of lying!"

He looked at her with that divine pity that is unisonous with the divinest love; had Goody Jones, dirty, crooked, and withered, propounded to him such heretical sentiments, perhaps a just and stern remonstrance would have been her portion; but Philemon Hall was a man, and Esther Dennis a beautiful girl, in deep distress. Parson Hall was wise too, as well as harmless; he made answer according to his light. "We will not guide the hand of God, Esther; 'what thou knowest not now, thou shalt know hereafter.' I want to give your thoughts a new direction; I want to set you to work."

Esther stared; with the unconscious selfishness of youth she had made her sorrow fill the world. She had thought it too much to suffer her wrong; she had not looked at any other creature's good or ill; given a thought to any trouble but her own. "Was ever sorrow like unto my sorrow," was her ignorant outcry. She was surprised and disgusted that Parson Hall should think of her as a possible help to anyone, so shipwrecked was her heart and soul.

But the parson knew better!

CHAPTER XV.

A CHANGE.

Look not every man upon his own things.

Parson Hall went on in his calm voice, "I know you must be considering how to take up your life when you shall leave Madam Stanley's house."

Esther looked up at him sharply: she had not given one thought to the future; she had not any idea of being a guest or a dependent, any more than a shipwrecked mariner who has been thrown up by the storm under the shelter of a friendly cliff, and lies gasping and placid in its shadow, thinks of going into business and making money; or of creeping back into the tumultuous sea.

"I have thought of nothing," she said, in a low, hoarse voice.

She meant, as women do mean when they say that, that she had only thought of one thing, and Parson Hall knew it.

"Think upon it now, then, Esther," he said, with austere gravity. "You are young, your life is yet to come, and to be endured if it cannot be enjoyed. The Lord hath work for each of us; and you cannot give all your days to mourning; you must awake and work to-day in the vineyard."

With his words Esther did awake; at least, partially; it flashed upon her that Madam Stanley had of late eyed her with disapproval, that Sybil since their conversation that night in the chamber had shunned her a little, and looked at her with an expression of fear as well as pity; these things returned to her now, a kind of moral palimpsest, coming to light as impressions do, received unconsciously, but yet stamped on her brain; a sort of terror seized her, she was so homeless, so helpless.

"What shall I do?" she exclaimed, in a tone of terror and grief.

"I have been thinking for you, Esther," answered Parson Hall. "I have talked with Miss Temperance Tucker of late; she came to Trumbull, sent for to hear the reading of Mr. Dyer's will, therefore expecting to be therein remembered."

Esther winced; here again her sin had found her out. Mr. Hall went on, —

"But being here she thinks to remain, if she can make it possible; our salt air hath a beneficial effect on her asthma; now Goody Green, who hath kept the dame school for the lesser children, is a mind to give it up and dwell with her daughter in Hartford, hereafter, being extreme rheumatical. It has come to me that if Miss Temperance and you, having about the same amount of worldly goods, should take Goody Green's house; and you were willing to teach the school, she doing the housework as her part, to make up for the further incoming of money on your part, from the school, that you would be doing a good work, and provide her, a lonely woman, with a home."

Mr. Hall knew Esther better than she did herself. Just now she cared so little what became of her, that had he based his plan on her own wants she would have turned away from it; her desire was merely to die, yet she shrunk from the contemplation of future wrath; and knew too well the doom of that rash mortal who should anticipate the Lord's time, and end life before He summoned his over-weary creature. But underneath Esther's impulsive, eager, passion-driven nature, lay a great, warm heart; a heart yet to be developed into its strength and loveliness; she began to consider favorably the prospect of helping another lonely and homeless woman.

"I will think of it, and I thank you," she said, slowly, as she rose from her seat, and went her way homeward.

Parson Hall sent upward an earnest, if silent prayer as he watched her languid, graceful figure disappear among the sand dunes and the glittering grass. He longed for Rachel to touch with her woman's tact the sore heart of this girl, and show to her the way of healing; never had he missed his wife so much as to-day; she had been so long his counsellor and helper that he undervalued his own penetration and his own power. But Parson Hall made a mistake; no woman, however wise or saintly, could have roused Esther as he had; in that time, women had not discovered that new gospel; to them a gospel, which sets woman on an equality with man; then, the old ordinance of God in Eden, the result and need of woman's sin and weakness after the fall, "He shall rule over thee!" had not been abrogated by the specious reasoning of the "strong-minded" sex! In those days, women did not head conventions, occupy pulpits, scour the country speechifying, or clamor in print as well as vocally to be put on the same plane with men. St. Paul had not been sneered and jeered at, and relegated to the days of darkness; and his fiat that "It is a shame for women to speak in the church," was not virtually omitted from the words of inspiration by the argument that times and manners have changed since then. Still, the ordination of God and the laws of His natural world made the man head and protector of the woman, and when to his native position he added the office of priest it was a foregone conclusion that his counsel would be authoritative and weighty.

Esther considered what Parson Hall had said, all the way back to Madam Stanley's house. It was hard enough for her to take up life again, but it was evident that she could not escape from that burden; she did not know Miss Temperance well; she had seen her during her mother's last illness, when her brain was reeling with Philip's desertion and her heart dull with impending loss; but she only recalled a short, energetic little figure, with wiry black hair brushed up over a small cushion, but so indomitably curly that it waved, and frizzed, and bristled out in a hundred resolute little quirls above the low forehead and snapping black eyes of the dark, shrewd face below.

Esther's bruised soul longed for some soft and yielding creature to comfort and caress it; her nature trended strongly toward indolence and enjoyment; with wealth and pleasure at command, she would have been a selfish sybarite; the sharp, wintry wind of sorrow was needed to arouse and develop her better nature, however she shrank from its discipline. She went to her room, and locked the door as soon as she reached the house. She must be alone to encounter her new idea, and resolve on her future course. More and more as she looked on Mr. Hall's plan, she perceived that it was not only wise and kind, but that there was no other way open for her. When she went down to supper, she had resolved to accept the position, and make the best of it, and was comforted against the hard look of Madam Stanley's cold steel-blue eyes by the consciousness that she should soon be out of their range, and freed from at least the daily obligation to her chilly charity.

After supper and prayers Esther laid her intentions before her hostess. Mrs. Stanley was pleased evidently.

"I think it a good thing, Esther: it does not become any of us to feel that we are vainly afflicted, or spend our days in mourning, when we pass under the rod of Jehovah. I believe this is an appointed means to help you. But I would have you to rememher that both my husband and I stand ready at any time to aid and protect the niece of our friend Joshua Dyer."

Esther stooped hastily, and put her hot lips on Madam Stanley's hand; but she said nothing. Sybil held open her arms, and the lonely girl laid her face against that fair cheek, still speechless. She knew the tender embrace was heartfelt and honest, just as she knew Madam Stanley's words were formal and unfeeling. As Sybil drew her down on the quaint old rush-bottomed settee, with its painted and gilded woodwork, that stood across the end of the keeping-room, Mrs. Stanley placed herself in a tall, straight-backed chair, took out her knotting-bag, and, anxious to turn the subject of her companions' thoughts, perhaps, also, conscious that Esther had felt her coldness, began to speak of the trivial happenings and hearings of the day. Presently she said, —

"I hear that John Stonebridge is coming to my uncle's at the Point. They will hold their Christmas revels there, instead of in the city this year. I would that these Puritan folk about us could at least respect that holy festival of the Church of England!"

Esther felt Sybil shiver. She saw in one swift glance that her face was colorless as the kerchief about her throat. She made no other visible sign, but clasped Esther's hand so tightly that there were deep, white marks left on the pink of that soft palm. Esther longed to clasp her to her own desolate bosom, and so express her sympathy, for she saw that Sybil suffered; yet her pity was not absolute, for she could not understand why her friend should deliberately deny and stifle her own heart for a mere difference of opinion, as Esther thought. Sybil's heart was wrung: it seemed to her that she could not meet John Stonebridge again; yet with the very spirit of a martyr she "betook herself to prayer," as the old chronicles have it, and in silent endurance and faith waited for her trial.

But before Christmas came, Esther had left the Stanley mansion; it was easier to Sybil to bear her apprehension when her friend's tender eyes and sympathetic voice no longer tested severely her self-control; she was in that cruel condition when "oil and balsams kill," when the cold eye and careless speech of Madam Stanley were better than consolation; were such a strength as the tense rope and the staves sunk in ice give to the traveller over an Alpine glacier; the chill unconsidered in the aid they give.

It seemed strange to Esther, when she now and then considered it, that she could so soon begin to interest herself in outside things: she did not know how her youth helped her.

Miss Tempy Tucker, too, was a person who was not to be ignored by the most pre-occupied mind: she asserted herself piquantly wherever she went, and had that rare faculty a few women possess of making any place she inhabited homelike and cheerful. The tiny house Goody Green had lived in was plain enough outside; within, boasting only of two rooms in front, and a long kitchen behind: it had once been a block-house, and its thick walls made pleasant seats now in the windows below stairs; a sharp-pitched roof, with dormer windows in it, gave room for two small chambers above, warm in winter from the heat of the great central chimney, and cool in summer from the draught of the sea breeze right across them from window to window.

One of these front rooms, approached from the green yard by an east door, was used as a schoolroom; the floor was bare of covering other than the white sand strown fresh every morning over the boards. Around the wall low benches were ranged, and in the open fireplace, hickory and maple logs simmered, flamed, and sparkled through the winter, to be replaced in summer by a big "bow-pot" of flowers, or leafy boughs, which it was the children's delight to furnish.

While Miss Tempy set the house in order, Goody Green still kept her young flock, and hammered catechism and primer into their shock heads in the kitchen of a neighbor, who was kindly enough to spare it for ten days.

"Now, Easter, lets you and me fly round," said brisk Miss Tempy. "I want to get to livin' again as soon as the law allows. I don't call it livin' to be a-visitin' round as I be, a-feelin' all the time that short stays make a long welcome; besides bein' in other folkses houses ain't noway to my taste. I'd ruther live in my own boughten hogshead than in another person's four-story mansion. You and me will be as snug as a bumble-bee's nest when we get fixed."

Esther smiled. Miss Tempy's voluble cheer was contagious.

"I am ready to do whatever is to be done, Miss Tempy," she said, in a steady tone.

"Well, first an' foremost, I wish 't you could settle to call me Aunt Tempy. I don't really hanker to have 'Miss' thrown at me continual. I know I've missed of a man so fur, — ef 'tis a miss, — and so fur forth I haven't, as I knows of, wanted one, but still 'tis a kind of a slur to be full forty-five and a onmarried spinster; besides, I'm sort of connected with you, if there ain't no relationship by blood, and it is real pleasant to make believe as though I had some kin to call me by name. Can you fetch your mind to 't?"

"I shall like to," said Esther, with a smile, touched by the loneliness and solitude the request conveyed.

"I haven't anybody either, Aunt Tempy; not any kith or kin in the world. I am glad to have an aunt."

Miss Tempy nodded with satisfaction, and, tying on her check apron, she soon introduced Esther into the busy work of arranging the house they were to occupy. Miss Tempy had sent for her furniture the week before. It had come safely on ox-sleds, for now the snow lay deep all over the land; it had fallen early, and it was well for Esther that she had occupation and exercise of another kind, now that her long walks were impossible. There was much rubbing and dusting and arranging to do, but the little parlor, which was to be the sitting-room, looked cheerful enough when it was at last in order. A great stuffed sofa, covered with a loose cover of red and yellow India chintz stood against one wall, and a long frilled cushion of the same chintz made each of the two window-sills, looking south and west out of small-paned windows, at once cheery and comfortable. Miss Tempy had sacrificed certain bed-curtains for this adornment. Bright fire-irons garnished the open fireplace, a low, wide rocking-chair, cushioned with red moreen, stood by the hearth on one side, and several tall, straight-backed rush-bottomed chairs were ranged about the room, while a claw-footed table, round, and shining with beeswax and rubbing, occupied one corner; a glass-doored cupboard filled the other, showing a small store of cups, saucers, plates, and pitchers of gay china, that to-day would be worth more than Miss Tempy could have imagined. There were no pictures on the walls, which were wainscoted half-way up, and above the panelled wood the wall was painted a warm yellow, and stencilled in a scroll pattern with dark red. There were shutters to the windows, which could be barred at night, and inside were nankeen curtains, gathered on a string and tied back with cord and tassels of scarlet yarn, evidently home-made. No carpet covered the floor, but half a dozen braided rugs lay about, one before the fireplace, where opposite Miss Tempy's rocker a low chair was set for Esther; and by either jamb a narrow wooden "cricket," as stools were then called, painted black, with green stencilling. It was a homely room in the primitive sense; and when candles were lit and the wood fire sparkled on the hearth, it had a peace and cheer in its aspect denied to Uncle Dyer's stately drawing-room, or the rigid splendors of the Stanley mansion; and when, after a look of satisfaction at the exquisitely clean kitchen, with its store of shining pewter and old blue delft displayed on the dresser, Esther stole up the little crooked front stair that clung to the chimney-side, and almost forbade the double outer-door to open fully, and crept into her dimity curtained-bed, she watched from her pillow the wintry moonlight making a path of melancholy glory across the heaving glittering sea, till a strange quiet, like that of a child that has sobbed itself to sleep, stole over her, and her eyes closed peacefully, lulled with the sense of having once more a real home.

CHAPTER XVI.

AGAIN.

> A child's kiss
> Set on thy sighing lips shall make thee glad;
> A poor man, served by thee, shall make thee rich;
> A sick man, helped by thee, shall make thee strong.

ESTHER dreaded the opening day of her school. She had no knowledge of her duties further than her remembrance of her own schooldays, and those were, she thought, doubtful as guides here; but Parson Hall had thought for her. He had sent a man to make a path through the snow to the schoolroom door, as well as the other doors; and before a child arrived he was on the spot, seated in a high chair by the fire. Esther took heart at once with such an ally, and smiled to see, as the rosy children trooped in, how every chubby face grew solemn at the sight of the parson, although his face was gentler and sweeter than Esther had ever seen it before.

When caps and cloaks and hoods were all hung up on the row of nails ready for them, and the children seated on their low benches, Parson Hall stood up beside Esther and said, —

"Children, this is Miss Dennis, come to teach you. I hope you will all be good, and mindful of her orders. Scripture saith that 'even a child is known by his doings, whether his work be pure, and whether it be right.' I trust there will be a good report of your doings."

Then he made a short, simple prayer, and bade them good-by, with a smile that reassured Esther, and gave her courage to begin.

It is not altogether a delightful task to teach the very young idea how to shoot, the received opinion of the poet to the contrary notwithstanding. It is drudgery of the most stupid sort to go over the alphabet day after day, in the vain endeavor to make a dozen or two little shockheads see the difference between M and N, or B and R and K; nor is the "Assembly's Catechism," which in Esther's day was a *sine quâ non* in all New-England teaching, a really exhilarating study for teacher or scholars; and the long daily strife with the natural restlessness of the little human animals was tiresome, all the more that Esther was young enough to sympathize with it.

Perpetual appeal to the water-pail and its tin dipper, nudgings of neighborly elbows, squirming on the hard benches, constant demands to sharpen slate pencils on the hearth, to have Patty reproved for a sly pinch bestowed on Nancy or Betsy Jane — all these weary trivialities would have sickened Esther and worn her out, but for one thing. Suddenly there awakened in her a passionate love of children; I say awakened, for it was really an integral part of her nature, but it had happened that she had never before been brought into contact with them. Mr. Dyer was not fond of them, and none frequented his house;

there were no children at the Stanley mansion,—happily for the children,—so that their society, "their tricks and their manners," were wholly new to Esther, and utterly delightful. She was one of those women who are born to be mothers, around whose knees little ones instinctively crowd and cling; had she lived to be the most ancient of spinsters, she would never have outlived that charm that the mother-heart gives to a true woman, or ceased to covet the caresses and companionship of children.

Eager as she was to do her strict duty by her little school, earnest as to discipline and instruction, there was a look in her eyes, and a sweetness on her lips, that gave confidence to every little bosom, and before she had held her post a week, the children all adored her; and her own heart, dead as she had thought it, awoke and thrilled with the purest of mortal joys at the soft clinging of tiny arms about her neck, the close pressure of round, childish cheeks against her own, the tender little kisses, the pleading of loving eyes, the sound of small, fresh voices lisping or shrill. Her heart-trouble was not gone, it lay like the rocks in a river bed, deep and dark below the stream of daily life; but she was comforted, and her thoughts diverted from herself, the first step toward cure. Sybil, who came often to see her, noticed that her eyes were brighter, her pale face tinted with a new glow, her voice more cheerful; but with instinctive tact she avoided speaking of it. It too often awakens a pain or a grief to be reminded that it is less potent than it has been, so curiously and sensitively strung together are the alternations of thought and sense, especially in women.

Sybil was content to witness and rejoice in Esther's quiet and peace, though she did not understand its source; for Sybil, though if ever she should have children of her own might love them, was too dainty, too reserved, too fastidious to love the tiny race merely because they were children; their noise, their untidiness, their quips and tricks, their headlong caresses, all repelled her. Esther was a woman to love even her husband with a maternal passion; to love him the better the more he needed her pity, her care, or her service. But with Sybil it was not so; she wanted and needed a king whom she could worship, to whom she could use the Miltonic formula, —

> "God is thy law; thou, mine. To know no more
> Is woman's happiest knowledge."

a phrase which found entire acceptance with her. She pitied Esther for the very thing that made the sweetness of her renewing life; but had tact enough to keep that needless pity in her own breast.

Indeed, the time drew near when Sybil's own mind was full of dread; and of prayer for strength to endure the presence of Colonel Stonebridge; for though Christmas as a religious or social festival was scorned and ignored in Trumbull, and but one family there were Episcopalians, or "prelatists," in the terms of the day, yet Madam Stanley had been brought up in the Church of England; and only in deference to her husband's faith and position in the colony went to "meeting," so that Sybil knew well when the holiday would arrive, and it seemed to her that the dark days flew like swift birds by her, so much did she dread their departure. For with all the strength and hidden passion of her intense but reserved nature, did Sybil Saltonstall love John Stonebridge; his keen wit, his courage, his worldly wisdom, his intellect, his fine, manly presence, his social position, all told on her pride, her ambition, her latent vanity, and his eager passion touched the very depths of her heart; but with her, duty ruled all things; the stern asceticism of her race and her education bade her give up and trample under foot every longing of the "natural heart," if it in any way thwarted the will of God, whose avowed and faithful servant she was, and would be, though earth should fail from its foundations and the firmament reel above her.

She saw from her window, the chariot of the Talcott family, John Stonebridge's cousins, drive past; and she knew it was going to the wharf at Myannis, a small town nine miles away, where sailing vessels touched on their entrance to the mouth of the Connecticut, to deliver lading, or such passengers as might prefer sea to land as the way to journey to certain points on the coast; she saw that same lofty vehicle pass the next morning with a leathern valise strapped on the rack, the black driver cracking his whip to urge the horses onward, no doubt in haste to warm his own chilly person, for the day was cold, sparkling, and beautiful to look at, but deathly in its bitter atmosphere, and the piercing north wind lashed the sea like a scourge, and drove it backward even further than the ebbing tide was wont to go.

Sybil shuddered with a deeper chill than the air could give her; she did not leave the house all day; and she knew that none would leave the Christmas revels at Judge Talcott's, though now she longed to have her meeting with John Stonebridge over. Still he did not come till the evening of the next day, and when Mrs. Stanley called Sybil to come down, she went with a certain desperate resolution that gave her cheek a color and her eye a brightness that had long since deserted them. She might well have passed for a crownless queen, regnant by natural rather than hereditary right, as she entered the formal drawing-room to receive Colonel Stonebridge; her gown of dark wine-colored brocade, figured with trailing vines of hop leaves and blossoms, fell away over a petticoat of deep green poplin, half covered by an apron of India muslin and Mechlin lace; a handkerchief of the same delicate and costly materials filled the low-cut bosom of her stiff bodice, and frills of the lace finished her sleeves at the elbow; the sombre richness of her dress brought into full relief her exquisitely delicate skin, her proud head with its high-piled coronet of pale gold hair, unpowdered, as she wore it at home, and seemed to enhance the singular clearness of her sea-gray eyes, as encroaching clouds heighten the lustre of the nearer stars.

John Stonebridge thought she had never looked so lovely, and his face expressed his thought as he received and answered her coldly civil greeting; ten minutes after he thought he had never seen her look so ill. The glow of resolution and will faded, he could see that the pale cheeks were thin, the temples hollow, the small, rounded ear, surest index of exhaustion, white as wax, and the arms half shaded by their wide laces were lifeless, nerveless, wasted; while the eyes that had now lost their sparkle were wide and sad as the melancholy winter moon; neither bracelets nor rings adorned those fragile wrists and fingers, blue veins traced their too prominent record along the transparent skin; John Stonebridge felt a throb of pride to see that she had really suffered, and suffered for him; that masculine pride which rejoices in power and disregards pain, when the power is theirs and the pain another's. If Sybil could have read his heart at that moment her own would have recoiled with the shock of the recognition, but, for good and evil both, we wear that organ hidden from the eye of our fellows, and she only saw the courteous grace of figure, the bold, handsome visage, and nerved herself afresh to resist temptation.

But John Stonebridge had known a great many women, and had plenty of love affairs; he showed no desire or intention to renew his addresses to Miss Saltonstall; he expected and intended to make her feel that she had lost a valuable prize; to awaken her deep regret, perhaps her jealousy; so he was fluent and graphic in his description of the city gayeties he had left to spend Christmastide with his relations. He filled Madam Stanley's delighted ear with accounts of the routs, the assemblies, the sledging parties, and the skating frolics of the wintry season just began; he described the beauties who ruled society, with evident appreciation and admiration, dwelling warmly on the charms of a certain French damsel a reigning belle in New York, who was by his own description as precisely opposite Sybil as was possible.

Petite, brunette, coquette; sparkling with wit; dressed with parisian grace and taste; dancing like a fairy and singing like an angel; Madam Stanley was convinced that all these charms had chained Colonel Stonebridge to the car of Mademoiselle Liotard; but the good manners and dignity of that day forbade any allusion to such a personal matter; so the good lady's thoughts were kept in her own bosom, but certainly John Stonebridge did his eloquent best to convey the idea to both of his hearers, that he was a willing victim to Mademoiselle's irresistible graces. But Sybil heard as one who did not hear; sitting upright in a high chair, whose heavy carvings of old mahogany threw her head and shoulders into beautiful relief, her wistful, lonely eyes sought rest in the world outside; she seemed to be present in the body, but far, far away in soul; with a slight start, a faint smile, she recalled herself if she were addressed; but the glowing pictures of city life and pleasure did not interest her; evidently, the pique and jealousy John Stonebridge hoped to arouse had no place in that pure soul; it was only saddened by a deepening consciousness that his life and hers were more widely separated than ever, that there was no unison in their aims or opinions, that only her own infatuation, an emotion that still caused her to thrill at his voice, to shrink from his eye, to feel that beside him she was utterly blessed, and to resist with all her strength, as a mortal sin, the instinctive worship her whole soul longed to offer him, bound her to him with a tie that must be broken, if at the cost of her life. For Sybil, innocent, young, and pure, could not see the hot passion that burned under all this talk of society and its leaders, hidden by this fluent speech of pomps and vanities; she did not know that the red glow in John Stonebridge's eye was the light of a fire that burned more fiercely than ever within him; never had he loved Sybil as he loved her to-day; to preserve the decent aspect of society, to carry out his plan of siege, he had to crush down with iron will the longing he had to clasp that delicate, exquisite creature in his arms and carry her away from the Puritanic world about her, to some far country where she would be all his own; yet never had he felt before as strongly that there was a barrier between them, slight but relentless as a thin sheet of adamant, through which he might gaze and despair, but which he could never break.

All unaware, Sybil was gradually impressing on her lover the fact that there was existent in her soul a vital and powerful principle of right, of duty, which he had never either believed in or accepted; he knew she loved him, he saw that fact written in fatal characters on fading cheek and sorrow-darkened eye; he knew it was her pining heart, her thwarted passion, that had worked its destruction on the fair flesh as well as the tortured spirit; and he could not but recognize that there was something more powerful than the master passion of humanity that could so defend and protect her from its strong assault; he understood at last, that there is a divine strength at the command of human devotion, which is mighty to save, even when the salvation itself is so as by fire. He said farewell with an echo in his voice that stung Sybil as if the adieu had been for eternity, but only a keen flash of anguish in her eye told that she felt that tone of despair; and as he strode away from the house with his wide hat slouched over his face as far as might be, a certain awe stole over that wild, bold spirit, a sense of some loftier Power in life than he had hitherto reckoned with, a consciousness, that like Saul of old, it was hard for him to "kick against the pricks"; not a feeling of submission, but of resistance and defiance, that followed him for many a weary day; but then Sybil's prayers followed him also, though he knew it not, and so entertained angels unawares.

Madam Stanley had heard and noted all that

Colonel Stonebridge had said, but she had not remarked Sybil's abstraction; it was the custom of the time for young people to be silent before their elders; for young maids to be shy and modest in the presence of gentlemen, strange as it may seem to the girls of to-day; and Madam Stanley thought nothing of her niece's speechlessness. She herself broke the silence first after the guest's departure.

"So it seemeth Philip Kent will not be among us this winter; I suppose his wife is little of a housewife; but it is not seemly to my mind that a married woman should gad abroad and be so gay as John Stonebridge telleth."

"I suppose it was her wont, before," said Sybil, gently.

"Then it should cease to be her wont now. Philip would do well not to waste his substance in riotous living, but come back to his own good house here, and teach his wife thrift and godly living."

Sybil smiled; she had seen Annetje Stuyvesant in Albany, and understood how far from that selfish nature were either thrift or godliness; but her face saddened again as her aunt went on.

"It seems they will make a country mansion of Joshua Dyer's house, and spend their winters in the city; so I suppose we may look for finery and fashion to alight in our quiet neighborhood when the warm weather is come."

Sybil thought of Esther, and the cruel trial it would be to her to meet Philip and his wife, to see their happiness, to watch the home, the heart, the life that should have been hers, all lavished on another. How could she serve or save her hapless friend? Like one of old she gave herself unto prayer, and prayer for Esther.

CHAPTER XVII.

REWARD.

The mills of the gods grind slowly.

IT is not always that evil deeds receive their punishment in this world, but doubtless they often do receive it in a way invisible to men. Esther's punishment was in her own soul, and day by day it seemed to burn in upon her more deeply. If she could have confided or confessed her sin, it would have been less a burden; but to do that would involve Philip and blast his character, for she was not subtle enough to imagine a way to blame herself and exonerate him. So she went about feeling that she was branded, though the brand was unseen of man; that she was a hypocrite and could not confess her hypocrisy, deeply as she repented it; this introspection might have turned her brain and ended her short record in a madhouse, but for the daily tender alleviation of her thoughts in teaching and petting her school children, and the growing affection with which she regarded Aunt Tempy; a woman gifted with that keen sense of humor and indomitable hopefulness that now and then springs up amid the stern gloom or the superhuman piety of New England records, like the cheerful and persistent glow of the "butterfly weed" on our sandy hillsides; a blossom gay not only with its own deep orange tint, the concentrated color of a hot sunset, but always alive and glad with the host of winged adorers its beauty and honey attract. Her odd ways, her quaint speech and thought, her interminable fund of apt proverbs and queer stories, amused and interested Esther, who inherited no small share of humorous perception from her father, and often beguiled her from the despairing consciousness of her own moral condition, as she considered it from her morbid point of view.

Philip was troubled with no such inward distress; he was too selfish and too fond of his own ease, to let his mind revert to any unpleasantness: what was done was ended, for him; he did not concern himself about the will; that, as he viewed it, was a mere matter of justice, and as for his love-making to Esther, what man of his type ever gave a remorseful thought to a mere amusement of that kind.

Indeed, are there many men of any type who think it harm to say sweet words and offer tender caresses to any girl who is willing to hear and receive them? I leave the answer to the experience of those who have been attractive girls, and the observation of those who have not..

But Philip's judgment came upon him, nevertheless, in a more open fashion. Annetje Stuyvesant's great charm to him had been her difficult, inaccessible manner; accustomed to see and conquer, Philip was not a little weary of conquests which were too easy to be exciting or interesting. He had not a mind capable of analyzing character, a perception quick enough to understand it instinctively. He found in the revelation of personal traits that the *solitude à deux* of marriage inevitably brings, that Annetje's coolness and pride were owing to a curious mixture of traits: a cold heart; a physical nature, self-indulgent and luxurious even to the verge of becoming sensual; an impertinent consciousness of being better than her neighbors; an indomitable will; and a prevalent intention of being the one person in the household to whom all its members should be devoted. Natural wit she had; a clear head, and a vivacious brain; as a man she would have been a little superior to Philip Kent, because she was quicker-witted, otherwise, the bent of their natures was alike; and their marriage became from its earliest days an individual conflict. And a conflict it was in which, naturally, the woman came off with flying colors; she stung Philip's self-complacency with sarcasms which made him wince, but which he could neither evade, ignore, or return in kind; and if he showed the hard side of his character, was unfeeling, inattentive, careless, her fierce temper broke out in a torrent of words, or she went into hysterics, a form of demonstration peculiarly unpleasant and subduing to a man who was not accustomed to that sort of thing. Or sometimes she lavished on him caresses that were like the caresses of a tigress, fierce and passionate, thrilling with the consciousness of talons beneath the velvet.

This sort of life was not agreeable to Philip Kent. He did not enjoy the doubt, after a time darkening into the dread, that assailed him whenever he went home from his business, as to whether he should find a sulky, an angry, or a shrieking and laughing wife.

That she sometimes shone on him like an appeased goddess, and clung to him like a really loving woman, did not atone to him for the general storm that clouded his days: he wanted to enjoy life, to have an abundance of this world's goods, to eat, drink, and be merry; and he was not only angered and distressed, but cowed and disheartened by this continuous disturbance. And, beside, his strong self-love and self-conceit were wounded to the quick to discover that he could not mould this woman, who was his wife, into the sort of person he would have her; she resented his educational experiments, laughed at his theories, and remained Annetje Stuyvesant in spite of being Mrs. Philip Kent.

It is only an inert or a weak woman, or, in rare cases, a very tender, selfless, and devoted nature, that a man can shape in his own fashion; and generally he becomes very tired of such a wax puppet, but Annetje was less "married than most women; she had her will and her way, and Philip might make the best — or the worst — of it.

Esther had her revenge, though she never knew it, in the repeated hours when Philip recalled her devotion, her ever-ready sympathy, her readiness to lay down her very life for him; her sweet, worshipping eyes; her soul-lit face, that grew bright or dark with his; her evident admiration for and pride in him.

Woe to the woman who feels above her husband in the slightest respect — if she lets him know it! From that hour he is averted from her, he resents the tie between them, he is injured and unrelenting. To wound a man's self-love is to kill all his other love forever. It is true that Philip was still outwardly devoted to his wife; he waited on her wants, watched over her intimations, guarded her from all the ills and inconveniences of life, and was remarked on as the most patient and thoughtful of husbands, — because he well knew that in this way only could he hope for, or expect peace in his own house, and beyond anything else he desired quiet, if pleasure were denied him.

But in the first two years of his marriage, he was more than once driven to the conscious acknowledgment that he had made a mistake, that Annetje was not the woman he ought to have married.

He would have liked to solace himself with the society of other women, for he was one of those men who enjoy the companionship of women more than that of men. The conversation and fellowship of average men jarred on him, because they did not acknowledge his superiority. He avoided those conclaves on the tavern "stoeps" in summer, or in the sanded bar-room, where the heaped logs and the high settles attracted other loungers; where the harsh cackle of the politician's strident laugh, or the more disgusting chuckle of the low storyteller timed the chorus of applauding listeners; he better liked to pose at the suppers of his numerous acquaintance as a devotee of women in a lofty fashion. Dear to him were the pathetic little confidences made to gentle souls about his low spirits, his failing health, or sundry griefs without a name; dear the pressure soft white hands allowed, the blush of sympathy, the eyes gleaming with pitiful interest, the tender voice of consolation and cheer. He knew that now he could go no further than these permissible indulgences, being a married man; that the kisses and embraces he had so often stolen in moonlight walks, or sleighrides, where the temptation was so near, could no longer be allowed him; but he soon found out that Annetje, for all her coldness, was as jealous as a woman could be; not because she loved him, but because she so loved herself.

It pleased him that she refused to return to Trumbull, not only for that next summer, but for nearly two years; he feared lest her wrath should light on Esther, with whom he fully expected not only to be on friendly terms, but to whom he meant to turn for comfort. He calculated acutely on those stringent customs of propriety, no less cultivated in those days in the country than in the town, which should bring Esther to his house, as at least a ceremonious visitor; and no less keenly he built upon her past devotion and her faithful nature as a guarantee that she would be ready to forgive and comfort him; so that he really longed to go back to Trumbull. During that first summer, after Esther began her school, he visited his old home once, on pretext of seeing to his business there, but he did not meet her. Delia still lived in the house, having fetched her old mother to keep her company; and Hiram, lodging elsewhere, attended to the garden, the horses, and the cow. It was an expensive business, this keeping up the old homestead; but Uncle Dyer, with the desire common to all men to carry out their will or wish after they are gone from the possibility of enjoying either wish or will, had made it an imperative condition with his heir that this place should be kept in order as long as Philip lived. He had the same feeling about his house that some men have about their places of burial, — a desire that it should not lapse into neglect and decay; but then it was not considered decent to allow the graves of kindred to be run over with weeds and briers; to openly leave their memorials in a state of disrespect and disorder. He needed no clause in his will to provide for such a contingency; but pining, as we all do, not to be utterly forgotten, entirely blotted out as one who had not been, who "had given up the ghost and no eye had seen" him, he left orders in detail concerning his mansion and premises which Philip could not evade.

Sybil Saltonstall, after the Christmas visit which Colonel Stonebridge made her, saw him no more for many months. She shut up her sorrow in her heart, and grew still more sweet and saint-like; indeed, her

Aunt Stanley's house and society were good training for a saint; but Sybil had no other home, and the customs of the day forbade her travelling about by herself, as independent young women do to-day. She also had a sense of duty toward her uncle and aunt, as standing in the place of her parents, that it would be difficult to explain to the girl of this period.

It was a great relief to her that her beloved Esther was to be spared the trial of having Philip at hand the next summer, and she hastened to let her know, in an incidental way, that he had lately written as much to her Uncle Stanley. As for Sybil herself, as long as Governor Stanley was absent so often on the business of the Colony, she was glad to have it needful for her to be at home on her aunt's account. She had friends in New York and Albany both, who would gladly have had her spend the winter and spring months with them, but she excused herself on the plea that she must not leave Madam Stanley alone, rejoicing that she had this valid reason for escaping any possibility of meeting John Stonebridge again; for Sybil looked upon their separation as final and eternal, and to see his face and hear his voice, was only a renewal of her burnt-sacrifice, and a fresh martyrdom.

So a year and a half rolled over the heads of these dwellers in a quiet New England village, with as little chance or change as life ever brings; the elements of woe and wrath and tempest were all there, but they slept. Esther went on her way successfully; her little pupils adored her; and if her experience corroborated her well-taught creed of "original sin," in the naughty tricks of little cherubs who looked all milk and roses, but were as sly, as mischievous, and as thorough little spitfires as kittens, and seemed to revel in "actual transgression"; still her belief in "total depravity," was something shaken, for she found them, even the worst of them, so easy to be coaxed into repentance, so wistful and woful after the ordained spankings, so ready with verbal contrition at least, that she laid their continuous backslidings to the door of their brief baby memories, and kept forgiving the small sinners, till they were half ashamed to sin. Miss Tempy kept the small house in exquisite order, and fed Esther on the most savory if not the most luxurious food; "the tricks and the manners" of modern or French cookery, were all unknown to this thrifty spinster, but her rye and wheat bread were perfect in their way; her pies crisp of crust and absolutely well-flavored; her "election cake" sought for far and near when the housewives about were straitened for help or expected company; though then it wore only the style of "raised cake," Election Day being a festival of the future. Nobody made such "sweetmeats" as Aunt Tempy; such pound-for-pound peaches, in syrup thick and golden like clover honey; such quart tumblers of red quince slices; such wine-colored currant-jelly, that cut like a solid; such great egg-plums, like spheres of clouded amber; or such damson cheese. Meat was not her forte; she did, I grieve to say it, fry her beefsteaks, but then she could roast a chicken to perfection, and her Thanksgiving pig would have made Charles Lamb cry for joy, so round, so crisp, so succulent was the porcine baby, untimely slain to celebrate what is now "a nation's holiday." And as for vegetables!—"I'm dreadful fond of green sass," Aunt Tempy candidly avowed. "Meat vittles I do not really set by a great deal; but now as for 'sparagrass in the season on't, I never pitied Nebuchadnezzar no great if that was the kind o' grass he lived on; and beans, why beans is good all the year round, biled or baked, and they're so fillin'! Then peas, good green or for porridge, 'pease porridge hot,' that is the porridge I'm give to; and corn, I wouldn't ask nothing better for dinner than roasted corn with a leetle mite of sweet butter and salt on to 't; and succotash is fit to set before the king, now I tell ye. Cabbage? well cabbage will smell; I lay that up ag'inst it; and you can't drive nor coax the smell on't out of the house noway. Onions is good, proper good, and dreadful hullsome; more so than what cabbage is; I've got to forgive their sin of smellin' on that account. Why raw onions with a mess of pepper 'n vinegar on 'em is a most amazing purifyin' to the blood in springtime; them and dandelion greens is better 'n a doctor, or 'Lixir Pro. I declare if we could have green things the year round, I shouldn't care if I never saw a bit of meat vittles, exceptin' a mite of salt pork, any more. But mercy me! there's nothin' but potatoes and parsnips eight months in the year that is green, and they ain't, really."

So the days and months went on, and the second summer coming in, brought back, not only Philip Kent, his wife, his infant son, but also John Stonebridge, who had all the past year been troubled with rheumatism, and had now obtained a long leave of absence to rest and recruit, and was coming to the Talcotts for the summer.

CHAPTER XVIII.

GRIST.

But they grind exceeding small.

As Philip Kent had expected, Esther knew that she must pay a ceremonial visit to his wife, or the village gossips would set all their tongues wagging with guesses at a truth nothing would tempt her to have revealed; like many another woman she had hidden her head and thought, as does the proverbial ostrich, that she was altogether out of sight, not at all aware that Philip's devotion and desertion were as patent to the eyes of the townspeople as to hers. Yet instinctively she was right in doing as she did; for the women who pitied her now would have despised her had she shown so little pride and self-control as to resent her wrongs openly. She did not even ask Sybil to go with her, she preferred to be alone when she should meet the new-comers.

Mrs. Kent kept her waiting some time; happily for Esther she was shown into the drawing-room, an apartment that held for her no especially painful associations; and it was not Hannah who opened the door at her knock, but a serving-man whom Philip had fetched up from his New York house to please Annetje.

When Mrs. Kent did enter she was not cordial but

courteous; nothing in her look or manner touched Esther's heart; the delicate, haughty face was a little worn, more with *ennui* than illness, and her languid, indifferent manner seemed to be rather natural than affected.

Esther was simple and civil; she put on nothing that she did not feel; asked after Philip, and heard he had gone to the Long Beach Farm, and, giving thanks inwardly that she was not to meet him, managed to keep up a slow conversation through the decent amount of time allotted for a call; and went away, encountering Sybil and Madam Stanley at the door as they came in. Sybil looked earnestly at her friend; she saw the tranquil face and was glad; had she seen it ten minutes afterward, pity and distress would have darkened all her soul, for just as Esther neared the gate of her home, Philip, in the old chaise, came up the road and stopped to speak to her. Poor Esther! She had felt so sure, so safe; she had seen this man in his absence as he was, not as her passion and imagination had endowed him with heavenly gifts; but now, here, the eyes that had drawn her soul out into his soul, the lips that had pressed hers so often, once more looking and smiling at her, for Philip drew up to speak as he passed, Esther knew that she loved Philip Kent still; shameful, sinful, horrid, as the past was, the wild tremors of her heart, the quick flush of delight, the forgetfulness of all the past, smote her like a flash of blinding light; she loved him! oh, yes, God help her! she loved this man yet, and another woman was his wife. Philip saw her agitation; she could not conceal the sudden pallor and the equally sudden rose-red blush that lit her beautiful face; she could not master the tremulous pathos in her voice, or darken the light that illuminated the mournful dusk of her great eyes; he was himself a little moved, and a little flattered; if Annetje had wounded his self-love to the quick, Esther healed it. She had grown far more lovely since Philip had seen her; her figure was stately and graceful, her taste modelled her dress as far as the stiff fashions of the day allowed; in her gown and petticoat of deep green paduasoy, with frills of quaint old English thread lace; a little white chip hat pinned on the high puffs of hair whose powdered rolls gave a singular charm to her glowing face and clear brunette skin, with cheeks that rivalled the garland of roses on her hat, Esther was indeed a beauty to have alarmed Annetje, who had only seen her quiet, colorless, and wearing a frigid conventional expression as became a formal visitor. Philip said little beyond the ordinary greetings, but his face spoke; his deep, gray eyes melted and glowed, his smile beamed on her with the old power and sweetness, she felt the divine madness of that dismaying emotion that before rioted in her brain possess and envelop her once more; and with a wrench of resolution escaped from his sight, and rushing up to her tiny bedroom, threw herself down on the bed, hid her face, and burst into a passion of tears.

I wish Esther had been a stronger woman, but I must paint her as she was, with a heart greater than her brain, an impulsive, undisciplined character, a creature who in the very nature of things could not escape wreck, and loss, and woe, if left to her own guidance; a girl to whom love was life and breath, but who loved as unwisely as such girls almost invariably do.

Not at first were her tears all bitterness, but rather a relief to her emotion; when she had thoroughly given way to them, a certain calm stole over her; she began to think of Philip instead of herself. Unselfishness is a good thing if it is not extravagant. When the Lord commanded us to love our neighbors as ourselves, He did not say more than ourselves, but made the measure of our neighborly affection and service the due self-love and self-respect which is every man's and woman's law of moral self-preservation. The mad passion that gives up life, character, honor, even decency for the sake of a beloved object, not only wrecks itself, but ministers to the shame and harm of that object.

It was well for Esther in that time, unguarded by a deep religious faith, the reserve and sanctity of a true home, and the tender omniscience of motherly love, that Annetje Kent was a resolute and jealous woman, whom Philip feared; and that Esther's daily life was among the innocent little children whose pure lips and clear eyes shamed her when she considered — as now and then she did — her own position.

Not in this fashion did Sybil Saltonstall suffer; she had a refuge and a strength unknown to Esther; it wrung her heart to encounter John Stonebridge as she was obliged to, often, since he had come to the Talcott mansion, but she held her soul far above in a diviner ether than the mists and clouds of earth; suffering drove her to prayer, and earth to heaven; day after day her face seemed to refine and sweeten, she grew lovelier in every word and deed; yet she had lonely hours of agonies when she felt sure, not being an Agnostic, that Satan tempted her to fall from her sad sanctity and taste the blisses of human love, the peace of a mortal home, the strength and guidance of a man's heart and hand; in those hours she asked herself — or an evil spirit put the question — why she needed to set aside the blessings made for a woman, and endure this gnawing self-denial, simply because her opinions differed from John Stonebridge's? Why, again, might it not be her actual duty to marry him and bring him by her example and her prayers to such a respect and love for religion, that he should enter its service? These terrible hours of casuistic question invariably followed a meeting with her lover, though it might even be a silent one; a little reflection on her part would have relegated the queries to Colonel Stonebridge's reproachful gaze, the dark passion of his melancholy eyes, rather than to the wanderer and devourer of men; but Sybil chose to refer all evil to its powerful source instead of his instruments; she could not invest her handsome, courteous lover with the traditional exterior of Satan, or ascribe to him the taunting and sneering suggestions that vexed her pure and tender soul, and tried the strength of her womanly courage.

To her, as to Esther, this beautiful and beauteous summer was a long torture; to Esther rather a tumult than a trial, for Philip made pretexts to see her, and used all his arts to awaken her sympathy for him that he might again gather her sweet consolations and condolings. It is true, he led a very uncomfortable life; Delia felt it for and with him. June was not yet over, the old white roses with saffron hearts that clambered even to Esther's window-sill, had still a few exquisite half-blown buds on the tips of their long slight branches, when one fine day, after school, Delia walked up the little gravel path and tapped at the schoolroom door, Esther opened it.

"Why, Delia!" she said. "How glad I am to see you. It is a long day since you came over my door-sill."

"I know it!" panted Delia, sinking into the arm-chair, and fanning her heated face with a bandana handkerchief of the most vivid yellow. "I couldn't noways help it, I've been busier'n a bee in a tar-barrel ever sence the folks come home, and I'm clear done over. I tell you what, Esther, I keep rec'lectin' old times the hull time. My land! 'twas like Paradise in them days, — only I didn't sense it. The Squire goin' in and out as pleasant as a picter, and when you and your ma came, you was jest as nateral as he was;

you was our folks right away, and Philip wasn't to call bad; he hectored some, and rid a high horse by times, but he wasn't nothing to complain of. But now! I tell you there's new times, and I can't stan' it. Sech things as she wants cooked up! Who ever heerd tell of puttin' a reason and a bit of citron into the middle of a riz nut-cake before 'twas fried, and then callin' of it a 'oly kook'? That ain't my kind of cook! Then there's her stuff she calls salmagundi; of all the messes! raw fish out o' the river, chopped up with green inions and mixed till its slimy with warm water! makes me spleen to think on't! — and that's her vittles. Then in place of real respectable chopped cabbage, she wants her'n cut into strings and wilted with hot water, and dreened, then she puts vinegar on to't. I should think them things was fit for swine. That ain't nothin' though, folks has different notions, and one man's meat is another man's p'ison as they tell; but she herself is worse'n her vittles. Now I don't never call myself stuck up, but I was always used well by folks I lived with, and respected when I done as I had ought to have did; but mercy me! she thinks hired help is the dirt under her feet! which I ain't nor ain't a goin' to be. An' 'tain't me only; you'd ought to see her a orderin' Hiram round! Ef he was two year old she couldn't ha' giv him more talk. He didn't mind it, not greatly; men-folks will take a sight from a good lookin' woman, but I don't feel to see him rid over, hoss and foot, like that. As for Philip, he's her little dog

Tray; he darsn't do nothin' of his own motion; ef he does she has the highsterics proper bad, and then he flies round! Well, I don't care such a lot about him, he a'n't nothin' to me. I arn my bread myself, and he's made his bed, now he's got to lie on't, be it how it's made, soft or hard; but I have giv' warning, the same house can't hold her an' me to the same time; I'd ruther set up in a hovil and go a berryin' for my livin'!"

"But, Delia! what are you going to do?"

"Now, don't ye smile, a mite! I'm a goin' to get married."

"What! married!"

"Well, I guess so." snapped Delia; "do you think I'm too humly to try for't?"

"Oh, Delia, you know I don't! I was so sorry for poor Hiram."

"I guess I shan't bile an' eat him," retorted the angry woman.

"But he will be so hurt at your marriage."

"I dono about that; I guess he'll be resigned," and Delia laughed; she began to appreciate the situation.

"But who is it?" asked the puzzled Esther.

"Well, now you're come to the p'int, I shouldn't think strange if 'twas reelly, — well, I guess it *is* — Hiram!"

"Oh!" said Esther, with an accent of relief.

"You see," promptly went on Delia, "I stood out quite a spell because he wasn't a professor, and I meant to keep up my end of the matter till he was, but I don't see no signs on't; he's good, real good, as fur as bein' clever to put up with, and havin' faculty, but I mistrust his speritooal condition is sort of duberous. Howsoever, I ain't so young as I was, nor so sot in my idees; I've kind of mellered down, and this bein' what your Uncle Dyer used to call a 'mergency, why I thought 'twould come amazin' handy to have a man round for good and all, and he'll be clever to mother, so I kind of giv him a leetle hint ye know, and my! he took it as spry as a robin takes a worm, and the upshot of the hull is we've took Hillside Farm of Philip, bein' as Robertses folks are movin' out west as fur as the York settlements, a takin' up land there for to clear and plant back of the river, and Philip was lookin' about for tenants. So we put in; I've got quite a little nest-egg, and so's Hi, and we reckon we shall be married next week, and go out to Hillside, bag and baggage. I want you to come over to the minister's house next Thursday, will ye? and kind of stiff me up? I haven't no idee how to behave."

Esther laughed and promised; Delia's justification of her changed plans was certainly a funny piece of sophistry; but when Esther told Sybil the tale, with smiles, it smote her heart with a dull pain instead of laughter; here was a woman who had held out as she had; yet at last been overcome and was about to be happy in the natural, womanly way; her sore heart cried out in sudden envy; it did not strike her that she and Delia were as incapable of comparison as a seraph and a hen, — that for her there was something higher than happiness reserved as a portion; the blessedness of a faithful spirit; the joy and the white robe of them that overcome.

CHAPTER XIX.

DELAY.

Speech is silver, silence is golden.

WHILE all these things were going on in that quiet that masks the inward strife and progression of earthly life, Mr. Hall was not unobservant or inactive.

He kept a tacit guardianship over Esther and her school; once a week he examined the children on their primer, and happy was the child who went through it without a stumble, from

> "In Adam's fall
> We sinned all."

to

> "Zaccheus he
> Did climb the Tree
> Our Lord to see."

for when the long alphabet of rhymes was correctly said, some edible reward issued at once from the pocket of the minister's broad-tailed coat; some red apple, some late sweet peach, perhaps a spicy nut-cake, or a gingerbread monster; and now and then Parson Hall had a field day in the most literal sense of the word, when he would unexpectedly break up the school, and take them, teacher and all, for a long walk in the woods, the meadows, or by the shore;

teaching them as he went, the uses of herbs that grew by the way, the difference in the growth, the foliage, and the bark of trees; the varying species of seaweed and shells; or when the soft autumn days shed their mists of fire over the woods, he took them nutting, or to gather wild grapes. All this time he was learning to love Esther with the strong, silent passion of a man who has not only suffered loss but been denied the human love that is so dear to men, the home and fireside so coveted, especially by those who do the world's heaviest work, — the attempt to teach and improve the race. Rachel had been an angel to him; Esther was a woman; her very faults fascinated him; the quick temper, the outspoken tongue; the brief anger, the sudden repentance on its heels; the capricious humor; the sweet heart of womanly affection for her little flock; each and all moved and bewitched him; but he knew well that Esther's undisciplined nature had been wrung to its centre by Philip Kent, and he could see that even yet it bled and moaned in the unhealed anguish of loss; he did not know that still Esther loved that false man, when he had given his name and his life to another; he could not have believed it had the thought come into his mind.

But one thing he did know, — that he must wait for this desire of his life; that to speak now would be idle; he must be patient, and content himself with giving her all the help and protection his office and position afforded; sure that time, enlightener as well as consoler, would at least teach Esther the falseness and selfishness of Philip Kent, and then perhaps that empty heart might turn to him for comfort.

But Esther had no idea of this. Day after day Philip contrived in some way to see her, not every day, but often; it was so pleasant to turn from Annetje's indifference or petulance, to the tender sweetness of Esther's voice and eyes; and she, fooled by her own heart, as myriads of women have been before her, grew to pity him more than ever for the unhappiness he half hinted, half confessed, and which Delia's revelations confirmed; she reasoned with that specious yet convincing sort of sophistry we all resort to when we desire to do a thing we ought not to do, that there was no harm in supplementing to Philip the deficiencies of his life at home.

She forgot his falseness to her before; his marriage which was a deliberate and voluntary step; the fact that he had made to her all the professions of a lover, and knew that she thoroughly shared what seemed his real passion. A mere woman, forgiving more utterly than a saint, Esther ignored all this, and hastened to meet her prodigal half way. They met in the old places, they lingered together on the lonely shore, when Annetje believed him inspecting his flocks and herds at Hillside: and gradually as before, Philip sunned himself in those warm eyes, held the soft taper fingers to his lips, cradled the dark head on his shoulder, and gathered kisses at his will; Esther all this while blinded by her re-awakened passion, filled with an absorbing love that covered its symbolic wings with the veil of the nun Pity, and wore the aspect of virginal innocence and pure affection.

To what irreclaimable depths this loss of self in utter devotion to Philip Kent might have plunged her, it is not best to speculate; there are thousands of other women who have dared these rapids and gone over the great fall to their eternal loss; it was the good hand of God that saved Esther on its very brink, and bade her shudder and recoil with the heavy consciousness and awful terror of sin premeditated if uncommitted, when in the after-time she looked back on the sweet poison of those hours.

In the meantime, some little merit is due to Philip; either his early training, his fear of Annetje, or his dread of popular reprobation, deterred him from taking the worst advantage of Esther; probably, he might yet have ruined and betrayed her had nothing interposed to prevent, but so far he had in a measure respected her friendless innocence, and understood the pure if mad passion which trusted him so utterly, and worshipped him so boundlessly, and which a worse or stronger man would have misinterpreted.

Parson Hall had been away from his parish very much this summer; a brother clergyman, failing in health in his charge in one of the Southern cities, but too poor to leave his home and travel, had come to Trumbull for a short visit to his mother, and was glad to earn a little by supplying Parson Hall's pulpit, while the parson went up to Northampton to partake in and investigate a state of things new to him, except in theory, now possessing the church of Jonathan Edwards.

It was the beginning of that wonderful interest in religious truth, and conversion to its faith and practice that swept over America from North to South at that time; under the ministrations of the New England clergy first, followed by Whitfield, Tennant, and various others.

Parson Hall had heard of this spiritual revival, afterward called the Great Awakening, and always alert toward heavenly things he would have gone to Northampton in its beginning but for the needs of his own people; he could not leave his flock with no shepherd, and loudly as his soul called for the refreshment of this new and lofty experience, he felt that his duty forbade him to go away, and in those days, duty was the dominant chord of every Christian man's life.

But when Mr. Atterbury came back to Trumbull, and confided to Parson Hall that he had fetched with him a goodly parcel of sermons, writ for and delivered unto his people in the Carolinas, and desired to find a parish where he might be hired for the summer, so to defray his modest expenses in Trumbull; the parson knew that his earnest prayer, that a way might be opened for him to share in the new light, had been answered.

He installed Mr. Atterbury, a slight, refined-looking

man with a fervent soul and a persuasive voice, over his congregation, and betook himself up the country, to sit at the feet of the great Jonathan Edwards.

It was while he was gone, that a great blow and a great deliverance came to Sybil; John Stonebridge, about the beginning of August left Trumbull suddenly. He had made no overt attempt again to soften Sybil's heart; it is true he behaved himself in her presence as one desperate and destroyed in hope and life; his eyes wore a look of gloom and evil, his lips a curling sneer; but she knew that he shared in all the junketings of the Talcott family and their gay friends; for hospitality and gayety were marked traits of the Stonebridge tribe to its remotest ramification; and being "church" people, as Episcopalians were sometimes styled in those days, they were not circumscribed by the rigid regulations of the Presbyterians, but took the position of dissenters awarded to all other sects but that one favored by the Puritans, and made the most of their freedom. Sybil knew that John Stonebridge danced ofttimes till the small hours of night; that he was an adept at the card-table, where he won fabulous sums of money; that he practised at "the fence" with his comrades, and was a keen sportsman. When he passed the house with other laughing and shouting men, comrades of the army, revellers from the city, armed for a hunt in the woods, his face wreathed with jollity and good fellowship, Sybil learned by sheer repetition the old lesson, that

"Man's love is of man's life, a thing apart."

But her pride and her piety both forbade her to acknowledge that

"'Tis woman's whole existence."

She tried feebly but honestly to divert her thoughts from their forbidden channel; she visited among the few poor that the thrifty village harbored, she waited upon the sick, she consoled the suffering, she learned how to make all the delicate viands that please or nourish invalids, and supplied them to cases of need and desert; she interested herself in the fervent and eloquent sermons of Mr. Atterbury; her head bent lowest in prayer, her voice rose highest in praise; she was punctual at every service; — yet against her convictions, her will, her common sense, she was haunted through all by John Stonebridge's face, as if she were a murderer and he a victim.

One still August day, when the sky was gray, the south wind blowing, and the sullen dash of long, dark waves beating the shore, Hiram drove up to Governor Stanley's house and asked to see Miss Sybil. She left the window where she sat looking at the water, and seeing instead a man's face, and went down. Hiram stood at the hall door, keeping an eye on his gig, which was the pride of his soul, and twirling his old straw hat between his horny hands.

He made Sybil an awkward bow and plunged at once into his errand. "Say, Miss Sybil, Delye wants to know ef you can come over to Hillside right off? there's a woman there seems to be sort of crazy-like, or somethin', and she's bound to see you; she's got your name writ onto a paper. I tackled up and come over for ye, and I'll fetch ye back ef you'll go."

"Yes, Hiram, I will go," said Sybil, with a faint, sweet smile.

She was often so sent for, and only staying to put some simple doses and a jar of gruel into the basket, she used for such purposes, she stepped into the gig beside Hiram, and a half hour's drive through the sad, sunless air brought them to the farm.

Delia came out to meet them, flushed and tearful.

"Land of Goshen, Miss Sybil; she's cleared out! She hes, and left the babe right here. I am beat!"

"How came she here at first?" asked Sybil.

"Why, she footed it over from Darby, right along the 'pike, so she told, and she was real footsore; but fust thing she come in, she pulled out a paper with your name on't, and asked real prompt, if you lived round here, and when I said you did, she was for goin' down to the taown right off, but I said Hi should fetch ye. When that he was gone, she set and meditated quite a spell; then she wanted some writin' paper, so I give her a leaf out of the back side of "Jinkses Devotions," and Hi's quill pen, and she writ a spell, and then she sort of folded up the paper and laid it onto the babe's breast, he lyin' asleep onto the settle-bench. I went out to see if my biscuits was riz, and when I come in she was gone, and she ha'n't come back yet. I don't know nothing what's come of her."

Sybil stooped to look at the sleeping child and saw

her own name on the paper, under one of its tiny hands. She took it from that slight pressure and opened it. This was written in it, —

"sibil Saltonstol. I heered John say that Name in his slepe; hee was Mine and You took him: now You can Hav his Childe: You hav stole One, take t'other. I hav no Concern to liv no More

"arbell."

Sybil shuddered and dropped the paper on the floor. This was the way that John Stonebridge consoled himself then. Her face grew stern and white, her pride took fire, her purity recoiled; traitor alike to God, to this creature, to her, John Stonebridge fell from his pedestal then and there. She loathed with all her soul the feet of clay that her idol stood upon.

"Is the' anything about the babe?" asked Delia.

Sybil did not answer her. The child was the sign and seal of guilt and sin. No instinct of womanhood stirred her pity for its evil fate, its hapless innocence.

"You can take it to the selectmen," she said, at last, speaking like an automaton; she did not even lift the paper from where it dropped, she drew up the hood of her light riding-cloak and went out to the gig, Hiram following. When he came back he said to Delia, —

"Say, she never spoke a word the hull way. I never see a human critter look the way she did. What upon airth did that paper say?" For Hiram's keen, marital eyes perceived that it was gone from the floor.

"Oh, land! a mess of stuff! The girl wanted for to have her take that child." For Delia sometimes reserved her confidences.

"Well, I shouldn't want no child o' mine to be took by one that looked like as she did. She ain't real kindly, now is she, Delye?"

"Well, she is, an' she ain't. She's proud as all possessed, and pious as all natur, and the' has ben times when she set by some folks like everything. But I guess she'll let that babe alone."

"What be you goin' to do with 't?" meekly inquired Hiram.

"Give it some warm milk," was Delia's dry response.

Sybil was once more alone in her chamber, dry-eyed, wan, silent.

Out on the lashing water, christened into that newness of life we call death, by the dripping rain, floated John Stonebridge's idle love, the mother of his forsaken child, — poor Arbell.

But Sybil lived to conquer and to serve.

CHAPTER XX.

JUDGMENT.

Sense endureth no extremities; and sorrows destroy us or themselves.

THE little village of Trumbull was thrown into wild excitement two days after Sybil's visit to Hillside Farm by the discovery of a young girl's body washed up on the shore close by. Delia at once suspected that it was her transient guest, and would have kept the surmise to herself, but that she knew Hiram, a real masculine gossip, would never be able to hold his peace on the subject, however she might exhort him. She judged him truly; no sooner did he hear of the discovery, than he avowed his belief that it was the girl who had left her baby with his wife, and Delia was at once sent for to identify the body. Poor Arbell! the delicate, rounded figure lay on a bench in a fisherman's hut just out of the village, its clinging garments torn from the strong white arms and marble bosom by the fury of the waves, the bare feet bruised and one wrenched cruelly, but the lovely face undisfigured, tranquil, but oh how ineffably sad! Its tender outlines were brought out by the mass of dark wavy hair that poured its wealth, dank and dripping, about the dimpled shoulders even to the knee, and

Delia's tears fell hot and fast as she looked at the hapless wreck of life and loveliness.

She had, with sudden prevision, thrown the note Sybil read into the fire, and when, posted by Hiram, the justice who presided at this informal inquest, a man of many small offices, being justice of the peace, coroner, hog-hayward, titheing-man, and town clerk, asked her what were the contents of the note, she answered him as she had her husband, that it was a request that Miss Saltonstall should take care of her baby.

"I 'spose," added Delia, astutely, "the poor cretur had heerd how good Miss Sybil is to folks, and havin' made her mind up to do away with herself, she thought to leave the babe in good hands. Its amazin' to me she didn't drownd it along with her."

The sole item of information beside this was the girl's own confession that she came to Trumbull from Derby, thirty miles up the country, but in the wholesome want of communication among the scattered towns of the colony, and the equally wholesome want of gossiping newspapers, Derby gave no sign, and it was nobody's business to go thither and hunt up information that could do no good; this waif of the world was buried in a corner of the Trumbull graveyard, and no stone told her mournful story, or even that her name was Arbell.

Madam Talcott had her own suspicions; she remembered that the day John Stonebridge left her house so suddenly, she had herself taken the few letters from the servant who fetched them, and that of the two John had, one was on regimental business evidently, from its outer aspect and peculiarity of address, while the other was directed in an unformed round hand, and in the corner was scrawled "Derby" after the fashion of old-time country postmarks. But Madam Talcott was a wise and a proud woman; she said nothing. Well she knew that the Stonebridge race thought little of what they termed "peccadilloes" of this sort; many a village girl before Arbell had rued the day when one of that family had noticed their rustic beauty and betrayed their simple faith. She hoped the matter might be hushed up and never come to Sybil's ear, for though she inwardly thought Sybil a stiff prude, she would have been glad to have her cousin John "settle himself" so well, as to wealth and position, and she held the ancient fallacy firmly, that a reformed rake makes the best husband.

But for Sybil all "love time," as the old poets call it, was over. Her pride, the besetting sin of her nature, was up in arms; she loathed the thought that ever she had stooped to care for an adulterer and murderer, for she looked the truth in the face, revolting as its visage was. And to fortify her pride, as Delia had said, came in her piety; she shuddered to think how near she had come to yielding her life and soul into the guidance of such a reprobate, and thanked God fervently that she had been enabled to fight the good fight of faith and lay hold on eternal life. Alas! it is a phrase of war that there are some victories that are worse than defeats; her purposes were indeed broken off, and an awful void, a sense of outlook into some horrid gulf from the edge of a precipice, such as haunts the troubled dreamer, showed her now that hitherto she had, unconsciously, cherished a little spark of hope in the future, of answer to prayer.

She did not in this first blank consider that all answers to prayer are not affirmative, or that John Stonebridge, with the scornful levity characteristic of the man, would resist and defy even the influence of the woman he loved best, if it tended toward a higher life than he led of his own will. But the release of Sybil also was the safety of Esther.

Jealous, without knowing where or upon whom to direct her jealousy, when Annetje heard the sorrowful story of Arbell, her suspicions, cruel and insulting as the suspicions of jealousy ever are, fell upon Philip; he was away from her a great deal on plea of business of course, and her own condition of health just now would not admit of her taking long drives; she put "this and that together," much after the fashion of a modern crazy-quilt, and worked herself up into a conviction, almost amounting to certainty, that Philip was the seducer of the suicide, and the father of the child still in Delia's care; for Delia had found it hard to part with the baby, who won its way into her childless tender heart, not only because it was a baby and motherless, but because it had all those infantile charms that make babyhood irresistible.

That the child was left at Hillside, and that Delia had kept it, confirmed Annetje in her belief: she did not really love Philip, but she loved herself intensely, and treason to her position was a dire offence. Angry and insulted, Philip at first refused to exculpate himself, but frightful hysterics on his wife's part, and a certain sense of guilt on his, as far as losing his affection for her and making love to another woman seemed to him guilt, at last drove him into a patched-up peace; but Annetje was determined to leave Trumbull at once and return to New York for her confinement, instead of staying near what she was pleased to call a "rival baby," and in the interim she would not allow Philip a moment out of her sight, and he dared not write a word of farewell to Esther lest it should fall into other hands.

So again he left her, as suddenly as before, and again with Annetje.

And having so left her it occurred to him that after all the situation had been embarrassing; he had now a chance to put an end to what might be a painful and weary relation in the future, so like a wise man he dropped Esther entirely; not one word came to refresh her tired and anxious spirit; she was again alone, with her own thoughts. This second desertion as it seemed to Esther, aroused her to a deeper knowledge of Philip's real character than she had hitherto possessed. She began to understand the overpowering self-love that was his dominant trait, and in the new pain of this second loss she also saw how false and wrong her own conduct had been. Severed from the eyes that had for her the real snake-charm; hearing no more the voice of tender passion that had fed her bewitched ear with phrases of love and appeals for consolation, Esther, like Sybil, stood in the midst of the wilderness, alone, but without Sybil's consoling consciousness of a victory over herself, and a stainless heart and life.

Shortly after Philip and his family returned to New York, Parson Hall came back from his three months' stay at Northampton. In his absence, Aunt Ruthy had gone up the country to see relatives, and the parsonage stood empty of life. Trumbull people were glad enough to see its windows thrown open again, and the smoke curling up from its great chimney; and Mr. Hall was equally glad to be at home.

His stay in Northampton had been a fresh and vivid experience to him; like most of his contemporaries, he had been educated under the precepts of the law of God, and the rigid demands of duty; the Gospel was set aside in those days as too mild a doctrine to use freely; and sinners were driven with scorpion lashes of threatening, fears of judgment to come, horrors of eternal punishment, to accept conversion instead of salvation.

But Parson Hall's nature, and the sweet charities of Rachel's religion had agreed so well, that long before he went to Northampton his belief had grown uneasy to him; he felt a deep need of something more comforting and healing than the stringent demands of the decalogue, and the aspect of God as an avenger and punisher. In the midst of the crowds at Northampton who were melted to tears or excited to joyful praise by the divine eloquence of Whitfield and Edwards, he too learned the lesson of the Gospel, that God is love, not in the sense of that feeble human love, that is weak, partial, and incapable of justice; but love that is spiritual, sacrificial, strong, and tempering its true judgments with heavenly mercy.

Full of this new light he returned to his charge, and soon the church at Trumbull was filled to its extreme capacity, for not only his own people, but those of adjoining parishes flocked to hear him, and the Great Awakening extended all over that part of Connecticut.

There were meetings thrice a week besides those on Sunday, the small gayeties of the town were suspended, shopmen closed their doors, fishermen left their nets to dry, farmers forgot their ploughing for winter grain; men, women, and children poured into the church, all sects and many of no sect flocked to hear the wonderful Gospel; a story old as ever, but forever new; and more than new in its rekindled aspect, and the heart-thrilled eloquence of him who now delivered it.

Hiram, driven by Delia to attend these meetings, when the baby kept her at home, soon came under this influence, and to his wife's tearful joy declared himself a changed man, and was admitted to the church.

"He was good enough afore," declared Delia, "as fur as this world goes; I hadn't never no fault to find with Hi; he's a good provider, and amazin' kind to his own folks, and dretful handy round the house. I dono as he'll be any better in them ways, but he wasn't a professor nor he wa'n't reelly *con*verted; didn't never read the Bible, nor pray, nor attend the Sanctooary reg'lar. I used to feel consider'ble bad when I thought about his future state, and the onsartainty of life, and such as that; for I set quite a little by Hiram; and its been borne in on my mind that mabbe I done wrong to him as well as to my profession by marryin' of him. I dono's I did, an I dono *as* I did; but it's all right now, glory halleluyer! an' thank the Lord!" and she wiped her eyes with her checked apron, for they were full to overflowing.

Even Sybil's rigid, pale face softened and glowed with sympathetic feeling as she too learned further of the love that had only worn to her the stern lineaments of dreary duty. Parson Hall had noticed two faces when he first went up into his pulpit after so long an absence, that made his heart ache; Sybil's, set in lifeless, icy endurance; Esther's, full of unendurable woe. For Esther's face was one of wonderful expression, it varied with every thought: when she was gay it absolutely sparkled, when she was sad all its lineaments were surcharged with grief so patent that even the little children of her charge stole to her side with mute caresses, and whispered wistfully among themselves. It wrung Parson Hall's heart to look at Esther; he had left her blooming and blissful, now she was the image of despair. He knew Philip Kent had left Trumbull somewhat suddenly, but he had only just heard it, and he shrank from attributing to this fact, Esther's unhappiness. Sybil's face pained him too, but she had never interested him like Esther. Sybil had the capacity for being a saint, but one saint at a time is as much as the best of men can endure as a companion; it was Esther's total unlikeness to Rachel that attracted Parson Hall; whatever life might bring to her of a new love or a religious experience, Esther would always be a woman; warm, jealous perhaps, faithful, loving, and impulsive; the sort of creature to pet, to caress, to be a companion; amusing and tender, "everything by turns, and nothing long," but never a saint; that sort of material was not in her.

The story of Arbell, too, had but recently been told to the minister, and he had his opinion of the matter; but it did not, like Annetje's, cast a shadow of suspicion on Philip, rather did it find confirmation in Sybil's wan and frigid aspect, the look of one who has lost all that made earth dear, and was not yet comforted by the peace of heaven.

But as the days went on, Esther was carried out of herself and her grief; her heart, sad and vacant, turned to the hopes of the gospel as a flower opens to the dawn : she saw no longer an angry and avenging God ready to visit her with direct judgment for her sin, but she perceived a redeeming Saviour, come to deliver her at once from its penalty and its bondage, and with all her enthusiastic nature she devoted herself to His service, and basked in the sweetness of forgiveness, the joy of a new spiritual life; she, too, with a crowd of others, stood up with Hiram to acknowledge her inward change and pledge herself to the Master, and Parson Hall bitterly rebuked himself that in that solemn hour he could notice the rapt loveliness of her countenance, the peace and glory of her beautiful eyes; he forgot that he was a man as well as a minister.

But Esther knew she was still a woman; even in those hours of prayer that filled her soul with the divine tranquillity that comes of communion with the divine, she could not yet pray for Philip; she felt her past sin with renewed poignance since she also felt that it was forgiven of God; and she felt, too, more bitterly, the sin and shame belonging to a man who, himself a professor of the same religion, could so belie his avowed faith by his walk and conversation. It was as yet impossible, even in the humility and joy of her own forgiveness, that she should forgive Philip or pray for him. She had yet to learn that forgiveness does not mean excuse or condemnation, but a fulness of superhuman goodness that

> "Like a mighty stream
> O'er all our sins divinely flows."

It was not so with Sybil; in the new uplifting of her already consecrated soul, she prayed for John Stonebridge as a cherub, image of wisdom and strength, might have prayed for a sinful man; without one throb of emotion or personal interest, but on general principles; just as she prayed for all the people of the colony, for heathens and publicans and sinners everywhere. John Stonebridge as a man and a lover was forever dead to her, and she had made "suttee" upon his memory, of this world's passions and hopes, as far as she had any share in them; but as a sinner among other sinners, still going astray and beguiling others into sin, he still lived and needed prayer. He would not have been flattered by his position in Sybil's mind; even if he ever should know it. Could it be true here too, that

"It was not love that went"?

CHAPTER XXI.

TEMPY'S TURN.

> An odd little god,
> Dan Cupid, is he!
> His arrows do fly, alow and ahigh;
> A wonder to me.

AMONG others who crowded in from the neighboring villages during this period, to hear Parson Hall preach at the "protracted meetings," was a certain little man of discreet age, who had met Miss Temperance Tucker before she came to live in Trumbull.

Deacon Ammi Hopkins was a short, fierce-looking, alert person; his gray hair was brushed as upright on his head, as if it were a bristle brush; his deep-set eyes snapped with determination, and his shaggy, heavy eyebrows gave him a perpetual frown; while his thick, red nose, and firm lips gave you the idea of a will and temper not easily moved or placated. But it was not so; it is true Ammi was a man of loud and aggressive speech, but at heart kindly, simple, and intent to do all his duty according to his "light."

He came in to call on Miss Tempy one night, after tea, and poured out his story to her sympathetic ear, for he had a story. The unlucky little man had just been admonished by the church in Pickering, where he lived, and his whole soul was roused with what he would have called righteous indignation.

"I'll tell ye jest how 'twas, Miss Tempy," he said, carefully depositing his broad-brimmed beaver hat on the floor, spreading his red and yellow bandana handkerchief across his knees, and pursing up his lips with a pleased consciousness that he had a tale of woe to impart.

"You see, Parson Dyer, he was a puttin' forth consider'ble strong doctrine one Sabbath day. I guess 'twas in July last; yes, 'twas; because I remember 'twas the sixth day of July, of a Saturday, I had bought a cow-critter of 'Minadab Sparks, down to Dog's Misery, 'n he'd got the better of me on the trade; for come to find out that cow was nine year old, ef she was a day, and I've faith to b'lieve he knowed it the hull time. Well, that sot me a thinkin' about the sinfulness of sin, 'nd how bad 'twas for other folks besides the sinner; and I fell back, as I hed ofttimes before, onto the myster'ous workins of Providence. I've always ruther consated that the' wasn't no good puppus in sin. I can't see none, and to look at it in a common sense p'int o' view now, how can the' be good to evil? It's a clear contradiction to my mind. I'd had it revolvin' around in my head all Sat'day evenin'. I'd read over the Catechiz, but that didn't p'int out any way of escape, as you may say, nor I couldn't find none in Scriptur so fur as I had time to study on't that night, concernin' the matter; and Sunday mornin' too, some. Well, I went to meetin', and there I sot, still consarned in my mind on the subjeck-matter, when sure enough, Parson Dyer he up and give us a most an amazin' discourse, wherein he went for to say that sin was a part of the dispensation of Providence, and ther'fore wasn't to be questioned about; nor no vain seekin' to be entered into about the cos or beginnin' on't.

"Well, I was 'stounded, so to speak, and clear put about; and I shook my head consider'ble smart, as who should say 'No! no! I purtest aginst that view on't.' I dono as I should have did it in meetin' if I had have considered the matter real thorough; p'raps I shouldn't; but I was took aback, and I sort of spoke in meetin'. There wasn't no speech nor language, as Scriptur says, but in the eye on't I sort of made as though I would speak, and Deacon Small he see me. Now, Miss Tempy, I should like to ask ye what's your onprejudiced mind on the subject? Did I do what I hadn't ought to hev did? Did I disturb public worship an rile the meetin'?"

"Well," answered Miss Tempy, briskly, laying down the stocking she was always knitting, and looking at him over her spectacles. "I'm free to say I dono wherein you done wrong. Who was to know you wasn't asleep, and a dreamin'?"

"Me!" screamed the outraged Ammi. "Me asleep in meetin'! Why, I'd ruther you'd said I had spoke my mind right out. Haven't I sot under Parson Dyer this twenty odd year and heered him down to nineteenthly every Sabba'-day, but one when he was off to his sister's funeral, and never so much as nodded?"

"Well, well. Sam Small might ha' mistrusted ye,

for all. The spirit is willin' ye know sometimes, when the flesh ain't. As fur as the doctrine goes, why, I ha'n't looked into it myself. I'm consider'ble taken up with my work week days, and Sabba'-days I feel as though 'twas the most I could do to listen to the sermons without tryin' to take 'em all in. Leastways I done so when I lived to Pickering; but here 'tis different. Parson Hall is a real searchin' and comfortin' preacher. He don't fuss much with doctrines and sech."

"Well, I make no doubt, Sister Tucker, but what he's sooted to your sect. The woman was in the transgression ye know, and ain't on an ekality with men folks. 'Milk for babes,' Scripter says, and it ain't strange that Parson Hall soots you; but I wa'nt so much inquirin' as to your opinion about the idea of sin bein' a good or no, as I was askin' ef you seemed to sense that I'd did enough to be called up before the meetin' and admonished."

"No; I don't," sharply replied Tempy. "I don't think you done a thing out o' the way. I dono why a man can't shake his head in meetin', if so be he feels to do it. Parson Dyer ain't the king, nor yet he ain't nyther pope nor bishop. I guess our folks didn't cross the water to get rid o' them church an state things to put up with 'em in these colonies."

The first spark of the Revolution snapped in Miss Tempy's black eye, and its battle-flag cast a red glow on her cheek as she spoke; yet she herself would never have dared to defy such a constituted authority as a minister's, — for herself. It was her womanly sympathy with Ammi; it was her womanly nature that made her add, —

"As to what you was a sayin' about 'milk for babes' ef my mind serves me, the' is a Scriptur about the 'pure milk of the word' and sech it is, to my thinkin', that we get from Parson Hall."

"Well, well, well!" testily replied Ammi, "that's nyther here nor there; the matter in hand is I was fetched up and admonished; and I don't fellowship that proceedin'. I shook my head a puppus; and I'll do it agin, ef I'm a mind to. I don't care a cornshuck about bein' admonished by 'em; the church has backslid in these latter days; its full of what the 'Postle calls false doctrines, heresies and schisms; there's the abominable doctrines of the Quakers down to Rhody; there's the Baptists sinnin' aginst light with their dippin' and what not; there's the Hopkinsites, and Sandeman's follerin', and the Lord only knows what else beside; Prelatists right here amongst ye, and Papists, for-'t-I-know; and you set light by doctrines. I tell ye, Miss Tempy, they're the bone an' sinner of the church of God; might as well build a barn 'thout rafters as a church with no doctrines nor covenant nor platform."

"'Tis said they're dispensin' with the half-way covenant mostly," put in Miss Tempy, with feminine evasion of the question.

"I guess they be, I guess they be. To my mind 'twas worse than nothin'; nyther fish nor flesh, nor good red herrin' as the say is. The Lord says, 'Come ye out of her my people!' meanin' the world an' its comp'ny, and comin' out is comin' *out*, 'ta'n't settin' on the fence and lookin' cross-eyed both ways."

"Well, we're havin' an amazin' season of refreshin' here, Deacon Hopkins," smiled Miss Tempy, her own snap having hospitably given place to the deacon's.

"Yes, yes, you be. I come over a puppus to see ef 'twas a real visitation, and so fur as I see it does appear to be a genooine outpourin'. I wish't Parson Dyer would have the mind to come along an' light his lamp to this burnin' bush."

Miss Tempy did not second the wish; she was more interested in her visitor than in Parson Dyer. She rose nimbly from her low chair and opening the door of the corner cupboard extracted from its upper shelf a goodly seed cake set on a plate of old china; a small decanter of currant wine, and two thin spindle-legged wineglasses, setting them on the table by the guest with an air of pleased hospitality. The deacon accepted a wedge of the dainty loaf, and Miss Tempy poured a brimming glass of wine.

"You've no need to be afraid on't, deacon," she assured him. "I made it myself, and your mother giv' me the rewl. The's loaf sugar into 't, and I picked the currants myself."

"I am extreme fond of seed cake," murmured the deacon, his mouth filled with a huge bite of that viand. "I haven't tasted none like this sence my first died: the second Mis' Hopkins she was sickly, ye know, and couldn't do round the house at all; she wan't nothin' but a bill of expense for them four year, and then I berried her; but I trust she's in glory; ef she is, I know she relishes it; yes, she relishes it; she lived in a poor dyin' frame, as the hymn-book says, all them years, and we didn't have real good hired help; our vittles wan't real relishin'. I used to hanker consider'ble for a biled dinner such as my first used to get a Saturdays. Then my third, she was a stirrer, I tell ye! dre'dful savin'; most too much so; but 'twas a good p'int, a good p'int. Ef so be I'd have come acrost her first time I should ha' had consider'ble more means; not but what I've got enough now, but more is handy, ye know. Yes, Almiry hed faculty, lots on't; but she was kinder sharp, had spells on't. So she bu'st a vessel one day in one o' them spells; sort of tempery she was, an' it ris her blood too fur ye see, and she dropped like a stun. Yes, I've be'n widdered goin' on eight months, and I'm some lonesome, I tell ye."

Here he took a long drink at his glass of wine, as if to recover courage, — or breath. Miss Tempy sprung to refill it.

"Things is goin' wrong with me ye see, Tempy." (she observed he had left out the formality of 'Miss') "I've got nobody but old Sally Steele to look after me; it's comin' on killin' time and who'll put down my pork and beef as Almiry did? I'm gettin' along in years too, and I feel to say a loud Amen to that Scripter which obsarves ' It is not good for man to be alone.' I had a leadin'; yes, a powerful leadin' to come over to Trumbull for to hear Priest Hall's tell about this here Great Awakenin'; but the minnit I sot eyes on you, Tempy, acrost the meetin' house I knowed there was another puppus in that leadin'. I've got means, and I'll give ye a comfortable home and a good livin', and be to you one that'll walk together with you in righteousness, the same as Isaac and Rebecca, if so you feel a leadin' to answer me accordin' as I would have you to answer," and the deacon wiped his lips with one corner of the big red handkerchief in which he had dutifully collected the crumbs of the seed cake, and fixed his little gray eyes on Tempy with the intelligent and questioning determination of that maligned animal, the pig, when it watches the apple or the ear of corn that a mischievous hand holds a little out of reach.

A dark, painful flush rose among and over Miss Tempy's wrinkles. "Why! why!" she stammered. "Why, I hadn't no thought of such a thing, Deacon Hopkins. Dear me! I dono what *to* say. I'd calkerlated to abide as I was 'cordin' to Scripter in the mouth of the 'Postle Poll."

"Marriage is honorable in all," answered the Deacon, solemnly. "Poll says, 'accordin' to my judgment,' in the place you kote; but 'tis an institootion of God, marryin' is; and there seems to be a clear leadin' to our'n, Tempy. Howsoever, I don't want to hurry ye none; marriage is a sollum thing, and I wouldn't hev ye to do it in haste and repent at leesure;

I'm willin' to hev ye think on't a spell, same as I have. I've got a little tradin' in critturs to do over to Niantic, betwixt meetin's, and I calc'late that will keep me here a hull week to the least. 'Tis Thursday to-day; you take a week to consider on't, and Thursday week I'll come back and see how 'tis."

"W-e-ll," said Tempy, almost reluctantly.

The deacon emptied his crumbs neatly back on to the cake plate, set down his glass, after draining the last drop, lifted his beaver hat from the floor, and with a frigid "Good-day," stalked out of the front door with as much dignity as his short legs would allow.

Miss Tempy sat down, threw her checked apron over her face, and first laughed and then cried.

This proposal was a mere matter of business to Ammi Hopkins; he wanted a woman to keep his house in order, provide the savory meat his soul loved, and prevent waste and unthriftiness in his household; a woman who would have no wages beside her needful food and clothing, and save him the money paid out now to an inefficient helper. He had his eye on two or three other women if Tempy should fail him, but he had selected her first because she had a small pittance of her own, certainly enough to clothe her, and pay her contributions to the sparse church charities which it was respectable to recognize.

But Tempy, poor Tempy! was a woman. In all her solitary life she had never before had an offer of marriage, and it came to her like a shock; pleasant, but startling. She had never read a novel in her life; nor had she the first idea of that over-mastering and headlong passion called love. Diligent as her life had been, full of little pleasures and small duties which Esther would have scorned to consider as either pleasures or duties, and Sybil would have simply passed by as trivial incidents, Miss Tempy had yet been happier in her dull round than either of these heart-wrecked young girls; though sometimes it had been a mortification to her, as it is to every woman in her position, to think that no one had asked her in marriage, or even approached her with such an intention.

But now her crown had come.

A sagacious but cynical old gentleman once counselled a "seeking" widower, in this wise; "Marry an old maid, my dear fellow, if you're resolved to marry. They're so grateful."

And the cynic showed some keenness of perception in the advice. If Tempy had once tried the experiment of marriage, she might have been less pleased and more cautious in this sudden prospect, but as she sat there, in the darkness of her check apron, she saw a vision of the pleasant old farmhouse at Pickering Centre, its goodly barns; its ample garden, stocked with vegetables and herbs; its orchards, red and golden with apples; the flocks of fat poultry; the herd of sleek cows; the pair of dapple-grey horses, that would carry her "to mill and to meetin'," and the warm respectable shelter such a house and home would be for her coming age.

She felt heartily grateful for the deacon's thought of her, a lonely spinster; and she thought no farther, — at least not yet; she would talk with Esther; she would consult Parson Hall; she would think and pray about this all the week. Honestly, she thought the question was yet to decide; the answer yet in her own power; she had never even heard of the sneering French axiom, —

> "Chateau qui parle, femme qui écoute,
> Tous deux vont se rendre."

CHAPTER XXII.

COUNSEL.

Ask, and ask, and spend breath o' the asking; then do what thou willest in the end thereof. 'Tis a woman's way, good madam, ever since Eve parleyed with the devil.

Miss Tempy considered it her duty to lay this matter before Parson Hall first, in his quality of her spiritual director; for the directorship of the Papacy was founded, as most of their rites are, on a knowledge of human character, and human tendencies, and it is and always will be as natural for a woman to have a confessor, be she ever so Protestant, as for a bird to fly. There is not the smallest country parish or the greatest city congregation where the average woman does not tell or wish to tell the pastor of the flock to which she belongs, her troubles, inward or outward; if she dislikes or distrusts him, her doctor fills the niche. Blessed is that woman who in place of either, has a devoted and sensible husband to shrive and advise her in all her mistakes and perplexities; her true and lawful confessor; the real priest of his own household.

But then there are so many widows and old maids: — and so many impatient or indifferent husbands.

Esther was too much absorbed in her own thoughts to notice how Miss Tempy blushed and fidgeted that night at the tea-table, and how silent she was. In her new life, full of bitter penitence and trembling joy; of the dawning hope that her sin was forgiven of God, and the shrinking consciousness that it was known in all its blackness to one man, — Philip Kent, Esther was unaware that she was selfish; yet she was; the "things of others" interested her no more; the time for that was not come. Life must rend and convulse us; shake our faith in ourselves and our trust in others; drive us to the roughest coverts with its storms of woe; and shatter the tabernacle of the flesh till it gives up its mastery over the spirit, before we know or act on the divine precept, "Love thy neighbor as thyself."

Miss Tempy felt a little hurt that Esther did not even ask if she were as well as usual, for her heart was pining for sympathy; but she smothered her sighs, and after the dishes were " sided away," betook herself to the evening meeting. She took a humble seat just inside the door, not from any impulse of humility, but because she wanted to see Mr. Hall as he went out; so she kept her place till the discourse, the prayers, the hymns were all over, and the pastor, after the fashion of those days, passed out before any of the congregation stirred. Miss Tempy however, being on the last bench, rose up and followed him to the porch.

"Can I speak with you this evening, Parson Hall?" she said, in a timid voice.

"Surely you can, Miss Tempy," he answered,

gravely yet pleasantly. "Will it suit your convenience to come to my study, or do you prefer that I should accompany you to your home?"

"I should like to see you alone, Mr. Hall; and I can't compass that to my house. Easter is there."

"True, true!" said the parson, as if he had not thought of that before.

He was an honest man, he would not lie, but there is an instinct in the heart of man or woman, that drives to subterfuge in the interest of passion, almost unconsciously. Not for a world would Mr. Hall have had Miss Tempy know that he had hoped she would ask him to her house, that he longed to see Esther in her home, to clasp her hand, and look into her beautiful, deep eyes; yet he did not formulate the thought to himself.

It was but a little way to Mr. Hall's house, and his study door opened from the left hand of the little entry-way into which they stepped from without; a dim oil lamp was burning on the shelf, and a great bow-pot of early chrysanthemums, "artemishys" Aunt Ruthy called them, filled the chimney with their yellow disks, and the air with their bitter, old-fashioned fragrance. Miss Tempy sat down on the rush-bottomed settee, and plucking at her bonnet-strings with nervous agitation, burst out at once. "You see, Parson Hall, I want advisement. I'm in a quandary, as you may say."

Miss Tempy's face grew redder and redder, even her funny upturned nose became red with her eager embarrassment, and her corkscrew curls seemed to quiver beside the bright snapping of her little black eyes. The parson smiled kindly, but said nothing. "Well, you see the fact on't is, Deacon Hopkins came down from Pickering to 'tend your meetin's; he thought he had a leadin' to come; and he naterally called to see me, bein' as I came from Pickering down here, and knowed him well before I moved. But, — well, — hm, — I, — that is" — Miss Tempy made a vigorous effort to swallow her confusion here, and wrung her old linen handkerchief into a screw from which it never recovered, being frayed and worn with the assault; but went on at last emphatically.

"Well! he finally concluded, when he see me, that the leadin had been tow'rds marryin' — me. I dono as 'twas; I don't want to gainsay it; maybe 'twas; but *I* hadn't had no leadin to sech a matter: I hadn't never thought on 't. I couldn't say amen right off, and so I told him. He agreed thet I should take a week to think on't, and to counsel with my friends. I haven't got any folks to ask what they think on't; so, 'cording as he said, I thought to ask you. Shall I ? or shan't I ?"

Mr. Hall did not answer at once, he was a little appalled at the question; in his straightforward, simple heart and his ignorance of feminine human nature, he really imagined that what he said would decide the matter.

He looked back and thought of his life with Rachel, seeking from experience the knowledge instinct denied him; it was as if one walking in the night should look upward to the sad and high stars for guidance to his stumbling feet; his life with her had been one of denial and sacrifice; he had married her from a pure impulse of lofty and spiritual feeling; a love that had in it no stain of earthly passion, and therefore was unfit for the needs of earth and man; that had even become irksome and galling at times, as he confessed to himself with bitter remorse when she had at last left him alone. There was nothing in such recollections to help him counsel Tempy.

Then he thought of Esther, whom he hoped and meant to marry; this was the warm, bright hearth-fire that comforts a man when he comes in from under the stars, and fills his daily life with charm and content, even when its first blaze of passion sinks into the smoulder and whisper of a gentle flame.

This did not fetch him near Miss Tempy either; he understood Deacon Hopkins's position perfectly; he knew the man, and he knew what he wanted; and, man like, Parson Hall ranked Tempy in the same category; he considered that marriage was to them both a cool, considerate bargain, the question being whether one or both would be bettered thereby, either in position or possessions.

He looked askance at Miss Tempy; could he suppose that under that odd, withered, yet pungent aspect, there still lived any sentiment? any warm emotion? Never! she was a capable elderly female, most inauspicious of countenance toward anything but hard sense and honest judgment; he spoke then.

"I suppose Deacon Hopkins is a man of some years, Miss Temperance?" he asked.

"Yes, he is; I expect he's five-and-sixty, if he's a day; but I ain't young myself."

"But in so important a step we should consider the future. You may have the care of an aged and helpless man on your hands, my friend, when you yourself need care."

"Well, what of that? Somebody'll hev to take care of him; might as well be me as the next one; and no young folks know how to nuss old ones. I took care of pa for ten year after he hed shockanum palsy, and mother was bed-rid fifteen year; I'm used to sick folks."

"But, my good friend, that is the more reason why you should have rest in your declining years. Is not your home now comfortable and happy?"

"Well, yes; but I haven't no assurance 'twill last. Easter's young, and reasonable good lookin'; what if she should marry? and I think likely she will."

A sharp thrill of dread smote the minister at these words. Tempy went on, all unconscious of their effect.

"And I a'n't reelly declinin', not yet; nor likely to. Our folks is long livers, and I'm as spry as most folks be, yet."

"That is true," said the minister, smiling, "but Time is going on, Miss Tempy, and his steps bear hard on us all. I take it Mr. Hopkins is a trusty and well-to-do man."

This was merely suggestive and complimentary in Parson Hall; truly, he was at a loss what to say to a woman who confuted as fast as he could offer it the advice she had asked him to give her.

"Well, he's all o' that; he's been a church member in good an reg'lar standin' sence he come of age; he's got a good farm, and int'rust money besides, and he's hed three wives thet hevn't never faulted him as I know of; good women they was too; but he ha'n't no livin' children, which is a blessin'. I shouldn't ha' give a second thought to't ef I'd had to mother other folkses children; tain't a thing to be did, to my mind; the' ain't no livin' woman ekal to it. But seein' he and me was both kind of lonesome, it did seem, the more I looked on't, to be a leadin' of Providence as he said. It's a forlorn thing, after all, Parson Hall, not to have a livin' cretur belongin' to ye; nor one to say why do ye so whatever you *do* do; leastways 'tis so for a woman; beshoo-she may."

A tear that glimmered on Miss Tempy's stubby black eyelashes enlightened as well as surprised the parson.

"My dear good woman," he said, warmly. "It is the best indication that God is leading you that he inclineth your heart to do this thing; and I can perceive that it is so inclined. I trust you may be a helpmeet indeed to Deacon Hopkins, and I think he will be a most fortunate man in that you do not say him nay!"

Miss Tempy beamed with delight as she shook hands with the parson for good-by and tripped out of the door. It is so charming to be advised to do that which we want to; so cheerless to go out on a venture of our own good will, but that of no other.

It was still hard to tell Esther, but she did not do it as a seeker for advice; as the two sat by the window in the warm October twilight next day, waiting for the church bell to ring, Miss Tempy took heart of grace and told Esther that she meant to marry Deacon Hopkins.

"Oh," said Esther, "why, Aunt Tempy! I wonder at you. When did all this come about?"

"Well, it come as it come; the Lord sendin' it I expect, Easter. 'Tis an amazin' thing that Deacon Hopkins should have took thought of me. I counselled with Parson Hall, and he favored it. It hain't but one thwart to't, and that is the idee of leavin' you. But, as I told Parson, you're young and good-lookin' and pretty-behaved, and its more'n likely you'd leave me some early day, so havin' a chance, it behooved me to jump at it. I shall hev a good home, and somebody to look after me, somebody that's got to, whether or no; so I shan't feel beholden to folks that ain't my folks, if I should live to be old and bed-rid."

Esther had no more to say; her heart sank at the prospect of this little home to which she was just growing attached, its kindly shelter, and safe peace, all to be swept away; but she would not mar Aunt Tempy's outlook with a suggestion of her own loneliness. She might maintain a servant, for her school increased each season, but she needed for a home, some friend, some companion; she felt lost and bewildered.

Safe in her faith that Esther would marry, Miss Tempy had no upbraidings of conscience about leaving her; and when on that fateful Thursday week Deacon Ammi appeared, punctual to the hour, in her small parlor, and said in a pompous and official sort of tone to the blushing old spinster, —

"Well, Tempy, have you pondered on the matter to be considered? and are you free to acknowledge 'tis the leadin' and will of the Lord?"

"I be," said Tempy, modestly but promptly, "the will of the Lord be done."

Deacon Hopkins having so settled the matter, was much in earnest to have his bargain fulfilled; "killin'-time" would come in November, or early in the next month, and if ever a man needed a capable, thrifty wife, it was when salting down, and trying out, hams, flitches, scraps, sausages, head-cheese, and souse, were the matters in hand; so Tempy's small preparations were hurried; her linen taken in hand; her gowns and petticoats re-fashioned; her winter bonnet, a goodly poke of grey beaver, pressed and new-trimmed; and store of towels of her own spinning and weaving brought from a great chest in the garret and "bleached up" from the yellowness of long lying; so about the third week in November, Parson

Dyer came down from Pickering for the ceremony on his Narragansett pacer, companied by Deacon Hopkins in his one-horse shay. Miss Tempy apologized to Parson Hall for importing the Pickering minister for this office, when naturally she would have had her own clergyman.

"You see, Parson Hall, I j'ined meetin' under his ministry, but I shouldn't have made no pi'nt of that as I know of, only he's always married Deacon Hopkins, and I thought he'd feel kind of strange if anybody else done it this time."

The apology was irresistible; so in due season Miss Tempy, arrayed in a gown of gray paduasoy, with frills and pinners of pillow lace, her hair rolled over a high cushion, a string of gold beads round her neck, and black lace mitts on her skinny hands, was united to Ammi Hopkins in the little parlor where he proposed to her; and after a decent refection of loaf-cake and hot flip, she took her place in the one horse shay beside the Deacon, her coat of blue camlet and the poke bonnet of beaver only half concealing the smiles and airs of the venerable bride.

It had added the last touch to this quaint wedding, that as soon as the brief ceremony was over, the Deacon turned round to Tempy and remarked with pompous deliberation, —

"See what a change! Five minutes ago you was nothin' but an old maid; now you are the honored wife of Deacon Ammi Hopkins, Pickerin' Centre."

Parson Hall took his brother minister off to dinner;

and apologized to him for Esther's want of hospitality by explaining that her school-hours, and her solitary condition now Tempy was gone, both prevented her from entertaining company.

"Doth Esther Dennis teach a dame-school?" inquired Parson Dyer in surprise.

"She has to do something for her support," answered Mr. Hall, "and this seemed the most available way so to do."

"But with all her property it seemeth she must have a frugal mind to labor so," went on Parson Dyer.

"But she has no property, brother."

"Where, then, is the estate of Joshua Dyer, my cousin? I was in these parts shortly before he died, and he told me then, concerning his will, that he had left a goodly portion of his means to Esther Dennis; both from good will and affection to her, and from an assurance he had that she was well-disposed toward Philip Kent, to whom he had left the lesser moiety of his goods; not thinking it seemly, he said, that a man should owe everything unto his wife. I well remember the will, brother Hall, and it was recalled to me to-day, in that he also left, as he told me, five hundred pounds to Miss Temperance Tucker; and I considered it likely Deacon Hopkins had an eye to that comfortable heritage when he selected the pert little spinster."

"That will was never found, Brother Dyer. Philip Kent inherited all, save a small sum left to Esther's mother, under an old will, made at Mrs. Dyer's decease."

"Sho! sho!" burst out Parson Dyer. "There is some iniquity to do somewhere. I was not at the funeral, being laid up with a fever for ten weeks; and thereafter sent to travel by sea for my great weakness; but I never heard more of the matter, and fancied it all as he told me. It is bad, bad."

"And beyond man's remedy now," sighed Parson Hall.

"Yes, yes, it must lie as it is, I suppose. Poor girl, poor girl!"

Parson Hall added a silent echo to the kind old man's exclamation; but he had only been confirmed in his own suspicions. He had always doubted the intent of that later will, and believed Esther wronged in its loss. Little did he imagine that Esther herself had wrought with her own hand this evil of her condition.

CHAPTER XXIII.

FINALITY

Unto all things that be cometh an end at the last; yea, even unto this small round world. Alas! that there should be so much beginning.

SHORTLY after Miss Tempy's wedding, there came to Sybil an unexpected access of fortune. An English relative of her father suddenly lost both his sons, and, being old himself, died of the shock, and his large estates devolved upon Mr. Saltonstall's heirs; represented solely by this young girl, the only next of kin. There had been a time when Sybil would have been glad to be rich; her natural pride, and love of power, would once have fed eagerly on those worldly advantages; but to her scathed and lonely soul they were now but ashes and dust. John Stonebridge, however, held such things in more respect, and hearing of this legacy, bethought himself to make one more effort to melt Sybil's hard heart. He had a sufficient property of his own to meet all his real necessities, and provide for him many of the luxuries of life; but when a man gambles, and carouses, and dissipates his money as well as his health and his character, continuously, it takes a very considerable fortune to feed all these outlets. He was already deep in the books of a certain usurious Dutch money-lender in New York, and a great fortune would be a good thing for him.

It is true he might have achieved a wealthy marriage more than once, had he so chosen; for his handsome person, his fine manners, his keen wit, and his *prestige* as an officer in the army won for him much admiration among the colonial belles of the day; but bad as John Stonebridge was, his heart still clung to Sybil Saltonstall. It is hard for a woman to realize that a man can deeply love her yet be absorbed in a thousand other things all the time; even be temporarily unfaithful to her, yet hold her image dearer and deeper in his soul than any other thing; but it is sometimes so. Colonel Stonebridge had more than once resolved to defy the power of this cold, proud girl over his life and happiness, but it was stronger than his will.

At the idea that there was now a reason of worldly wisdom, a valid excuse for once more tempting his fate, the old slumbering passion awoke in fresh strength and swept him to her feet.

Sybil would have refused to see him, but the servant who admitted him was a new comer and garbled his name; he was shown into the familiar withdrawing room, and stood looking out on the wintry sea, grey, cold, and foaming under the rush of the northwest wind, when a slight rustle roused him from his revery; he turned and faced Sybil.

She stood motionless as some pale pillar in a dim-lit church; the white gown garnished with black ribbons which she wore in honor of her dead yet unknown relative, made no contrast with her paler face, her very hair had faded from its natural glitter, and hung limp and dull in loose ringlets over her shoulders; her dress, in the phrase of the day, was a dimity "*negligée*"; *negligée* indeed was the wearer's aspect.

"Sybil!" hoarsely cried John Stonebridge, "I have sworn to live without you, never again to tempt your scorn; but my love has prevailed against vow and oath. I have come again. I could not forbear. Sybil, have you not one kind, one hopeful word for me? Will you ever find another heart that adores you like mine? Can you refuse me again?"

She raised one hand as if deprecating any such wild language, and looked at him like one who gazes from a mountain peak at some far distance invisible to the watcher below.

"Never!" she said, in a low, strange voice. "I have no hope, no thought to give you, John Stonebridge."

"Never?" he echoed, "why is it never? I swear you loved me once, Sybil; cold as you are, I believe you once held me in your heart."

It was an instinctive appeal; he scarce believed what he said in his own mad anxiety.

"If ever I did," she answered, in the same low, distant tone, "I shall never do so more. There is one who will forever stand between us, and fix there a great gulf over which can no man pass."

"Who the devil dare cross my path like that?" he answered, wild with passion.

She looked straight at him; her voice was like a knell. "Arbell!" was all she said.

Furious words rose to his lips, but he could not utter them; he would have replied to any other woman with a scoff at her use of such a weapon, but the awful lustre of those sad eyes, clear as the ice that seals some crystal spring that, still pellucid, has lost its living sparkle; the pallor of her wasted cheek; the pathos of her wan lips half parted over the shining teeth as if she could hardly breathe; the sense of that angelically severe purity which penetrated her voice and her look like a diviner atmosphere than he had ever dreamed of silenced him. For once in his life, John Stonebridge felt a pang of shame, and it stung him like a whiplash; he dropped his head on his breast, and hid his face in his hands. It was a dumb confession.

When he lifted his face, Sybil was gone; never again, in life or death, did they meet; and both of them knew their parting was final.

Esther, meanwhile, went on her solitary way as best she could. She established a decent middle-aged black woman in her kitchen, who went to her own home after her daily service was done, and left behind her that terrible and oppressive solitude that only a woman can comprehend. Yet not all women comprehend it; there are many who live out their lives in such loneliness and do not suffer from its terrors; but Esther was nervous, imaginative, and heart lonely; to her, the solitude had its own dreadful voices; its evening apprehensions; its dumb, midnight oppression.

She began to feel in another sense than it is used in Scripture, yet no less true, that "it is not good for man to be alone." Her meals, frugal and scanty, went off the little table uneaten, sleep ceased to refresh her, it was so broken and so brief. She had been many a time annoyed by Miss Tempy's little notions, her fuss about nothing, her incessant flow of talk, quaint and piquant as it was; but now she would have given anything to see again that round cheery face opposite her at table; she was absolutely homesick for her companionship. Sybil did what she could to cheer her friend, but Sybil herself after her final interview with Colonel Stonebridge had fallen into a state of languor and melancholy that made her cheerfulness forced and unnatural; so that Esther was even more dispirited after their interviews than before; for she knew John Stonebridge had been in Trumbull, — had come and gone in the same day; and from her own experience she interpreted her friend's melancholy, and made shrewd guess at its cause. When, in the course of the winter, advices from England made it needful that Sybil should go over to see to some affairs concerning her inheritance that could not be transacted without her personal presence, she begged Esther to give up her school and accompany her. Governor Stanley was to escort his niece, and

Sybil would much rather take with her a friend and companion than go alone with her uncle, a taciturn and self-absorbed sort of man. But to Esther, inland born and bred, a sea-voyage had unspeakable terrors; not even her love for Sybil could tempt her to undertake a voyage of six weeks across that treacherous tumbling water which was to her mind the very sea of death.

Nor could she, either, have left her little school with a clear conscience, since in so short a time as she would have for preparation there could be no one found to take her place; so she made this her excuse. But to Sybil the sea had no terrors; she had always lived beside it and loved it, and even to her well-disciplined soul it was pleasant to think she could at least escape the scenes of her life's worst anguish, the place so crowded with painful associations. She was obliged to drive out to Hillside Farm on an errand for her Aunt Stanley one day before she left, and, as she entered the door of the keeping-room there was Arbell's child sprawling, in the delight of its freedom from crib and go-cart, on a comfortable Delia had spread across the floor. A pang shot through Sybil's heart as the bold, beautiful infant looked up and laughed in her face; there were John Stonebridge's dark splendid eyes; mobile and expressive lips; the very dimple that cleft his imperious and determined chin. A pang of disgust and repulsion made Sybil shudder; and Delia, with feminine acuteness called a woman who was at work in the kitchen to take the child away.

Women are curious anomalies; some among them would have gathered the fatherless baby into their tender arms, and ignored its unconscious sin against them; but Sybil was not of that mould; she did her errand; bade Delia and Hiram a kindly and stately farewell, and ordered Moses, the Stanley coachman, to speed his horses as fast as might be safely done, for she must hasten home.

When at last the Stanleys sailed, Esther felt her desolation settle down about her like a cloud; it was with a sense of relief and gratitude that she opened her door one cold February evening to admit Parson Hall, who hung his furred cloak and cap upon the high nails in the entry wainscot, and coming in smiling, sat down before the fire in the big chair which Esther placed for him. A quiet, friendly talk ensued; a discussion of the church and its prospects, and queries concerning the school and its success; then in a natural way Parson Hall asked Esther if she missed Miss Tempy.

There was a suspicious glitter in her eyes as she answered, "I do, truly. I have much solitary time, and lacking her cheerful countenance it is lonely indeed."

"And Miss Saltonstall hath deserted us also."

"Yes, that was the last blow. I sometimes think there is not another woman so utterly lonesome and set apart as I am."

"There is another man, Esther, who hath endured the like experience. Think you not that my hearth is also cheerless; and my home lacking smiles and company?"

Esther looked up at him with tender sympathy in her eyes; the parson's lips quivered, his voice was broken and tremulous as he reached his hand across and grasped hers, though his speech was manly and straightforward, and full of simple dignity.

"Esther, my friend. I have come in hither this evening of set purpose to ask you to come and be my partner, my friend, my beloved wife; to share my home and put away its loneliness; and to find rest and companionship in my true affection. Will you, my dear?"

Esther trembled, her hand quivered in his like some fledgeling bird in the grasp of a schoolboy; she was surprised, frightened, agitated beyond self-control; the woman's refuge came to her, she burst into tears.

Parson Hall was moved and pained. "Dear Esther," he said, gently, "I meant not to startle you; I thought it might be you had read my countenance somewhat, and were aware of the way my heart hath tended for a considerable season."

"I — I never thought of it," sobbed Esther.

"Think of it now then, dearest girl. I would not have you hasty in decision even to relieve my great suspense. I have held you in respect and affection a long while, Esther. I have delayed seeking my heart's desire until it seemed to me you needed solace, and affection enough to consider this matter. I am older than

I should be, my friend, to mate with a young maiden, perchance; but my heart is young and beats still with warmth and keen emotion. But consider of it; it is all I ask. I could serve for thee seven years, my beloved, even as Jacob served for Rachel, if so I were sure of thee at the last."

Esther wiped her dim eyes, and looked shyly at the parson.

"I cannot think it!" she said, naively. "Oh, sir! I am noway good enough for you."

The parson could not repress a smile, but it was very gentle, as he answered. "Dear Esther; it is not thy province to judge of that. Verily, there is none good, no not one, the Scripture saith; but it is not mere goodness the human heart asks of its fellow; it is love, sympathy, care, comradeship, that a man craves from his wife. Can you give none of these for my asking?"

Esther's heart sank; well she knew that no other man would ever awaken in her breast the keen absorbing passion she had given to Philip Kent; it was a bitter recollection in this hour; she remembered too, how lost to all other earthly things she had been in the new delight she found in his love; nothing like this filled her soul now; no rush of overmastering emotion; she was surprised, grieved, humiliated to know herself so all unworthy and irresponsive when a man so saintly, so noble, so far above her, asked for her heart. Confused and distressed beyond expression, she rose to her feet and clasping her hands in a gesture that was half an effort at calmness, half entreaty, she said, —

"Oh, I cannot, cannot tell! I am not in my right mind, I think. I can't believe it. Will you — will you leave me for a little? I am confused. I cannot think."

The parson was a gentleman in the noblest sense; he rose directly.

"I will leave you, my friend Esther. I have been over hasty with you. Farewell, my dear; when you will send me a word of welcome I will come again. But hasten not, Esther; ponder well on the matter; it is for life, death, and I trust Eternity."

The girl looked up at him with such pitiful trustful eyes, such an honest and pure desire to do the right evident in their expression, that a sudden change, almost a spasm of emotion passed over the parson's face. With all the strength of his nature he longed to fold her in his arms, and kiss away the tears that bedewed her blushing face, for he loved her as he had never loved before, with all the might and passion of a man's nature; but his self-control was greater even than his nature; like a giant it constrained love and longing to hide their heads and bide another day; he did not even clasp the little hand that was half offered to him; he only said, "Good-by, Esther. God be with you," and as the door closed behind him she flung herself down on the sofa, and a tempest of tears put an end to thought or consideration for one while.

When it was over, Esther took up her candle, raked up the fire, and went up to her bed. Was it to sleep?

CHAPTER XXIV.

A CONFLICT.

> Shall I then end this life
> Of solitude and strife
> And live a happy lie?
> Or leave my love alone:
> Go make a wordless moan
> Lay down my head and die?

No, there was no sleep for Esther that night. Her bed gave her no rest; she sat up in the darkness and held her cold hands to her burning forehead. She had to face her life as never before; the past, which she had thought concerned herself alone, turned and rent her now; for it was not her own any longer; it was a matter of deep concern to Parson Hall. She had never felt more lonely. Philip and she were separated forever, not merely by the separations of time and space but by that all-powerful barrier, the knowledge on her part that she had not loved him, but instead loved an ideal and called it by his name.

She had begun to see in this past year how utterly selfish he was, and to feel as a modern writer puts it that "Selfishness is the fault most impossible to forgive or excuse, since it springs neither from an error of judgment nor the exaggeration of a generous motive . . . it is the result of a cold-blooded, self-concentrated system of calculation, which narrows the sympathies and degenerates the mental powers."

Nor had Esther even that fellow-feeling for the fault that makes us all "wondrous kind" in excuse and forgiveness. Unselfish and devoted herself, she could not understand how another could be so utterly regardless of her and her wounded heart as Philip showed himself. Her impulse now was to put a barrier between them that he would not dare to pass over in order again to make her the amusement of his idle hours, or the too-ready consolation for his comfortless home life.

She felt that Parson Hall's wife would be safe from any such intrusions; and safe even if the traitorous heart within her desired once again to capitulate.

She longed to be protected against herself, for while her reason told her all this hard truth concerning Philip Kent, her weak soul knew that his look, his touch, his smile, had still power to thrill her to her heart's core.

But then another aspect of the case stared her in the face; Parson Hall was honored, respected, beloved, by every person in Trumbull; had she, a thief, any right to link her stained life to his?

However firmly and gratefully she believed that God had washed out her sin by the free grace of redemption, she knew that toward man her fault still wore its blackest aspect. She felt that she had robbed the parish of a newer and more ample place of worship, simply to aggrandize, Philip Kent; and how could she, a sinner, so deliberate and dreadful, marry a saint like Parson Hall?

If she could only tell him! but, alas! the secret was not her own; it would be betraying Philip; which she had no right to do, to save herself; no, not to save, but to set her soul free toward this other man. For Esther felt sure that Parson Hall would regard her only with profoundest scorn if he knew how she had fallen.

Yet again the other side of this question confronted her; here she was, lonely, helpless, poor; life lying before her as a barren desert, a long, weary journey, which she had no right to shorten. She was naturally indolent, and the idea of working all her life was intolerable to her; though she did not know it, she had been physically weakened by the sad and tragic experiences of the past few years; her weary body tired the over-worn soul; the prospect of a home, of care, of faithful tenderness, tempted her; but to be a living lie all her life seemed to her horrible.

That it was a sin to marry without absorbing love for the man one married, had not occurred to her; she was both innocent and ignorant, and in all the world there was not a creature to whom she could go for advice; Sybil was out of reach; Esther was that loneliest of all human creatures, a motherless, friendless young girl.

At last the sophistry of weakness and inclination got the better of her; she said to herself.

"If I never tell Parson Hall, Philip never will; he dare not for his own sake; I shall have a home where I belong, a good, kind man to take care of me. If he never knows how wicked I have been, what harm is it? I will be good now. I will not think of what is gone. I will marry Mr. Hall."

Poor Esther! as she rose wearily from her bed at sunrise, set on this resolution, she forgot, nay! she knew not at all what lay before her, a life of deception and terror; the haunting of that blackest of all black cares, an evil secret. Poor, poor Esther!

All day she went languidly about her work, many a misspelled word was all unnoticed, many a whisper, pout, mistake in geography, or blot on copy book passed by; the joy of requited love, the first sweet breath of the new-born Cupid, the "purple light" that should have illumined all things, were not for her. She had made up her mind as one resolves to begin a long journey into an unknown country and takes up his abode there; and her soul was oppressed with the same dread and inquietude; she had chosen one of two evils, not extended her hand to pluck a great joy; no wonder her eyes were sad, her face pale and drawn. She was not at all in the same position that Miss Tempy occupied when she went to Parson Hall for advice; that little spinster had been so pleased with the prospect before her that she had in her heart resolved to accept it even before she opened the parsonage door, though she had not formulated the resolution to herself; but it was a foregone conclusion. Esther was alone; she had not yet learned to ask help where it is given willingly, convincingly, and without upbraiding. Indeed, had the idea occurred to her she would at once have thought that it must be God's will that anybody whom Parson Hall asked to marry him should do so; the man was such a saint; she did not know that saints are made saintly by denial and deprivation; nor did she yet know that she herself was to help make Parson Hall more saintly still.

As she sat in her chair of rule the day after, having achieved a little more self-control, an objection occurred to her that seemed more valid than any yet; an objection she thought even Parson Hall would consider ought to prevent her marrying at all; who would take her school? A throb of joy shot across her heart as she thought of it; a throb that would have enlightened and convinced a more introspective woman. Never had those rosy little faces seemed so dear to her as to-day; even the thwart aspect of the black lambs in her flock moved her with pity rather than wrath. She brought out to them at recess her bowl of fresh doughnuts and distributed them with divine impartiality to all. She warmed in speech and face toward every youngster among them; she gathered the tiny girls into her arms and about her knees with a tenderness that overflowed all their faults and follies, and the children responded with clinging arms and fond caresses.

No! she could never, never part with them! But it was a girl's "never."

That night she wrote and sent this quaint, shy little note to Parson Hall.

Reverende Sir,—I have given some Thought to the matter Off which we held converse. I think i had Forgot my littel Charge of Children. i know not Howe to leve them withoute a Teacher. Therfor I think We wille speak of this Noe further.

Y'r ob't humble serv't to command. Esther Dennis.

Yes! it is misspelt; but so were greater people's letters. They lived and loved, and were great and good in those days without spelling well. Strange, but true!

Parson Hall smiled and sighed both over the little note. He perceived in it only the maidenly shyness and the desire to do right of a sweet, conscientious young girl. It was something deeper than he knew; a want that he felt, yet could not express, that made the sigh follow the smile. Between those formal lines lay a desert space that chilled and disheartened him as he read; yet like any other man he ignored the warning instinct, and was rationally pleased to think what a helpmeet this woman would be, who could so tranquilly set aside love for duty. He did not know Esther!

But her heart sank as she read the answer.

My Beloved Esther,—The Obstacle of w'h you speake I have alreddy Provided for, if there Bee no other. I can fill your Place in the School, but not in mine owne Hart. I wait withe some Impatience but A resolved Sperit for your favore-

able Answer. May You be guided by Devine Providense is the Prayer of your atached Friend and Humble Servant,
PHILEMON HALL.

Esther's heart sank as she read this short but purposeful missive. She, too, read between its lines the steady, powerful nature that indited them; the strong if kindly will that had laid its hand on her, and would not lift it; and Esther was a typical woman. The legend of Paradise, "he shall reign over thee" was imprinted on her nature; even resisting while she obeyed, she would still obey. She sat down in a sort of desperate calm, did her daily work as steadily and as stupidly as a machine, and endured with voiceless dread the sharp rush of hurrying hours that brought Mr Hall for his answer.

It was evening when he came, and as before, Esther let him in. There was no one else to do so. Awkward enough was the situation; her face was rigid, her eyes cast down. A statue that had locomotion would have been as encouraging a hostess!

Only the most meagre commonplaces passed the lips of either. It is true the minister's heart beat loud and fast. An ordinary man would have come with more confidence, for well Philemon Hall knew that to be the beloved and chosen partner of a minister was in those days a high honor, but Parson Hall was not an ordinary man; he felt in his pure, manly soul that the heart and life of a young girl were a great gift to ask, and that he or any other man was scarce worthy to receive such a blessing; and moreover he loved Esther far more that he had loved Rachel. It is possible for a man to love twice or thrice with the same fervor and freshness. Alas! it is impossible for a woman; but no man knows it. At last, after all the commonplaces of the time had been exhausted, the Parson, as became him, spoke first.

"Esther," he said, "I am come for my answer. Is it yes, or no, dear?"

Esther trembled like a tall lily in the wind; she could not speak, her face was wan with trouble, her eyes uplifted. The parson had risen as he spoke, and she too rose with a slow gesture of delay, as if she were about to ascend a sacrificial altar.

"Esther?" he asked again.

She stretched out her hand to him, slowly, and he clasped her in his arms. Esther shuddered.

"Look at me, dear," he said, misinterpreting the tremble that ran through her frame. Men before and after Parson Hall have mistaken a chill for a thrill!

She lifted her eyes obediently. Philemon Hall had once looked into the eyes of a woman who loved him; he knew the deep, immortal flame that burns with a true love's breath, but these great hazel eyes were like those of a shot dove; and his heart fell before their sad and mute appeal. Was this his triumph? the hour of his pride? Is fruition ever as satisfying, as bewitching, as hope?

It was to be again the old story of one who kisses, and one who offers the cheek.

The parson, if he did not understand women, was a gentleman. He released Esther from his embrace, and quietly replaced her in her chair, moving his own beside it, so that she need not be conscious of his eyes searching her downcast face; and then he began to talk gently of the future. He explained to Esther that Aunt Ruthy was becoming stricken in years, and no longer able to work as she had done; so it was his plan to send up to Wethersfield for a recently widowed niece of hers, who would be glad to increase her small income by means of the school; and then Aunt Ruthy could establish herself in the house, as Miss Tempy had done, and keep her independence, and occupy her time by caring for the small dwelling that, inhabited by two women only, and not obliged to open its doors to a succession of guests, like the parsonage, would not require a tithe of the care and work which the dear old woman had hitherto undertaken.

Esther listened and acquiesced like one in a dream, she could not imagine herself in the new position; she already shrank from contemplating the future; she tried to be passive, to forget; to accept all things as they came, and believe they were right. Parson Hall, man-like, admired her silent modesty; if he would have liked better a little more demonstration, a tender glance, a blush, or a pressure of the small hand when at last he left her, he still respected her girlish coldness and reticence, and thought how sweet it would be to melt that thin, beguiling shimmer of frost, to teach that virginal heart its rightful beating, to melt the chilly sadness of those eyes into a real glow. He forgot that he once thought she had loved Philip Kent; he did not know, would he ever know? — how she had loved him. If the parson had ever seen those eyes, those lips, that radiant face as Philip had seen it times without number, would he have doubted his own power to rekindle the spent fire? Probably not; he was a man, if he was also a saint.

But no such idea disturbed him to-night; he left Esther early, after having asked her to drive over to Pickering with him on Saturday and make a call on Mrs. Tempy, as he himself had some clerical business with Parson Dyer. Esther assented, and the parson gravely raised her cold fingers to his lips as he said "Good-by." She was glad he went. Poor Esther.

CHAPTER XXV.

DOWNWARD.

> Full easy is it downwardly to go;
> But to ascend, what labor! and what woe!
> So saith the Latin poet; but, ah me!
> Some in this doleful countering world there be,
> Who dread descent, and linger on the way,
> Yet needs must go, howe'er they long to stay.

SATURDAY came, cold but clear; the last day of February was even more wintry than the first day of December. Esther put on her cape of soft old marten fur over her serge-lined camlet cloak, and tied her red quilted hood under her chin, put a small heated soapstone into her muff, and filled the tin footstove with hickory coals well smothered in ashes; the fire was raked up in the chimney, the chairs set back from beside it, and she was ready in every detail to set out on her drive when Parson Hall drew up his steady, sturdy old nag before the door. Esther, since she had laid her hand in Mr. Hall's as a tacit acceptance of his suit, given more because she did not know what good reason to give for refusing him rather than of ready will and joyful assent, had begun to recoil from the shore upon which she had allowed herself to drift; she awoke to the consciousness that she had promised what she never meant to promise, but her morbid conscience forbade her to break her word.

All the night after that decisive interview she tossed on her bed, sleepless and wretched. Utterly alone since Sybil sailed for England and Tempy had gone to Pickering, Esther had felt that terror of solitude, that eager longing for some one to speak to of her own trouble, that is characteristic of a woman of her temperament. To Sybil, solitude was native air; she enjoyed its calmness and repose, but to Esther it was torture.

Left to herself to face what she had done, she became wild; Parson Hall's tender, strong heart, would have been wrung to its depths could he have seen her restless figure, her head buried in both hands, or turning to and fro in distress; her face streaming with slow, hot tears; or heard her stifled cries, her sobs, the low piteous wails like those of a young bird deserted in its nest, facing all the terrors of darkness. Ah! how Esther needed a mother now.

But there was none to comfort her; she grew more composed as the grey dawn slowly crept over the wintry sea and lit her chamber with its wan and wistful shining; she made up her mind to that pitiful subterfuge so common to women, that she would not think of the matter any more than could be helped; she would pretend all was right; deceive herself into peace; and follow the path she had chosen to walk in, as calmly as she could. Had not she and happiness bid each other a long farewell months ago? Yet, under all, that subtle tormentor a trained, ironclad, relentless, unconquerable, New England conscience, told her that she was sinning anew; that her victory over her own inmost convictions was worse than a defeat. But she would not listen; she busied herself about her house, she threw herself more heartily than ever into her little school; she went out among the parents of her scholars to take tea or wear away the long evenings as she had never done before; so that even in the few days intervening between Parson Hall's momentous visit and the Saturday's drive she had attained in some measure to the

"Glissez mortels! n' appuyez pas,"

of the French philosophy; whatever depths lay under the surface of her life that surface was smooth and glittering — if it was ice — she would slide on tranquilly. So she presented herself at the door when she heard old Dolly's jingling bells stop before it, and Mr. Hall helped her in so carefully and tucked the buffalo robe about her with such attention that the color rose softly into her pale cheeks.

It was well for her that this man whom she was about to marry without one particle of the love which is the only reason or excuse for marriage was the man he was, a thorough Christian gentleman. All the way to Pickering he treated Esther with a grave courtesy most unlike a lover, which set her entirely at ease; the least demonstration of feeling would have made her long to escape from his companionship then and forever; so sore, so harassed was her wounded girlish heart. Parson Hall had not forgotten that at one time he had supposed Esther to be in love with Philip Kent, but with a man's usual ignorance of women, he thought it a girlish infatuation that had long passed away; indeed she had no doubt gotten over it as soon as Philip's marriage made it a sin for her to think of him in that way. It was a natural conclusion for a man and a minister. What did he know of that force of a first passion that defies the proprieties, and refuses to leave the heart it rends and tortures, even when the conscience arrays itself against its indulgence? He had loved his wife well and truly; he had given up all that makes wedded life dear to a man to prove his unselfish love for her; he had sacrificed his youth to become the nurse of a helpless invalid, with a divine Quixotism ingrained in his nature; and lo! here he loved Esther even more than he had loved Rachel; why should Esther not learn to regard him as she had Philip Kent? But he thought she was timid and sensitive, and he would not startle her with expressions of affection that must be strange to her innocent ears; he talked to her of the day, the exquisite half-lights the clouds shed upon the tossing water as they veiled the cold winter sun with hurrying fleeces driven by the north wind; he pointed out to her the blue shadows of the drifts, the picturesque outlines of the snow-laden old cedars that crowned the cliffs along the shore; he told her stories of his childhood in the inland country where she too had been a child; he made her laugh over his boyish pranks; he took her out of her life in Trumbull away back into a world she had wellnigh forgotten; the days when she too had cracked nuts and roasted apples by the open fire in the kitchen, and been terrified by the pumpkin lantern her father had made to amuse her. For there was much of the child left yet in Esther, nor was she of that selfish sort who are so grappled and absorbed by their own sorrow or their own concerns that they cannot be diverted from their conscious contemplations of themselves by anything in heaven or earth.

Esther was impulsive, generous, gentle, in spite of her quick temper and rash self-devotion; a real woman after that most perfect description of woman that ever a man made, —

> "One in whom
> The springtime of her childish years
> Hath never lost its fresh perfume,
> Though knowing well that life hath room
> For many blights and many tears."

So by the time they drew up before the south door of the farmhouse in Pickering, over which Miss Tempy "that was" now reigned, Esther was like her old self again, gay, smiling, rosy, and ready to return heartily Tempy's warm embrace.

"Dew tell if it's you! Well, well, I dono as ever I was more glad to see a livin' cretur in all my born days. Why, ain't you agoin' to 'light down, Parson Hall? Goin' over to the minister's, be ye? Well, you come back to dinner, we'll have some vittles for you I guess, 'tain't none too often we get sight of anybody here in sleighin' time, seems real folksy to see ye."

The parson laughed as he answered, "I cannot promise, Mrs. Hopkins; you know Brother Dyer is a positive man, and if he says I shall stay with him I know not how to escape. But if I return I will be here on the stroke of twelve."

Neither Esther nor Tempy knew that he was so considerate of Esther that he meant to leave her alone with her old friend as long as he could.

Esther was led quickly to the kitchen fire and her wraps lifted off; then Tempy set her in an old armchair well cushioned for Ammi's benefit, and drawing up another for herself, began the expected flood of questions about all the people and things in Trumbull. Suddenly she broke off the queries, and said sharply,—

"Easter Dennis! what have you b'en a doin' to yourself sence I came away? You're about as fat as a hen's forrid! you looked kind of prompt and rosy when you come in, but now you're real white; what's the matter of ye?"

"Nothing, Aunt Tempy," said Esther, wistfully.

"Yes the' is; I expect though, the Lord only knows, and he won't tell!"

"You don't look as well as you did, either, Aunt Tempy."

"Well, I dono as I do. Fact is, there's a sight of work to be done here. Deacon Hopkins he's a real driver; I had all the hog-killin' to see to, ye know, after I come; sassage, an' souse, an' all that; and there's the butter, and the hens; oh mercy me! tain't all sugar 'n honey-pie now, gettin' married, Easter, you better believe. I expect if you're goin' to do it, whether or no, you'd better begin young; it's hard to learn a old dog new tricks. Not but what the deacon is a good-disposed man; he's as pious as they make 'em; goes to meetin' reglar, and is a hero at prayer; beats all! But you see I was consider'ble old to fall into new ways, and it's wore on me some. He's pleasant enough, but he's kind of pernickity 'round the house, wants to hev the pork-barrel jest in that corner, and the pickle-pot in t'other; he's lived by himself a spell ye know, and got notional.

"But he's as good as th' everage, quite as good as th' everage; ef he is a little near, and I couldn't pick and choose. I've got a comfortable home, and I calc'late to make the best on't. He's quite a little older 'n I be, and ef he dies fust, why I shall be well-to-do; and ef I do, I make no doubt but what he'll keer for me, as fur as is needful, to th' end, and put up a stun for me."

Esther's heart sank as she listened to this confidence. Was this all then that marriage offered? the patient drudgery of a housewife?

"But Aunt Tempy, after all aren't you glad you married the Deacon?" the girl asked, with a sort of quiver in her voice.

"I dono. P'raps I shall be when I get used to 't. I some think the 'Postle Poll was right when he said, 'it is better if they so abide,' — meanin' the onmarried. Still, 'twas dreadful lonesome to look forrard to livin' and dyin' alone."

Esther's heart said "Amen." She too dreaded the solitude of a single life.

"Well, I think so, too, Aunt Tempy, and I — I — you see I am just as lonely as you are. There is no one — so — oh, Aunt Tempy! I am promised to Mr. Hall!"

The last words came with a rush. It was so hard to say them!

"My blessed lamb! you don't tell me! well of all things! Why, now I can say like that old cretur in Scriptur, I can't recall his name, — 'now lettest thou thy servant depart in peace'; my dear, my dear!"

And here Aunt Tempy fell upon Esther and hugged her with all her old energy. The tears stood in the girl's eyes with pleasure and pain both. She had committed herself now past redemption; but it was so good, so sweet, to have Aunt Tempy's tumultuous congratulation!

"And I never even surmised of it. I thought his heart was berried along with his fust. But bless me! ha'n't the deacon had three before me? and to hear him talk you'd think I was the best of the lot. I feel set up good when he gets onto that string. Well! well! he'll be proper good to ye, Esther. He's a good man, one of the best, — not but what he's a man. They don't put no angels into Connecticut meetin'-houses, whatsoever they may do elsewhere; and I'm glad on't! I don't want no perfection round where I be; a little of th' old Adam is as good as salt into a huckleberry pie. Well, I be set up now. I've had ye on my mind, dear, this long while. I couldn't see how I come to leave ye all alone so; but, bless me! women-folks hes to give in when a man comes round; they're such masterful critturs. I spose I thought 'twas best to marry the deacon, but I expect my own will had a leetle something to say to 't; and his'n had a heap more, twan't all reasonin' of it out.

"Goodness! 'tis most noon-mark and I haven't took a step towardst dinner. Well, the deacon's gone over to New Haven to.day, so you and me can have a pick-up; there's some hung beef, and we'll put the p'taters in the ashes, and I'll stir up a short-cake; and if I didn't make apple-pies yesterday! so I'll clap one down to the fire to crisp it up; and what with cheese and some saxafrax tea we'll make out, I guess, if the parson doos come."

But the parson did not come; the two women enjoyed their savory little meal together. Esther's heart was lighter than for many a day: it was another strong rivet to her resolution that Aunt Tempy should so vehemently approve of her engagement, and express such entire confidence in Parson Hall's goodness, and the comfort of Esther's future with him.

So when the parson came back for his companion, he was greeted with a shy, sweet smile, and Aunt Tempy rushed on him with such eager and fluent congratulations that his heart warmed as his face flushed beneath them.

It is so good to have the cordial approval of our fellows in anything we undertake! So sweet to hear the voice of cheer, that fills us with hope and courage; restores our self-respect; and thrills our hearts like the gay trumpet-call to the battle, that inspires to victory even before that victory is assured.

Was it not one of the elements of His speech who "spake as man never spake," — this loving, hearty interest in the individual life of every soul on earth? Is it not one of the examples that His followers make too little account of? One powerful way to do good?

"But stop a minnit!" screamed Mrs. Tempy, after the two were at last securely tucked into the sleigh, and just as the parson lifted his whip to advise Dolly that they were ready to leave.

"I forgot, I was so took aback by good tidin's, to ask if you'd heered anything from Sybil Saltonstall? Did she get acrost safe? or don't ye know?"

"Not yet," answered the parson; "but I had it from a sure hand yesterday, that the "Lady Fletcher" hath been spoken off the harbor of Manhattan, and I think there will be a frost by Monday night."

"Well! well! 'twas a ventur'some thing to sail acrost the seas like that. Now, wa'n't it?"

"The Lord hath the sea in the hollow of His hand, my friend," answered the parson, reverently.

"'Mm, I s'pose 'tis so; but that don't argoo that

He won't let it slop out sometimes, and drownd folks."

It was rather a mixed and irreverent metaphor, and the parson had some trouble in keeping his face straight. Retreat was his only refuge, so he smacked his whip, and Dolly plunged into the drifts at a smart pace

CHAPTER XXVI.

THE LAY SISTER.

> With even step and musing gait,
> And looks commercing with the skies,
> Thy rapt soul sitting in thine eyes;
> There, held in holy passion still,
> Forget thyself to marble.

It was not till toward the middle of the next week that the mail which the "Lady Fletcher" brought from England was, so far as Esther's share of it went, delivered in Trumbull by the post-rider. Esther was overjoyed to get a letter in Sybil's firm, legible script, not only because it was from Sybil, but that it was her first letter from over seas, and had about it a sort of foreign atmosphere, as if from another world. For in those days people did not talk familiarly of the "herring-pond," or "going across." The majesty of that sinful and storm-tossed ocean still asserted itself. It was a perilous and solemn journey of long weeks, and "a man going to sea" was prayed for from the pulpit in much the same phrases used for a man dangerously ill; the chances of living through either ordeal seemed nearly equal. Sybil's letter had an interest for Esther, however, that she had not foreseen.

It ran thus; —

"MY BELOVED ESTHER, — It seemeth to Me long since I Beheld thy dear Face. I had a prossperus Voyage the Captin of the Vessel said; but I was soe tossed Withal, being driven up on Greate and Mightie Waves and downe again into appallinge Hollowes, that my Soule was affrighted, save when I could command my Thoughts to fix them upon Him who said unto the Sea 'Be Stille' and it obeyed Him. I had lived so long Tyme upon the Shore, I had looked upon the Oshun as my Frend; but Lo! it turned and Rent me, and I think I shalle Never cross it more.

"I have found goodlie Lodginge in a house of this Citye of London, hard bye where that Godly Woman, the Lady Huntington, liveth; and being alone as to Kindred and known Frendes, and abel to Lette the Countrie-House left unto Me, I purpose to Abyde here amongst the Saintes, and live as a Servant waiting upon my Master for the Remnant of my Daies. For thou knowest, Esther, that my Purposes of this Worlde are broken off, and it may be that it was for Good; that it was the Hidynge of His Power soe that I should be sett for Service. I have no Mynde to Marrige. I think it is better so to Abyde even as I am; and there is Place and Meaus here whereby to Serve my Generation.

"I miss thee, Esther, but my Aunt Stanley hath given me to wit that Thou hast a new Life before thee; and we shoulde have been Separated had I Stayed in Trumbull. I am glad if it be so, Esther. Mr. Hall is a Good Man, rooted and Grounded in the Faith; Steadfast, always Aboundynge in the Worke of the Lorde. Thou hast chosen well; there is Woe on Woe for her who fixeth her Harte upon an Evil Man, who regardeth Himselfe above all Lords and Gods. It is a bitter thing to give the Harte where the Soule may not bear it Companye. I rejoice that you will have a Comrade and a Helper toward the Holy Citie. Forget not in thy Prayers thy poore loving Sister in Christ. SIBIL."

Esther was indeed surprised; she was not aware that Mrs. Stanley's sharp and inquisitive eyes had long since penetrated Parson Hall's feeling for her; and that she had advised Sybil of her discovery in the very first letter she had sent abroad. It never entered Mrs. Stanley's mind that Esther could refuse such a good match; one that the governor's proud lady considered far above the desert or hope of the lonely schoolmistress. She would have characterized Esther curtly and pungently as "a devilish little fool!" had she known with what hesitation and apprehension she at last consented to be Philemon Hall's wife; for Madam Stanley was a thoroughly worldly woman, and women of her station in her day did not stand upon ceremony as to words when they meant them to be expressive.

But if Esther was surprised, she was also delighted to have Sybil so warmly approve of her engagement. Had there been any to oppose or object, her feminine nature would have risen in arms at once, and she would have hurried on to her fate in the warm haste of perversity, but since there were none to blame or try to prevent her, except her own inward distrust and shrinking, she was glad and thankful to be encouraged. As she laid down the thick sheet of coarse paper, she perceived, under the fold where the seal fastened it, a few lines more.

"Post Scriptum. I have sent thee by the hand of a Friend, One hundred Pounds Sterling. Take the half of it for thy Wedding Gownd, from thy Sister. The other Moeity I would have thee give to Delia at the Hillside farm, to keep in Store for the Tyme when the Babe she hath taken may have need of a Neste Egg."

Esther was astonished indeed. What was that child to Sybil? The nameless offspring of a self-murdered mother; a fatherless waif; why had pure, proud Sybil stooped even to notice its existence? But she remembered how good to the poor and the friendless her friend had ever been, and laid this bounty to that charity and sweetness that had so long distinguished her. Then came the question, how should she get out to Hillside? But, though Esther did not know it, Sybil had been provident enough to write a little note to Mr. Hall, and ask him to see that Esther was taken out to the farm to do an errand for her which Sybil could not entrust to any other hands. Mr. Hall was glad of another opportunity to drive out with Esther; he greatly desired to accustom the shy girl to his presence, to wear away the strange reserve in which she wrapped herself, and which hurt him to the heart as she daily became sweeter and dearer in the promise of wifehood.

But with instinctive delicacy he did not tell her of Sybil's note; something in its tenor made him conscious that her agency in the matter was not to be known; so he simply asked Esther if she would drive out with him toward Hillside and allow him to leave her at Hiram Perkins's while he went further on among the hills to make one or two pastoral calls. Esther's eyes shone as she assented, and the quick color rose in her cheeks. Alas! the parson rejoiced in his heart to see these tokens of what he thought, naturally enough, was pleasure at going with him, whereas it was only pleasure at finding a way so soon to do Sybil's errand; since she had received the night before from Governor Stanley, just returned on the vessel that brought Sybil's letter, a package of gold and notes that she did not like to keep in the house till Delia's share was safe in Delia's keeping. So once more she seated herself by the parson and sped away to the sound of the tinkling bells up through the ill-broken tracks, and the moments were too short for one of the pair, for Esther, pleased to do her errand, and simple as a child in her impulses, without one thought of what her aspect and manner might seem to mean, was brighter and sweeter than the parson had seen her since their new relation.

Delia was brought to the door by the sound of sleigh-bells, an unusual sound since winter had practically blockaded the farm.

"Why, 'tain't you, is it, Esther? I can't skerce believe my eyes. I should ha' jest as soon thought of seein' a ghost!"

"But, Delye dear, it isn't any ghost," laughed Esther. "Ghosts don't hug folks, do they?" throwing her arms about the good woman's neck with a hearty affection that made the parson envious.

"I guess they don't! nor they don't look so rosy. Won't ye come in, Parson Hall?"

"I thank you, Mrs. Perkins, but I have further to go. I will return in an hour or so."

And with an effort the parson turned Dolly's head from the door; he had seen how Esther could look at one she loved; — he knew she had never so looked at him.

"Set ye down, dear," said Delia, with an assiduous and tender voice and gesture that made Esther happy, for Delia was the only other person beside Tempy Hopkins left to her of her old life, now; and she loved her with a warmth natural to her age and character. Servants in the good old New England days were a part and parcel of the family and deserved so to be; now they rule the house with a rod of iron, and despise their submissive victims.

Delia was both surprised and pleased at Sybil's gift.

"She is so good," said Esther. "Delye, I know not of another woman who would think, so far removed from her old dwelling, of a solitary orphaned child."

"Don't ye?" said Delia, with a keen sparkle in her eye; and just then the child crept toward them and lifted his face; he had been playing near the corner of the hearth and had picked up a bit of charcoal with which he had smeared the lower part of his face till it looked like the darkness of a beard that needed shaving.

"You look at him, good!" said Delia; and as Esther turned her head, she gave an involuntary start; there was John Stonebridge's face before her. The bold, brilliant, dark eyes; the full audacious forehead, crowned with short black curls, the mobile lips; the heavy, deep-shaded jaws; the cleft chin. Now she knew why Sybil's charity flowed this way; she looked at Delia with a look of pained surprise. Delia nodded.

"You see now. She couldn't abear to touch the youngster, nor to look at him nyther, when she was here; but I expect she's sorry for him, 'tis jest like her; she's a sight too good for this airth, she had ought to be one o' the saints, and I expect she will be in the Lord's good time. But she no need to ha' sent that money. Hiram he got fifty pound last January; well 'tis last month, ain't it? and a line to say 'twould be paid reg'lar for the boy's use so long as he lived, but for God's sake to fetch him up strict, and make a good man of him. Well I knowed who writ that letter! I ha'n't lived in Trumbull the hull o' my life with shut eyes. But how he could hev hed the solid impidence to even himself to Miss Sybil, beats me. Comes of bein' a man, I s'pose; they do think, every man-jack of 'em, that ef they say 'snip' to any livin' woman, beshooshemay, she'll say 'snap' and be tickled to death *to* say it. I suppose the Lord made 'em so, and I haven't no call to fault 'em; but I do hate to see creturs so consated. Look at Adam now, the very fust of 'em! 'stead of standin' up like a honest feller when the Lord took him to do about eatin' of the apple, why he sneaked under Eve's apern; didn't have the grit to say, 'I done it Lord, an' I'm sorry for't,' but kinder whined out, 'the woman whom thou gavest to be with me, she gave me of the tree and I did eat!' Mean! meaner 'n a hoppin-toad! and men take after their pa all the way down. I solemnly b'lieve ef that I could corner Cunnel Stonebridge this minnit, about this matter, and ask him 'Why done ye so?' he'd lay it to that poor miser'ble critter that went an' drownded herself in the harbor!"

Esther listened with a shocked, almost a terrified face. She understood now the whole of Sybil's letter. She had known that for some reason Sybil had once and again rejected John Stonebridge, and had wondered deeply why; but Sybil was reticent always, and Esther had, judging her friend by herself, concluded that Sybil did not love him very profoundly.

Nor had she before connected Colonel Stonebridge with the tragedy of the drowned girl. She had been horror-struck at the occurrence, but never questioned its cause, or talked about it. Esther's mind was so essentially pure that sins of the coarser sort never seemed to dwell in her memory; they slipped away from contact with a nature that had no affinity for them. Now she shuddered, as for the first time she understood the depth of Sybil's trouble, and the anguish of her final loss; for well she knew what such a sin would be to proud and high-minded Sybil; death itself could raise no more impassible barrier between her and John Stonebridge than this.

And Esther returned with deep gratitude to that phrase in Sybil's letter wherein she spoke so earnestly of Mr. Hall's goodness; she contrasted him with her friend's lover, and felt a warm pride steal into her heart. Poor Esther! the rush of overwhelming joy, the utter disregard of all adjuncts, all reason, all doubt, that had filled her soul when she loved Philip Kent were all wanting here; at best, she was trying to excuse herself to herself for forming this new tie from which in her secret heart she shrunk with a cold terror she dared not recognize; but could not ignore. She found herself thinking that Sybil's part was best; that to be through with all the troublous joys, the irksome duties, the deceptive hopes, the futile expectances of this world; to live a life of devotion to God and uplifted benevolence to man was of all lives the sweetest, the most desirable. To be "a pensive nun, devout and pure" like Sybil, suddenly seemed to her the apex of life for a woman. When Parson Hall came back for her he felt that some subtle change had passed over her; her eye was cold, her face pale, her aspect rigid, and she only answered him when he spoke to her, she had nothing to say. Her thoughts were all with Sybil in her passionless devotion; her retreat from a weary and unsatisfying world; the mood absorbed her, and, for the time, she acted under its spell. It was one of Esther's charms, that varying moods possessed her, that her "infinite variety" interested and excited both her lovers and her friends; it was this that had kept alive Philip Kent's flickering ardor; that had made her so attractive to Parson Hall, though he did not understand it. But the mood of to-day had no charm for him, the keen wind seemed keener; the long, blue-white drifts more pitiless; the whole face of nature more ghastly and severe, because the sparkle had died in Esther's eyes, and the glow fled from her cheek. He did not approve of nuns; he did not like them either. However, Esther was not made for such a destiny. As well might one make the brown-thrush that flits from one swinging branch to another, and pours its wondrous flood of joyful song along the summer air till the hearer can scarce believe such delicious madness is not human and expressive of sentient joy, into a cooped barn-yard fowl, that crawks, and cheeps, and knows no other delight than to peck its corn and brood above its embryo offspring, as put Esther into Sybil's life with the prim and pious women who formed Lady Huntington's coteries, and hung on to the skirts of Whitfield and Wesley! Her real life had not yet begun, but Sybil had found her "sphere." She went on her saintly way, set about with prayers and good works, cloistered in her own holy thoughts. Even when she learned that John Stonebridge had fallen in the duello, slaying a brother officer as he fell himself, sent into another and an unknown world without even the short shrift of him who found mercy

"Between the saddle and the ground."

Sybil showed outwardly no sign of woe. Her creed forbade her to pray for that soul gone forever beyond the reach of hope; and who was to know that she passed night after night with wide opened eyes and clasped hands, staring into the darkness that symbolized to her the condition of the man she once so passionately loved; praying for the submission and resignation against which her whole nature rose in rebellion, like the tides of an angry sea?

Nuns must endure in solitude; not always with angels to minister unto them; for what consolation can those divine messengers bring to the first awful passion of despair? They can but look on with sacred pity, and await the silence of the storm when it sobs itself into acquiescence, and does no more futile battle with the rock-bound shores of fate, — or Providence.

CHAPTER XXVII.

A CLIMAX.

Much must be borne which it is hard to bear,
Much given away which it was sweet to keep ;
God help us all! who need, indeed, his care.
And yet, I know the Shepherd loves his sheep.

THE time came on too fast now when Esther had at last been persuaded to fix her wedding-day. To be married in May was, according to the old saw, to "repent alway" and earlier than that she could not think of, nor would Parson Hall consent to wait much longer. He felt sure in his own mind that once irrevocably pledged to him he could and would win Esther to love him. He knew that Rachel had almost adored him, and he did *not* know what a difference there is between "love's young dream" and the acquiescence of reason to a fate that seems unavoidable. If at the very last moment Esther had suddenly been left money enough for her comfortable support, she would have gone away secretly and silently from Trumbull, and from Mr. Hall, and made for herself a home elsewhere; in spite of her loneliness she might have lived by herself with the adjuncts of servants and luxuries and society, but poverty and solitude, too, had coercive terrors in their prospect. She had to content herself with delaying the dreaded finality as long as might be, and when at last it was fixed for the second week in June, she resolutely set herself to work at her preparations. "Can a maid forget her ornaments? or a bride her attire?" It is mercifully impossible. All the arguments against mourning fall useless before its power to distract the stunned and wounded soul with its persistent triviality, to bring back the thoughts that else would go wandering down the abysms of darkness, to the wholesome externals of daily life. So Esther, perplexed and distracted by the coming crisis, with no one to warn or advise her, welcomed with a relief that was almost joy the needful preparations for her wedding. She made with her own deft fingers the modest store of linen that was necessary, and edged its bands and hems with narrow English thread lace that dear Uncle Dyer had bestowed upon her from his dead wife's abundant stores; from the same source she also owned two goodly gowns of paduasoy with brocade petticoats and stomachers, one black, and one dark red; neither of them unsuitable for the wife of the parish minister, but yet too dark to be married in. To lighten the black gown, which was of flowered Italian silk, she bought herself a pale rose-colored petticoat elaborately quilted, which would at times take the place of the black brocade one, and she laid in plenty of rose-colored ribbon of the same soft shade, deftly tied in love knots, wherewith to garnish the sleeves and bodice. There were chintz and dimity skirts and short gowns for daily wear, and Mrs. Stanley sent her a gown of white linen embroidered all over in crewels, done by her own hands and her tambour frame, in birds, and blossoms, and creatures meant to be animals, but unlike anything in the heaven above or the earth beneath, or the waters under the earth; but very gay, and harmonizing well with the brocade petticoat that was a tangle of all-colored flowers, equally conventional and unrecognizable as earthly blooms, on a deep blue ground. Esther smiled over that gift with astonished amusement; it did not seem appropriate for Parson Hall's lady to wear such a gaudy and giddy costume as that, but she thanked Mrs. Stanley prettily, and laid the garment away in the press for the benefit of her descendants.

She was a little anxious about her wedding-dress, which she meant to have creditable to Sybil's generosity, yet not so fine as to be useless. White was not *de rigueur* in those days for a wedding, especially for a widower's bride, so after much deliberation, and many doubts, she entrusted the village draper to fetch her certain samples from New York, whither he was going for his spring goods, and hit upon one that suited her; a pale silver-gray, almost lavender colored levantine, with white brocaded figures sparsely scattered across its gleaming surface, for the gown, and a thick rich white satin for the petticoat, with frills of English lace for the tucker and sleeves. No accomplished French man milliner of to-day could have devised a dress more exquisitely fitted to the wearer than this, in its moonlit tones of light and pearly shadow, and when Esther on that eventful day piled her dusky hair high over a cushion, and frosted it with powder that made her great dark eyes and delicate brows darker and more distinct than ever, and set off the unusual and burning flush on either cheek, and the quivering scarlet of her full lips, she looked as she had never looked before. The square-cut neck of her gown showed the round white throat and its exquisite set into her shoulders, but the lace tucker was high and modest as befitted a bride, and her fair white arms were also half-covered by the deep frills at her elbows; no bracelets or rings marred the symmetry of those beautiful arms and hands; her only ornament was a cluster of the half-blown creamy buds of the old white rosebush that grew beside her door, set in their own clean blue-green leaves.

Tempy Hopkins had come down in the chaise with Parson Dyer from Pickering Centre, as the parson was to perform the ceremony for his brother minister, and at Tempy's request they had come early, that she might offer help and criticism to the friendless bride; but help Esther did not need, and Tempy's criticism was all admiration.

"My goodness gracious!" she exclaimed, as, folding her mittened hands over her flowered muslin apron, she made a tour of inspection about her friend after the last touches had been put to her attire.

" You do beat all, Easter! That gownd is jest like a mournin' dove's wing, and the sattin ain't nothin' but moonshine; seems as though you was too good to

A CLIMAX.

look at. I'd like a pictur of ye drawed out this minute, for to hang up in my front room."

Esther laughed, and the little dimples that stirred and deepened her glowing cheeks, and broke up the calm of her scarlet lips, made her still more lovely. Tempy drew a long breath.

"Well, you look as ef the Lord had jest made ye; and I can't say no more. Come down now; they're a waitin' for you, and Aunt Ruthy has set out the cake an' wine on to the table."

Very slowly Esther descended the narrow, crooked little stair, her train rustling behind her; she seemed to be in a dream, nothing was real to her, not even the friendly face of Parson Dyer or the placid benignity of Aunt Ruthy's lovely old countenance, full of anxious feeling. But her color did not waver; she spoke to them both quietly, and, directed by Mr. Dyer, took her place beside Philemon Hall without even looking at him.

The service was long, and awful in its solemnity. Had Esther and Mr. Hall been about to go to execution the next moment they would hardly have received less exhortation and warning. The deep tones of Parson Dyer, as he exhorted the wife to obey, respect, and serve her husband; to receive him as her priest and king under God; to submit herself to him in all things, and strive to train her family in the same paths, sounded like a knell of doom in her ears; she had scarce heard the injunctions he gave to Parson Hall, but of these to herself she missed not a word;

they pierced her very soul. What! was this what she had undertaken to do? Was she who expected to provide for herself by this marriage a considerate friend and a quiet home, bound instead to slavery, to submission, to that lowest form of servitude that involves the body but not the soul? She had looked on the whole matter in such a theoretic, dreamy, exalted way; exalted because her innocence and ignorance afforded no other standpoint; that when the actual and practical view expounded in Parson Dyer's lecture and prayer burst upon her, she felt as if some awful fate grasped her breath and stopped her pulses. She grew paler and paler, her great eyes stared at Mr. Dyer with a look of woe and horror, but an intruding sunbeam fell across his spectacles and he did not perceive her expression, nor did he notice, in his zeal to fully perform the rite, that Esther never bent her head even in assent to his questions; he only thought her modest and timid, as a good girl should be. As for Parson Hall, standing there at her side, he could not see her, and during the long prayer which followed of course he closed his eyes properly. But for Esther the hour seemed interminable ages.

Filled with a mad desire to escape, to deny, to retract, she dared not open her lips even to sigh. She had been brought up in a religious awe of the clergy, as the very messengers and vicegerents of the Lord God himself; what they said and did must be right. It was against her own ignorance and weak stupidity, as she now saw herself, that she so angrily and desperately rebelled. Oh, what could she do? whither fly? Never, never! could she fill this place, perform these duties. The illusions that had hitherto veiled the way before her were swept off, as with a very besom of destruction; her heart beat so heavily and so fast that it choked her; her head whirled; her brain seemed to be on fire; she neither heard the amen nor the benediction. When her husband turned to embrace her she swayed heavily forward, and it was Priest Dyer who caught her in his arms and laid her at length on the sofa, pale and cold, as if Death had been her bridegroom.

"You go into the keepin' room," said Aunt Ruthy to Mr. Hall, who stood in his place, shocked and bewildered. "It's a swound; she'll come out of it. Mis' Hopkins, can you fetch the camphire?"

Parson Dyer led his friend away into the next room, and brought him a glass of the home-made wine that stood ready there, and then left him; for he was a wise man, and knew how little our best friends can intermeddle with our joy or grief.

Pretty soon Esther came back to life, with one long, sobbing breath, and as soon as consciousness returned hid her face in her hands, and gave way to a flood of hot tears.

"That's right, deary;· cry away; 'twill do you good; tears is like the balm o' Gilead, sometimes," I know well," said Aunt Ruthy's kind old voice at her side, and before long, what with sniffs at the "camphire" and a liberal dose of sal-volatile, she recovered her self-control enough to give Parson Hall one piteous smile when he was summoned to come in; and let Tempy tie on her long mode satin cloak, and round hat with its cream-white scarf, so that she was ready to enter the chaise and drive over to the parsonage, where she was at once to take up her abode; wedding tours being unknown to any but the *haute noblesse* in those days. She had forgotten that the children of her school were gathered at the door to see her, each with a little spray of blossoms; and her heart fell as she went out into the rosy crowd she had loved so much and yet given up of her own will. She put forth all her will-power to return their smiles and kisses, and they half smothered her with the knots of heartsease, idle name to her now, the posies of lad's love, and ragged robin; the red button roses, and loose-leaved spiderwort; but most of them brought long stems of the great, pure June lilies, and she held a perfect sheaf of them as she drove away; never again did she inhale that languid odor without a grip at her heart that seemed to bring back her wretched wedding day. The parson helped her from the chaise, and when they entered the cheerful, flower-decked sitting-room, carefully untied her cloak and hat, and saying softly, "Welcome home, my wife!" folded her in his arms.

A long shudder ran through the girl's whole figure and a sob that was half a shriek burst from her lips as he kissed her; again she fell to the floor, cold and lifeless.

"Good God!" said he to himself, in an inaudible whisper. It was an appeal and an agony together.

Only a few moments was Esther unconscious; wild hysterical outcries and restless motion succeeded her partial swoon; it was well for her that the parson knew what to do, his long service with Rachel had given him the knowledge and tact of a nurse. Esther shrank from his touch, but he persisted in loosening her stiff bodice, and then made her swallow a mild narcotic. By and by she became more quiet, but she turned her face to the wall and uttered no sound; and he could only sit and watch her as a patient mother watches her child, with love greater than grief or anger; but dreading to ask himself what all this meant. It was well for both of them that they were alone in the house; some delay had occurred in getting the woman who was to do their housework, and Esther had chosen to wait rather than provide another; the sun was westering now, its low rays entered between the ill-closed shutters, and presently Mr. Hall saw that Esther breathed more calmly; the narcotic had acted soon and strongly on her healthy organization unaccustomed to medicine, and soon she turned over on her side as a child turns when sleep at last overpowers it, and her pale, tear-stained face showed in every subdued line that slumber held her fast. Mr. Hall drew a shawl over her very softly, he dared not close the open windows, lest the noise should rouse her; then he sat down again and looked at his bride with his heart in his deep, mournful eyes. There she lay on the couch where Rachel had spent so many long hours; but this beautiful, undisciplined, woful countenance was utterly unlike the divine calmness of his lost saint's, or the look of heart-deep love that Rachel had always turned on him, even to her dying hour. Rachel had loved him; this girl shrank from his lightest touch.

An awful dread arose in his mind; was this marriage, also, to be a mockery? Had he wedded a woman who could only fear and repel him? What had he done to be so visited? The Bible that had been his guide and counsel so long gave him words now to express the terror that seized his soul.

"All Thy waves and billows have gone over me," he murmured softly as at last the sunshine left the earth, and darkness fell upon all things as well as on his heart.

He stole quietly to the side door and sat down upon the step; cold moonlight just began to glimmer over the sleepless and restless sea; there was no sound except the gentle break of waves on the near shore; he was alone with this new sorrow — and with God. But God does not always demonstrate to us His presence; never, unless we are eager and ready to perceive it; and just now Philemon Hall's soul was chaotic; his whole nature aroused to bitter rebellion; he arraigned in his thoughts the very Master whom he had so faithfully served, and said, with Job's impatient wife, "Curse God and die!"

Far into the night he fought this one-sided battle with the Power that seemed so wantonly to thwart him; the moon rose high and paved the sea with silver scales along a shining track, but for him all was darkness and silence, gloom and despair, till suddenly a weary sob smote his ear. Esther was waking, he must go to her.

CHAPTER XXVIII.

THE CURSE OF A GRANTED PRAYER.

> My Lord! How longe I askt this Gifte of Thee,
>   With Harte full sore.
> And now, beholde! Thou givest Untoe me
>   That verie Store!
> But Lo! my Loafe is stone, both Hard and Colde
>   Oh, Master! Why?
> Is this Thy Breade? Is this the Thynge I wolde?
>   Then, Lett me Die!

THE doors were open through from the south room on whose doorstep he sat, which was the state parlor, into that behind it, the sitting or "keeping" room where Esther lay; the parson struck a light from the tinder box in the fireplace corner, and went in where his wife was, with a sinking heart.

Esther looked up at him with vague, wandering eyes, as he shaded the candle with his hand, and passing by her set it on a tiny stand behind the head of the couch. Then he came back and stood before her.

"Esther!" he said, with cold restraint in his voice. "You are ill, and over-worn. I would have you go to your chamber now, and betake yourself to rest. Your box of clothing is there, and your chest of drawers, with certain of your garments that Ruthy arranged within it. Turn the button, so you shall feel secure from disturbance; if you knew me, it need not to say that; but we are still strangers."

Esther rose slowly to her feet, half asleep, wholly bewildered, yet her ear had taken in her husband's words with the curious mechanism of that organ that seems to store up sounds to which the mind shall afterward give meaning; and seeing that she was yet unsteady, Mr. Hall led her like a child up the tiny winding stair to the landing above, and reaching out his arm pushed open the chamber door and put the candlestick into her hand.

"Good-night, Esther!" he said. "The Lord bless thee and keep thee. The Lord lift up His countenance upon thee, and give thee peace."

His voice sounded in her ear, clear, sad, and steady; but even yet she did not take in the situation; mechanically she closed the door and made it fast with the big wooden button, and still under the influence of the narcotic took off her dress and stays, and flinging herself on the outside of the bed fell asleep again before she was aware of her waking; yet all through her troubled rest the sad face of her husband seemed to be watching her, and over and over again she heard his deep, melancholy voice say, —

"But we are still strangers."

No such rest awaited Philemon Hall; when he turned to go, he knew that sleep was not for him; he took his hat, shut the outer door behind him, and with rapid steps made his way to the shore. He knew that Esther was safe in her solitude, for no tramps had been imported then to terrorize the quiet country, and neither rogue nor masterless man had disturbed the homes of such tiny villages as were strown along the Connecticut sea-beaches; so he went his way along the low bluffs till he reached a lonely headland that jutted out into the sea and was crowned with a few stunted cedars, and between them and the precipitous edge with some square yards of short, dry turf. Philemon Hall had been here before; it was an oasis where oftentimes he halted in the midst of his cares and duties to rest his tired brain in the silence of solitude, for at least a mile intervened between it and the last house of the village, and it was hedged in from intrusion landward by the thicket of low cedars that ran down to the sandy dunes beyond and behind it. Here was no sound but the dash and whisper of the waves, and as the heart-wrung man flung himself down on that slippery brown sward, the aromatic cedars seemed to breathe a caress on his burning forehead, and the strong, bright moon veiled herself with a fleecy cloud and soothed his hot tear-burned eyes. For, man that he was, Philemon Hall had given way to a few tears, wrung from the depths of his soul; tears that never fell, but were only hot and stinging to his eyeballs. He had come out here to face the second battle of his life, and from the first moment he knew it was to be the hardest. With his face earthward, prone on the parched grass, his soul met its Maker with wild anguish and bitter reproach; had there been voice given to his thoughts they would have said, —

"Why hast Thou done this? Have I not served

Thee faithfully all my days? Did I not give up my life to make the love of my youth happy? Have I not taken up my cross and followed thee? Lord! I am a man, not a saint; a man with human passions and affections; hast thou given me these to be thwarted and stifled forever? Did I not pray to thee long months for this desire of my heart, alway adding, 'If it be thy will!' and lo! now it is in mine hand, and it is bitter ashes! Lord, art thou not our father? where, then, is thy pity and compassion? Oh, God! how can I bear it!" and he clenched both hands into the dry, loose sod, as if that grasp of earth might assure him that the creation was stable and sure, however the Creator denied and thwarted him. It was to be noted, had any critical ear overheard his wordless arraignment of the Lord, that he took it always for granted that Esther was to be respected in her mistaken position; and neither forced or persuaded into accepting her relations with him except nominally.

Philemon Hall was not only a gentleman by nature but also by the grace of God; to him every woman was sacred, under any circumstances. He had sacrificed himself to Rachel, but it had consoled and inspired him to know that she shared the sacrifice, and loved him both passionately and purely; to him it was the visible hand of God that had put an adamantine barrier then between him and the sweetness of family life, so dear to every true-hearted man; so especially dear to him who was without a near relative in the world. But now —! Was this also of God? Was it not that devil, in whom he believed as firmly as in his Master, who had deluded him through Esther, and was now urging him to deny and defy his Lord and God? Whatever modern speculation has to say in its plausible and shallow fashion about the existence of a personal devil; however the feeble philosophers of to-day may sneer and jeer at the idea of such a being, and throw aside as "symbolic" and "typical" all the revelations and declarations of Scripture on this subject, it is notable that under that belief grew up the strongest and most steadfast of theologians; the most pure and righteous of men. Why this was so it is not in place here to discuss; the fact is historic; but certain it is that the moment Parson Hall grasped the idea of a spiritual opponent making him the medium of treasonable and abominable defiance, his loyal soul sprang up from the dust; it was a cry to arms, and the faithful soldier and servant obeyed it. He lifted himself from the ground and stood erect in the broad sad moonlight; it shone on his white, worn face, and dishevelled hair, and lit them with a ghastly distinctness as he lifted his clasped hands toward heaven and cried out with a hoarse voice, "Though He slay me, yet will I trust in Him!"

A light wind rustled in the cedars behind him, sighed, and died away; it seemed to him the echo and seal of his renunciation; as if earth bore witness to the vow he offered unto heaven; and worn out with the conflict which had lasted for hours in a maddened repetition of the words here recorded, he crept a little closer under the stunted cedars, laid his head on the turf and fell asleep. Deep and tranquil was his rest, for mind and body were over-worn, yet it lasted but one hour, for then the day broke in its June gladness and splendor, and the earliest rays of the new-risen sun dazzled his opening eyes; the carol of birds had awakened him at first, thrush, and song-sparrow, blue-bird and robin poured out their sweet exultation among the sheltering boughs, and as Philemon Hall slowly rose to his feet, the whole warm glory of the sunrise burst upon and enveloped him. Long familiar words came to his lips: "Which is as a bridegroom coming out of his chamber, and rejoiceth as a strong man to run a race."

He involuntarily shivered, but laid hold on his thoughts with a strength greater far than that of the runner, and setting his woe aside with the hand of power, recalled the fact that he must get back to his house, — would it ever be his home? — before the village awoke. He bathed his face in a tiny, clear pool left by the retreating tide, brushed the grass and moss from his clothes, and walked rapidly along the beach, and among the sand-dunes, bright now with glittering grass, meeting no one, for the fishermen had come in late the night before, and would not go out on the ebb; and the farmers were all at breakfast. He let himself in by the shed, and kindled the hearth-fire for their own breakfast, then he listened at Esther's door; she was stirring, so he went down again into his study, and opened the Bible for his daily reading. It seemed to him a direct ordering of God that the first words on which his eyes fell were these, — "But thanks be to God which giveth us the victory through our Lord Jesus Christ! Therefore, my beloved brethren, be ye steadfast, unmoveable, always abounding in the work of the Lord, forasmuch as ye know that your labor is not in vain in the Lord."

Who shall say that it was not such an ordering? The phrases fell upon Philemon Hall's soul with divine comfort, for they re-assured him that he had not taken up arms without the strength to wield them in a courage and power from on high; and the calm earnest exhortation to be steadfast in battle, to abound always in labor, the strong assurance that neither battle nor obedience should be futile, aroused him like the soaring cry of a trumpet that calls to war, under a mighty commander; his eye kindled, his face glowed; it seemed little at that moment to give up all human consolation, all sweetness and refreshing that life below can bring; he was ready to die for the Captain of his assured salvation. Alas! he had yet to find how much harder it is to live for Him!

He heard Esther come down the stair, but he did not stir. She had been instructed in the ways and means of the kitchen some weeks before by Aunt Ruthy, one day when the minister had gone out of town to an association; and she knew that kindly parishioners had stocked the pantry and storeroom with supplies; she was not ignorant of her duties, she set the round table for two, and soon savory odors of "saxafrax" tea, shortcake blistering before the fire, rashers of frizzling bacon, and eggs frying in the pan, mingled with the breath of damask roses and spicy pinks that came in at the open windows. It was a breakfast to make a modern hygeist shudder, but in those days men and women were unconscious of their stomachs, and the sufferer from what we call dyspepsia, was merely considered bad-tempered. Are they still convertible terms?

The minister entered the dining-room at Esther's timid call, and bade her "good-day," gravely; then he asked the accustomed blessing, but asked it with so solemn a voice and in such an unusual phraseology that Esther felt her awe of him increase. Breakfast was eaten in silence, — it might have been apples of Sodom to Parson Hall rather than staple and indigestible viands, for all the savor it had to his palate, and Esther too had lost her healthy appetite.

Who can eat on the brink of a crisis? Our digestive apparatus resents inattention as perversely as a child. When one is deeply and painfully absorbed in some important matter or some awful and possessing grief, it is worse than useless to eat; yet we all try to go through our recurrent meals and keep up a pretence of hunger. It is one of the painful conventions, far better set aside than observed.

The minister went in again to his study while Esther removed and washed her dishes; but as he rose from the table he said to her in a calm and strenuously gentle voice, that almost stopped her heart's quick beating, —

"Esther, when the morning duties of the house are finished, will you come into my study for a brief time?"

"Yes, sir!" gasped Esther, in a pained, childish fashion. She was frightened, and grieved, and fully conscious that she deserved severe reproof and remonstrance; but that consciousness did not make the prospect of such a visitation any more agreeable to her. She delayed her work as long as she dared, polished her few china dishes till they shone again, chased every speck of dust she could spy out with eager energy, and took a long hour to set her own apartment in order.

She was not physically tired, for her rest had been long, if troubled; but she was mortally afraid to face the interview before her. She felt like a prisoner at the bar, already convicted by the jury, who awaits the coming of the judge to declare that sentence. But at last she could find nothing to do, and with her heart in her mouth, trembling knees, and short-coming breath, she stole down the queer little staircase, and passing by the dim parlor redolent of the great *potpourri* jars on the hearth and a faint scent of camphor from the Indian matting, she knocked gently, but distinctly, at the study door.

CHAPTER XXIX.

A COMPACT.

Patience! patience! though heart should break, contend not with God in heaven.

PARSON HALL opened it. He set a chair for her on one side of the quaint, many-legged ebony table, on which lay his books of daily reference, and his sermon paper, and said at once, in a gentle, constrained, yet steady voice, —

"Esther, my friend, you and I have made a grievous mistake. I would you had told me that you were not prepared in your mind to be my wife."

"Oh!" said Esther, in a piteous tone, "I was wrong! I had nobody to tell me, and I was so lonely!"

Mr. Hall heard between the faltering words far more than they said.

"Nay, my dear! I was most to blame. I let the strength and sweetness of human affection hurry me on, not regarding your youth and solitude, as was fitting. Esther, we have laid our hands upon the ark of the Lord, hastily and carelessly, and He hath smitten us; we have taken upon us solemn and awful vows, and for me there is no release, for I took them with full understanding and purpose; but you knew not the thing that you did. It was even as you say, there was none to advise or warn you. By the authority of my ministry I release you from the promise made in your ignorance, so far as it is repugnant to your soul. I shall no longer ask you to love me; but I cannot free you from the outward bond that fetters us. Give me the respect and obedience you can give to a minister of the Gospel of Christ, to whose flock you belong, and I will ask for no more. I will treat you as a dear and honored friend, and respect your wishes in all things. We cannot separate, we must bear our sorrows together. I dare not afford occasion for the enemy to revile by the scandal of putting you away. Neither man nor woman must intermeddle with our life. It savors of deception, I well know so to live; but I see no other way to take, and I have prayed earnestly for divine guidance. Shall it be so, Esther?"

The girl bent her face on her hands and sobbed bitterly. By one of those strange, inexplicable revulsions of feeling, peculiar to women, she had never come so near loving Philemon Hall as now when he virtually divorced her. He stood there, strong and calm, his face lit with spiritual beauty, almost to her like some angel of judgment uttering her condemnation, and putting her beyond the confines of hope and joy for all time. Her sobs wrung the parson's heart, but he dared not attempt to console her, lest his own self-control should be shaken. He repeated the question.

"Shall it be so?" and his voice was stern and cold.

Esther lifted her tear-stained face and bent her head. In her simple gown and carelessly arranged hair, with that tearful countenance and those quivering scarlet lips, she looked like a sweet chidden child, and the longing to clasp her in his arms and comfort her, rose so fiercely into Philemon Hall's heart that he turned suddenly and left the room, well knowing that in every conflict to retreat is sometimes more needful than to fight.

Esther stole away to her own chamber and sat down to consider what must be done. She knew very well that after dinner one and another of the parish women would drop in to congratulate, inspect, advise, and inquire, and she must be ready to receive them, but first she must adjust herself a little to the situation; she prepared the apartment she occupied for her husband, it had always been his room; and she unpacked and removed her own possessions to another back of that one, where Aunt Ruthy had formerly slept. She had observed, with feminine quickness, that Parson Hall had never even implied a possibility of change in her or in himself; given no hint or intimation that in all time she might ever learn to love him, or he forget how she had deceived and wounded him. It was best so; yet as she looked forward to this dreary life of continual pretence and loveless intimacy, her girl's heart shuddered at the prospect, and she sighed often as she went about the house, and thought of the monotonous, untrue, harrassing days she must spend there. But there was work to be done, she could not sit down and vex her soul; work! the one blessing of life, lay close at hand. Work! the too-well-disguised angel of daily life, the comforter that makes living possible to the loneliest soul, the most desolate heart: the blessing in disguise that kept our first parents from dying of home-woe for their lost Eden. Who shall sing its praises fitly? Who canonize Saint Labor? Who raise a *carmen triumphale* to that which humanity miscalls a curse?

In the vindications and revelations of another world, we shall know that of all mortal blessings and balms the power and opportunity to work was the greatest, but here we are blind, because we are mortal.

Mr. Hall spent the morning in his study after Esther left him. He poured out his soul on his sermon; never before in all his ministry at Trumbull had he written such a discourse. It had for its text the verse to which his Bible had opened that morning, "Be ye steadfast, unmoveable, always abounding in the work of the Lord." He wrote on and on in the fervor of his experience, and could scarce bear to leave the work when Esther called him to dinner, but according to his custom as soon as the meal was over, he went abroad to visit some of his parishioners who were ill or sorrow stricken in the outlying parts of the parish. It had been one of his dreams that Esther and he should take these long drives together through the beautiful country in its fresh summer leafiness and perfume, but now he preferred to walk; the new chaise, the gentle, swift horse provided for her pleasure, might stay in the barn; he could not yet face a solitary drive; he must weary himself with sharp bodily exercise, the better to control his inward grief and disappointment. He walked at his best pace; the shining grasses of the shore never caught his eye, nor did the soft plash and whispering recoil of the rising tide attract his ear; he gave no heed to the young lambs frisking on the salt meadows, nor when his long road turned into the inner country, did he observe the crowds of mild blue sand-violets with golden eyes smiling upward to the kindred blue of the June heaven, nor yet the tiny thickets of gray-green sweet fern, full of young brown catkins; the clear red of oak-sprouts beside the wood path; the shimmer of emerald light downward through new leaves of maple and birch; the velvet-banded boles of old gray-barked beeches leaning forward toward him. All these he passed unheeded, even the round innocent pink buds with here and there a calm, open blossom that were clustered on the apple-trees in their abundant promise, and the long rods of roseate bloom on late fruiting peach-trees, or the snow of stainless pear-blossoms were all vague to his eye; he saw nothing but Esther, dove-like and womanly in her bridal garb, or childishly, piteously sweet, in her flowered chintz skirt and white short gown, burying her face in her hands, or lifting it again with tearful submission.

It almost seemed to Philemon Hall that he was

haunted by that lovely ghost of the past and the future. He bared his burning head to the summer breezes as he went, and sent his whole soul upward in prayer for help. The very effort to lift his thoughts beyond himself had its own power to quiet them, and bodily fatigue gave a certain languor to his weary soul that made it easier to control. Had he stopped to philosophize, now was the time to inspect and wonder at the curious admixture of spirit and matter that goes to the make-up of human beings; but Philemon Hall was a simple, direct, earnest man; simple in the way that Fenelon eulogizes: he would not, could not, dissect his own spiritual nature, "peep and botanize," thereon to satisfy his curiosity; he had duties to fulfil, and war to wage with the world, the flesh, and the devil; the solitude of these lonely country roads was the mountain-top where he must meet and fight the enemy; it mattered nothing to him that he was himself fearfully and wonderfully made; that was God's doing; his part was to put on the whole armor of God and "having done all, to stand."

While he was striding over field and hill, Esther was making ready for the inevitable visitors. It was most in accord with her feelings to put on the black dress that had been Aunt Dyer's; but it looked so sombre that she could not forbear lighting it up with a bunch of June pinks pinned on to her stomacher; she had brushed all the powder from her hair, and its dark rich masses made her pallor more apparent, for except in her lips there was not a trace of color in her whole countenance. She seated herself in the window and took up a small tambour-frame; she could not sit idle, she dared not; she was afraid of her own thoughts. Soon after she had assumed her position, a chariot rolled up to the door, a footman descended, and a smart knock heralded Madam Stanley. Esther dropped a formal courtesy as she ushered the gorgeous and stately lady into her low parlor.

"Well, Madam Hall," began Mrs. Stanley. "I am pleased to be the first to congratulate thee; but where is your maid? It is scarce seemly for you to attend the door yourself."

"I have no maid, Madam Stanley," said Esther with quiet pride.

"No maid? tut! tut! child; this will never do. I had thought the Hadsell wench was coming to thee."

"She is not," replied Esther, curtly.

"Hum! airs and graces already! Child, thou art over-proud for a parson's dame. And where is Parson Hall?"

"He hath gone to visit some sick ones over Hillside way."

"Not that brat of John Stonebridge's?"

"Nay, madam; somewhat further I think; he hath gone toward Dog's Misery to see the farmer at Chuckster's Mill."

"Methinks he is more than lawfully quick to go about his business so soon. Doth not the Scripture say that, — 'When a man hath taken a new wife, he shall not go out to war, neither shall he be charged with any business, but he shall be free at home one year, and shall cheer up his wife which he hath taken.' Parson Hall needeth to rub up his Old Testament, eh, child?"

Esther colored hotly; she did not like Madam Stanley's overbearing ways; she had never liked them; but she also inwardly resented the feeling that made her herself so warm in Parson Hall's defence. Why should she care what was said of him. Yet she answered as a wife should.

"Madam, Mr. Hall liveth not under the former dispensation, he is a preacher and liver of the Gospel of Christ. I think none will ever find him neglecting his duties for" — she hesitated a moment — "his civilities!"

"Hoity, toity! so one must not say an ill word of the husband, little Grizzel! 'Tis sportful to hear the chicken cackle so like an old hen. But to be serious, chick, I think thou shouldst have a maid. Respect thine office; the parson's wife hath a position. And it is not well that you over-work."

"Nay madam, I enjoy work. I think we will continue even as we have begun."

"Well, go thy way; if wilful will to water, wilful must drench; but when there come other cares to fill hands and arms, the maid will perforce follow."

Esther blushed an angry crimson; she liked neither the allusion nor her own consciousness of playing a part; and as Mrs. Tempy came bustling in just then, Madam Stanley, after inspecting the room through her glasses, with the frank impertinence of a great lady, bade Esther farewell, proceeded to her carriage, and rolled off.

"Proud as a pie, a'n't she?" said Tempy, with a sagacious nod. "'Tis the old story; she'd better rek'lect the pit whence she was digged; her granny was a French papist and her grandsir a 'pottecary. Set her up for a great lady! And what is the time of day with thee, Easter? Alack! my sweet; thou art but a sad-colored bride. Why didst put on this black gown? Sure as you're born 'twill bring misfortin. What a tell! a bride in black."

Esther smiled wistfully. "Will luck hurt a parson's wife, Aunt Tempy? Yet maybe I have had it already; for I forgot to ask the madam if she heard from Sybil by the last ship. Madam Stanley is sharp of speech and I had much to hear that I misliked, so I remembered not my dear Sybil."

"Well, child, there comes another time; Mr. Hall will ask for thee. Where is he to-day?"

So again Esther had to explain; and over and over again to the good women and gossips who came in, all that long afternoon, and wondered why the parson had left his young wife to receive the parish alone.

They had expected to see a gravely smiling bridegroom, ready to welcome them, by the side of a blooming bride; but here was only this pale, quiet girl in a black gown, that might have become her mother.

One and another queried about her domestic affairs in the kitchen; some applauded her thrift; some deprecated it; the few young girls who came, said almost nothing; she was not of their kind; they only stared and went away.

It was well after sunset when the parson came back, tired and haggard; and Esther's face had not even the glow of welcome in it; she was weary, spiritless, and angry with herself; all the covert allusions and matronly warnings of her well-meaning but not well-bred parishioners, through the long hot afternoon had not only disgusted her maidenly nature, but filled her anew with the bitter consciousness that she was a living lie.

Poor Esther! more unhappy parson! for if her conscience was sore, he had not only his personal conscience, but that which pertained to his office to keep spotless, and he had stained both. The sinner had, after all, led the saint astray!

CHAPTER XXX.

DAILY.

> A grief without a pang, void, dark and drear
> A stifled, drowsy, unimpassioned grief
> Which finds no natural outlet, no relief,
> In word, or sigh, or tear.

VERY monotonous were the days that now made up Esther's life. She had her household duties, but they were light, and to her youth and strength rather amusement than work when she became used to them. She could take the chaise and drive herself wherever she chose to go, but she never did. In order to keep up appearances, Mr. Hall now and then drove out with her to make his parochial visits, but the drives were as formal, as lifeless, as appearances always are. When they spoke together, it was of indifferent subjects, and they spoke little, for with that pensive, lovely face close beside him, it was hard work for Philemon Hall to keep his voice from betraying the anguish and passion of his soul. He could only hope that in the course of years he might become, through habit, as cold and calm as befitted the situation, but it was too new now for him to stifle within him the feeling he dared not outwardly express.

For Esther the matter was far easier; she had no love to hold down, no longing for any nearer relation;

her trouble was that her life was one of constant deception and gnawing regret that she had in her selfish desire to change her solitude for the peace and protection of a home, placed so noble a man in a false position. For, as the days went on, she could not but admire and respect her husband more and more.

His fervent prayers; his devotion to his duty; his courage in reproof of evil; his tenderness to all grief or want; his charity and his truth; all reproached her, yet bade her wonder and admire a man whose like she had never known.

And with each silent tribute her heart rendered to the excellence of his life, and the strength of his religious faith, came the stinging thought that she had given occasion of offence to this pure soul, and caused it to dissemble and pretend.

Left very much to herself, for in spite of her opinion of him, Parson Hall was by no means a perfect man, and involved in his own war with his inward nature forgot that his wife might have her own troubles to face, and so left her alone to face them, Esther encountered a new danger; she began to think of Philip Kent. He had been very far from saintly or perfect, as she knew to her cost, but she had loved him! In spite of herself her solitary heart turned back to those hours when life had been so rapturously sweet to her, and her weak soul was consumed with the bitter regret of a hopeless recollection. She knew this was wrong; she knew that one strong reason for her marriage had been that she would thus put a barrier between herself and Philip for all time; but, as the French proverb says, the effort to forget only made her remember.

She shuddered when she found herself thinking as she sat by her lonely fireside at night waiting to give the parson his supper after his long day of visitations far and near, how sweet it would be if it were Philip coming in; how joyful to meet tender eyes and clasping arms at the door, and give back the warm welcome, wait on his needs, and then, sitting on his knee, demand and receive the story of his day's occupation.

Ah! how wicked all this was! What could she do to avoid it? How get the better of these perilously blissful dreams? She prayed with all her soul for help; she read her Bible with eager diligence; she went about to visit the sick and the poor; she took down the volumes of history and theology, ponderous and few, that formed her husband's library, and tried to read them, but they were as dust and ashes to her girlish mind. Often she went over to the school and disturbed its order with her presence, for the children still worshipped her, and when they found she had not gone from them, or ceased to love them, they began to haunt the parsonage, to find their own way to the jar of spicy nut cakes in the pantry, to discover the dish of sugar cookies and revel in its treasures, to pluck posies in the formal garden, and dispute with the robins and orioles the reddening currants and the ripening raspberries.

Their little rosy faces, their innocent, saucy prattle, as once before were a balm to Esther's sore and tired heart.

Aunt Ruthy watched her as she went about among them, and sadly noted the wistful and woful curve of her lips, the darkened eye, the melancholy of the smiles that awoke the dimples in her still rounded cheek, and the good old woman's heart ached. She loved Philemon Hall like a son; she had watched with the deepest pity and reverence his devotion to Rachel, his smitten wife, and she had hoped and prayed that in this second marriage he might find recompense for all his goodness in the past; but she knew something had, gone wrong now. Silent, but observant, she had perceived Parson Hall's love for Esther before he had been conscious of it himself, she had seen its strong and ardent growth, and, though she believed the woman did not live who would be a perfect mate for this man, she was wise enough and old enough to know that no one can guide or govern a man's predilections in the case of a woman he elects to love, or, rather, loves without electing. She had also been aware of Esther's liking for Philip Kent, but not of its extent. She thought it was but a girl's fancy, and believed that when Esther discovered the false and selfish character of the man, and contrasted him with Mr. Hall, steadfast, faithful, and generous, her early passion would vanish like an autumn mist before the sun. She could not now picture to herself any possible hindrance to the new and happy life that ought to blossom in the parsonage, but she distinctly saw that it did not exist; and knowing well that she could neither help or hinder it by any mere human means, she betook herself to prayer, for in those days there were men and women who accepted the Bible as their guide, believed in the Triune God, and made their lives blessed and beautiful in that faith and its fruits. Then there was no open reaching after a new religion, that should conform its theories and demands to the reason of man instead of the wisdom of God; the creature rested in his own place, and adored and trusted his Creator with childlike confidence and manly reverence, anxious only to work out his own salvation, knowing that it was God working in him to the loftiest and purest results.

So the summer wore on, and before its end there came a new interest into Philemon Hall's life.

At the time of which we write there was a legalized union of church and state prevailing in the colony, and no other church than the Congregational was allowed to exist; or, if such a schismatic organization or conclave persisted in existing, its members were punished by fine, by extortion, by imprisonment, and by branding. Even the neglect to attend "the public worship of God in some *lawful* Congregation," for the sake of "worshipping in separate companies in private houses," was visited by a heavy fine.

Perhaps it was this stringent prohibition, and an inheritance of the old spirit that drove their fathers across the sea in search of "freedom to worship

God," that worked in the bosoms of certain good and godly men, who read their Bible with a different understanding of its technical phraseology from that of the Congregationalists, and so induced them to declare to the world that baptism by immersion was necessary to salvation, and therefore they must form a separate, and a Baptist church for themselves. Years before this time such an offence against the stringent ecclesiasticism of the Colony had been made by law a serious matter, involving severe fines, and to the clergyman who dared administer the communion to such a flock, "corporeal punishment, by whipping, not exceeding thirty stripes for each offence." It is painful to record this illiberality on the part of those whose national history began in a protest against the tyranny of ecclesiastical power; whose immediate ancestors had suffered the loss of all things for the sake of spiritual liberty. Yet it demonstrates a fact that should be a powerful incentive to charity of judgment toward our fellowmen under any and all conditions or actions, the fact that human nature is akin the world over, subject to the same passions, the same prejudices, the same narrowness of outlook, and cruelty of conceit in 1620 as in 1748 or 1889.

At this period of which we write, men who avowed their faith in the Baptist "heresy" were persecuted with little mercy; they were not hung, or shot, or drowned, but they were cast into prison, stripped of their substance, reviled and despised, and, as a natural consequence, increased and flourished in the face of their enemies; for that "the blood of the martyrs is the seed of the church," is a truth for all ages and nations.

Early in the winter following Parson Hall's marriage, just when the gloom in his heart seemed deeper and his position more unendurable than ever, since the cold without put an end to his long walks and drives and forced him into daily companionship with Esther, in all her gracious, if pensive beauty, her gentle household ways, and tormentingly delightful presence, he received a message from the Baptist church in Watertown, the adjoining town to Trumbull, saying that Doctor Bellamy, a well-known divine of the "established" church, had preached to them to their great acceptance and comfort, for in the "great awakening" this little church had been aroused to deep religious concern, and therefore their pastor had invited certain of the clergy of the orthodox denomination, who were considered to have caught some of the spirit and power of Whitfield's inspired ministrations, to preach for his flock, "Observing that as to the internals of religion they could heartily join with them, though not in the mode."

Now in Watertown the Baptists had been treated more mildly than in the neighboring villages; and by advice of the governor of the colony, who seemed to have some especial reasons for favoring the Baptists in that town, (perhaps because Mr. Milliken, their pastor, was his cousin by marriage, and Madam Walcott, the governor's wife, was reputed commonly to be "the power behind the throne,") the assessments made for the support of the legal church were remitted in behalf of these schismatics.

It may be that Parson Hall was aware of their peculiar immunities in Watertown; it may be that he was not; in the light of following events one thing is manifest, that such knowledge, or the want of it, would have made no difference in his course; he was pleased at the invitation, for while he did not in the least accept or favor the peculiar dogmas of the Baptists, his spirit had been filled with indignation at their sufferings and persecutions; for he considered them fellow Christians, honest and righteous, if mistaken in their non-essential points of belief.

He spoke of the letter he had received from Parson Milliken to Esther with keen pleasure; once more a spark kindled in his eye, and his voice recovered for a moment its old ring. While he had never hesitated to express his opinion concerning the treatment of the Baptists by his own church in terms of forcible distaste and denunciation, he had never yet had an opportunity to prove his words by his works; and the spirit of the man roused to the occasion; he knew that he might, nay, that he doubtless should, encounter some opposition and reproof, but it was a matter of conscience with him to feed his Master's sheep in whatever fold the door was opened for him; and having written his acceptance and appointed an early day in the next month to occupy the pulpit, he set about him to find some one who should fill his own place on that day, and then began to consider on what verse of Scripture he should hold forth to this hungering and thirsting crowd of strangers.

He selected for his text the curt and tremendous sentence "He that is not with me is against me," and filled with the immensity and awe of that declaration and all it implies, he sat down at his study table and wrote like one inspired. For once he utterly lost sight of himself and his troubles in burning eagerness to set before men their destiny and their freedom of choice; the absolute impossibility of being neutral; the inevitable necessity of avowing their position, since whatever they said their lives would deny or assert the truth in spite of their elusive words. And from this he drew fearful pictures of the hypocrite, and the open opponent of God; and with heartrending pathos described the penitence and acceptance of the convicted sinner, and the divine peace and strength of the saint, who, when the griefs and losses of life come upon him like a flood, can exultantly declare "The Lord is on my side! I will not fear; what can man do unto me?"

It was indeed a wonderful sermon, but the astonishing part of it to Philemon Hall was its reflex action on his own soul. In endeavoring to bring others to this standpoint he had arrived there himself, and in the glow of his enthusiasm, and the shining of this immortal truth, his own sorrow seemed to be but a passing shadow driven off by a keen, strong wind; he recognized the brevity of time, and the awful issues of eternity in their true proportions, and felt a sort of noble shame in that he had not better endured hardness as a good soldier of Christ Jesus.

It was an illustration of the Scripture "he that watereth shall be watered also himself," and though Parson Hall wrote far into the night, he slept peacefully thereafter, and not even Esther's fair, tormenting face looked in upon his dreamless rest.

CHAPTER XXXI.

IN THE BEGINNING.

> Mortal! who standest on a point of time,
> With an eternity on either hand ;
> Thou hast one duty over all sublime,
> Where thou art placed, serenely there to stand.

PARSON HALL's sermon was wonderfully acceptable to the Watertown Baptists; they were moved to the depth of their hearts by its earnestness and fervor, and it was so strictly unsectarian that it might have been preached in St. Peter's at Rome, and given no offence to the Pope himself.

It had always been characteristic of Mr. Hall's preaching that it was devoted to the essentials of religion, and ignored the trivialities and absurdities of man-made dogmas and assertions.

He said one day to Parson Dyer, who at the instance of certain old rigidities in the congregation undertook to remonstrate with him for neglecting the stringent doctrines of the day, such as election, predestination, free will, infant damnation, and the like.

"Brother Dyer, 'necessity is laid upon me; yea, woe is unto me, if I preach not the gospel,' and I cannot think that these things be needful unto salvation. I am a mortal man, and who knoweth at what hour I may be called to put on immortality? It behoves me while life lasteth to know nothing among you save Jesus Christ and him crucified; I leave to him who alloweth us to see but as in a glass, darkly, the administration of his government. I know in whom I have believed, and that is all I do know."

"Well, well, Brother Hall, I know you are one of the New Lights, but be it said they don't seem to see through a millstone any better than the old sort, I cannot but think that the grappling of the mind with speritooal problems hath an effect to strengthen its hold upon invisible things. It rouses the grit to endeavor to reconcile the ways of God to man, for it is hard, yea! it is hard."

Philemon Hall's brain suddenly evolved before him that June morning when he too found those ways hard as adamant, and impossible to understand, as he lay prone on the cliff wrestling with the will of God, even as Jacob wrestled with the angel at Peniel, but alas! unlike Jacob, had not prevailed, but had submitted. He drew a long, sighing breath.

"Yea, Brother Dyer, it may be so, but that is not my calling. 'To every man his work.'"

Parson Dyer cast upon him a sharp glance from under his shaggy brows, but said no more, and Philemon Hall thence and thereafter preached in the simplicity of the Gospel; but the elder men of the ministry kept an eye on him, half of doubt, half of distrust.

He left Watertown on the Monday morning with a glowing heart, for he felt that he had done some worthy work for his Master, and though the chill shadow of his personal life fell upon him again as he opened the door of his house and received Esther's shy and formal greeting, he could rise above the clouds to-day, and rest in the serene atmosphere of a higher and purer existence, "hid with Christ in God." Wonderful words! more wonderful truth. As he went on toward his study, Esther followed him with two letters in her hand, which she had just taken down from the keeping-room shelf.

"These were brought by the post-rider but two hours after you were gone, on the Saturday night," she said.

He took them from her silently, and laying them on the table proceeded to take from his bookcase certain books of reference with a view to his next sermon, and then seating himself, broke the seals of the epistles. They were both postmarked from Watertown, where he had just been; the first he opened was a short missive signed by forty-two men of that town, desiring him not to preach to the Baptists there. They gave no reason why he should comply with their request, except that they wished him to do so, and he cast the letter aside, intending to destroy it, but on second thought took it up from the floor, folded, and dated it on the outside, and opened the other. This was equally brief, but came from a brother clergyman, the Reverend Mr. Miles, of Eastport, a town of the consociation to which Trumbull and Watertown belonged, advising him in a friendly but peremptory way, not to preach in the Baptist meeting-house in Watertown.

Philemon Hall laid this letter upon the other, and resting his head upon his hands fell into deep thought.

Why should he not preach to these few sheep in the wilderness? he said to himself. He did not thereby aid or endorse their peculiar doctrine, or help to extend it among the townspeople; they were anxious sinners, hungering and thirsting for salvation, and what reason was there that he should not point out to them the Way of Life? He thoroughly studied the *pros* and *cons* of the matter; in a measure he perceived what lay before him; he knew that his brethren disapproved of his course, and would oppose it with all their power. They could make his position very uncomfortable at least; possibly, he might suffer at their hands the same indignities they had inflicted on several of the Baptist preachers. But ought he to consider his personal gain or ease in the face of so manifest a duty as this? He dared not decide for himself; he knew that in his seemingly quiet and mild disposition the spirit of the church militant was strong and eager; he distrusted his own candor in a point where his soul sprang up like an armed man zealous to fight for the Lord against the foolishness of men. Perhaps his native combativeness, so long and so well kept under, not only by the restraining grace of God, but by the strength of self-control his bitter disappointments had taught him, might now unduly influence him to set at naught the warnings and wishes of his brethren, because to him they seemed idle and futile.

It did not once occur to him that he could be influenced by the popularity he might acquire among his Baptist people, for he was not a vain or a conceited man. He was honest and self-distrustful, and there remained but one thing for him to do, — to ask counsel from on high. He slipped the button across his door, and on his knees laid the whole matter before God, in humble confidence, asking for guidance from that wisdom which sees the end from the beginning, and is given liberally, without upbraiding, to whosoever asks in simplicity of faith.

There is a calming and elevating influence in the mere attitude of real prayer, that brings the soul into an atmosphere whose tranquil clarity shows the things which make up our strange lives in their true relation both to this world and another. In the face-light of Divinity our souls see how small are the things men count important; how awful and how lofty those eternal truths we daily neglect and ignore.

Philemon Hall in that presence-chamber perceived at once what his duty was; how clear, how direct, how needful to be done. And as his future course opened before him, with all its rough possibilities and alienations, he was not daunted; for there flashed through his soul the words that had before guided him to the battle: "Be ye steadfast, unmoveable, always abounding in the work of the Lord, forasmuch as ye know that your labor is not in vain in the Lord."

He could have cried like the Roman emperor, "*In hoc signo vinces*," for he felt that the Lord had spoken to his soul in the word of Scripture; and he arose from his knees, having his commission and his password therein.

It may not be as æsthetic, as rational, or as philosophic to believe in the Bible as in the "religion of nature;" "hysteric Boodhism," as a small child aptly misnamed the new Asiatic cult; or that denial of all things, that says in its heart 'there is no God'; but it certainly is not as helpful or satisfactory to trust in any of these refuges of lies, as in the God of the Bible, and the Christ of the Cross. To them what myriads of desperate and wretched human souls have fled in all recorded time, and found help and hope; what death-beds have they comforted, what lives inspired, what sinners reclaimed, what civilization wrought, what social reforms inaugurated! "By their works shall ye know them!"

Parson Hall went to his daily duties with a resolute and calm countenance. The dark expression that had deepened his eyes and set his lips was gone. He had told the Watertown Baptists that he would preach for them on the ensuing Sunday, and now in the new courage and ardor of his soul he began to write the sermon so promised. This time it was as unsectarian as before, but more tender, more pleading, and it flowed like a joyful stream from its fountain, from the good words: "God so loved the world that He gave his only-begotten Son, that whosoever believeth on Him should not perish but have eternal life."

Again the earnest hearers were moved and melted; many of them professed to be converted by one or the other of Mr. Hall's discourses, and seemed of a truth to have begun Christian lives, so that his heart rejoiced as he said over again to himself: "Forasmuch as ye know that your labor is not in vain in Lord." But the trouble he had expected followed fast on the heels of his rejoicing; he was, the very next week, complained of to the Consociation of Congregational Churches of Newport County, as a disorderly person, in this formula, —

I, the Subscriber, do signify, by way of Complaint to this Reverend Consosiation, that on ye 10th day of January last past, the Reverend Philemon Hall did enter into ye first Society in Watertown and preach in a Disorderly Manner in Contem'pt of ye authorety of this Consosiation without ye consent of ye Revd mr Wappinger, Pastor of sayd Society, contrary to the Act of ye Milford Counsil, contrary to the Act of this Consosiation, and contrary to ye Desire of two naybouring Ministers, and a grate Number of Church Members in Watertown.

PETER HALE.

Parson Hall was grieved deeply by this first shot from the ecclesiastical batteries of his own church. Hitherto, he had enjoyed the friendly intercourse of his brother clergymen extremely. In the denials and endurances of his earliest home life, and its social solitudes, — for Rachel's extreme suffering at times, and her chronic helplessness, forbade her either to receive guests or to visit; and her husband thought it best not to indulge himself greatly in pleasures she could not share, — he had looked forward to the meetings of the Consociation as a sort of mild dissipation, which he could enjoy, and yet feel it was his duty to attend. Then his personal friendship for some of the very men who felt that now they must reprove him and expel him from their society, had been, — nay, still was, — very strong and sweet. It would be as the severance of David and Jonathan, should two or three of these take up weapons of war against him. And now that his private griefs had once more taken possession of heart and hearth, he had looked forward to these meetings with his brethren as occasions where his weary soul should be refreshed, and his feeble knees strengthened. This hope he must relinquish. How glad he would have been now to carry his troubles to Rachel, and from her perceptive mind and loving heart draw the sympathy and consolation men so invariably demand from the nearest woman fitted to give it.

Could he, should he, tell Esther?

The cold silence of their daily intercourse daunted him in this stress of vexation and dismay, but he must speak of his new position, in justice to her. He began to feel that, as his wife, she had certain rights; she ought to understand what he knew now would be the consequence of his following out his ideas of duty before the knowledge should be spread abroad in his own church or the town. So, before he replied to the accusation of the Consociation, he sat down by the fire one evening instead of going back from supper and prayers to his study, and laid before her, as plainly as he could, the results of his course.

"And will you go on preaching to the Baptists, nevertheless?" she asked timidly.

"I shall, Esther. I have considered the matter with much prayer. The Lord's commission unto his disciples was, 'Feed my sheep,' and who shall say that these few souls, hungering and thirsting after righteousness, are not his?"

"But you may have to leave this church and your own people, if you are steadfast in this matter."

"Ah, Esther, do you think me so poor a creature that I cannot abide the wrath of man, when I can see the face of God? Nay, I feel that by his grace I could take joyfully the spoiling of my goods. I must, indeed, lay the matter before my church, to whom I am bound by ties not lightly to be broken. But if the worst you or I imagine shall come upon us, have we not the promise that the Lord will provide? Yea!—" and here his voice rose clear, ringing, and triumphant, and his face glowed as Esther had never seen it,—

"Yea! 'Who shall separate us from the love of Christ? Shall tribulation, or distress, or persecution, or famine, or nakedness, or peril, or sword? Nay! in all these things we are more than conquerors, through him that loved us!'"

He turned away and went to his study, half ashamed of his outburst of feeling, though it was involuntary. But his wife sat long and late by the fireside, thrilled with an indescribable tumult of feeling.

Why was her pillow wet with tears that night?

CHAPTER XXXII.

A SURPRISE.

> There comes a resurrection of the dead,
> Before this world and all its folk have fled.
> Past deeds, past words, past thoughts arise, and call
> With living voices, that the soul appal.
> We know, aghast, that nothing ever dies
> But, soon or late, shall from its grave arise,
> Confront us, like a spectre, from the tomb,
> And fill our souls with fear, remorse, and gloom.

Soon after Parson Hall preached his sermon to the Watertown Baptists, and received the remonstrance and complaint of Peter Hale, from the hands of the Consociation, to which it was sent, he returned to that body the following vindication:—

To the Reverend Consociation of Newport County,
— I, the subscriber, having been duly notified that a Complaynte hath been sent you that upon ye 10th day of January I did, in a Disorderlie manner, in Contemt of ye Consociation and withoute Consent of Revd Mr. Wappinger, preache ye Gospel unto a Convocation of folk commonlie called Baptists, said folk Inhabitynge within sayd Wappinger's Society. I would hereby state, 1st, that ye Honble John Walcott, Governor of this Colony, hath not pressed ye sayd Baptists for their ministerial Taxes; therebye Implyinge that they have Ecclesiastick rights and Privileges of their own. Also, 2d, the Publick Authorities of ye Colony send unto them their Annual Proclamations of High Days even as unto other Churches, which implyeth the same as Aforesayd. Moreover, 3d, I entered not Rev'd Mr. Wappinger's parish; but discoursed to a People in no wise His. And 4th, with respect unto my preachinge contrary to the Advyse of

two Ministers and numerous church members of **Watertown**, I am constrained to say that I know of no Rule in the Word of God, neither in the Saybrooke Platform, which Obligeth me to comply with such Advyse and Desires. Nor do I see any right Reason therein. And 5th, I see not that this Complaynte accuseth me of any Violation of ye Divine Law; or of doing anythynge contrary to the Word of God.

PHILEMON HALL.

While the Consociation, confounded by this sharp rejoinder from a man generally held to be so peaceful and reasonable as Parson Hall, were still meditating on their duty, or their intentions in the case, singly, or in private council, Parson Dyer was making a toilsome journey toward the city of New York. He was getting on in years, and began to think that his duties as minister of a country parish involved too much hard work for a man of his age and ailments. He was racked with rheumatism, that scourge and torment of the New England climate, and every year grew more unfit for the long rough drives required in his scattered parish. To be called up in the dead of night to attend a dying parishioner four miles off, the thermometer below zero, the northwest wind blowing, or the northeast driving snow like clouds before it, exasperated all his aches and pains; and he had no longer the strength of youth to help him bear them. His hands, too, were becoming stiff, and his eyes failed him; he had a little money saved from his poor salary, and a little that he had inherited. He did not want to live in a city, for he loved all natural sounds and sights; he would have pined with homesickness among brick walls and noisy streets; his idea of life now was to buy a farm, and lease it to some man who would either take it on shares, or take him, the parson, to share his home as a compensation for the use of the land. Looking about him for some such place and person he hit upon Hillside farm. It was good land, having arable fields, wood lots, pasture, and grass lands, and the house was large and comfortable; Hiram and Delia did not use it all, a sunny spare chamber and the parlor below it were even yet unfurnished; so having ascertained the willingness of the present occupants to accept him as an inmate on the terms he proposed, Parson Dyer mounted his Narragansett pacer and set out for New York to transact, if possible, the purchase of Hillside farm from Philip Kent. After a night's rest following on his tedious journey, Mr. Dyer betook himself to the stately house fronting on a green common of small size, on the further side of which the sea broke gently on the beach, and sprinkled the grass with salt spray.

Philip Kent was at home, and came into the richly-furnished library where Parson Dyer sat, with his usual smooth and courteous manner.

He was not a generous man, though he liked well to spend money on himself, so it took him long to arrange terms with Mr. Dyer. He was glad to sell the farm; he would have liked to sell all his uncle's property in Trumbull, for he did not want to own such comparatively unproductive estate; but he wanted to extort the last farthing from the purchaser. Parson Dyer, however, inherited and had been trained in all the thrift of a Yankee, and he kept up his part of the debate with as much keenness as Philip Kent, and they were no nearer the end, apparently, when an idea flashed across the parson's brain.

"I think," said he, looking straight at the other man, "that had this property gone whither my old friend meant it should, into the hands of Madam Esther Hall, I should not have had so many words about it."

Mr. Kent's face suddenly darkened, his eyes grew confused, his voice shook, he looked furtively about him, as if to collect his wits for an answer; then he said.

"You speak of things I know not, Parson Dyer nor was I aware that I had driven a shrewd bargain for my lands."

"I was but recalling the fact that very shortly before his death, mine excellent Cousin Dyer, late of Trumbull, confided unto me that he had made a recent will, leaving unto his niece, Esther Dennis, a goodly, yea, the greater share of his property, which was not small. I wonder what became of that will, Mr. Kent."

"How should I know?" said Philip, with an angry flash in his eyes.

That was enough for Mr. Dyer; he could not prove anything more against Philip Kent than he could have done an hour before, but in his own mind he was fully convinced that the disappearance of the document lay at the door of the only man whom it profited.

"How should you, indeed?" answered Mr. Dyer, gravely, his eyes still fixed on Philip's.

"Let us return to the subject we had in hand," Philip said, moving uneasily, as if those deep-set eyes had pierced his flesh as well as his spirit.

"There is little more to say on my part," answered the wily parson. "I have offered for the farm of Hillside what I can afford to give, and what seemeth to me a fair value for the premises. It remains with you, Mr. Kent, to take up mine offer or to cast it away."

"Well, well, Parson Dyer, I do not desire to be hard upon the clergy; I must even abide by your price I perceive. I will have the deeds drawn up post haste, and send them to you by a trusty hand."

"And I will then remit unto you the needful moneys by your own messenger."

"Well said! Let us strike hands upon it. And now will you walk into the dining-hall and share our poor dinner?"

"I thank you, but I may not tarry here so long, sir. Nevertheless, I thank you for your hospitality, though press of time forbid me to enjoy it. My respects to Madam Kent. I wish you a good-day."

And with that the parson walked away, secretly chuckling.

But no such agreeable emotion diverted Philip Kent's perturbed soul; here was a surprise indeed; here had a man arisen suddenly who knew the real tenor of Uncle Dyer's last will! What if he should tell Esther? Why, oh! why, had he himself been such a fool as to sell him Hillside? Because he had been confused and shaken by Parson Dyer's unexpected speech was that any reason he should so have lost his presence of mind, and not only retracted his demand for the sum he fully intended to acquire, but perhaps shown in both face and speech that he was not only surprised, but troubled?

But for the thought that Parson Dyer might suspect still more, he would then and there have followed him and cancelled the bargain, but he dared not, as it was.

Why had he not spoken of his offer to Esther of pecuniary aid? Why had he never thought of at once proposing to share with her the property that should have been hers? He felt that the first instinct of an honest man, on learning the fact that his uncle's will had been made to benefit Esther, would have been to give up a possession that never should have fallen into his hands. But he had not even hinted at such a possibility; he had done just what a guilty and conscious person would do; abruptly turned the subject, and showed his perturbation by closing up a bargain he had so strenuously refused even to consider a few moments before.

"Curst fool that I was!" he ejaculated to himself, walking up and down the library floor. "What's to be done now? for sure he suspects me of somewhat; I saw it in his eye. Gad! it shone like a wild-cat's from a thicket, under those bushed brows."

But no counsel of any present avail came to him; long did he walk to and fro on that costly Turkey carpet, in the solitude of his goodly library, well-filled, for that day; but with books that chiefly came from his uncle's house in Trumbull.

He could arrange nothing, trust to no scheme of immediate device; he could get no further than a fixed intention to see Esther, whom he had never looked on since some time before her marriage, and try to find out if Parson Dyer had been as communicative to her as to him. But he could not do it soon, gladly as he would have set his mind at rest thereby; just now Parson Dyer would be moving to Hillside, and his road from Pickering Centre lay along the turnpike that passed through Trumbull; he did not want to meet him again at present.

There was nothing he could do; yet strangely enough Esther's face, her voice, the soft delicate touch of her little fingers, the cool fragrance of her lips began to haunt him; he had but made of her a passing pleasure, as one plucks a rose, enjoys its odor, lays it against hot eyes or burning cheek for its balm and breath, and then drops it as carelessly as a weed! But oddly enough — for a man — now that he knew she was out of reach he began to prize her.

For many a day he was snappish to clerks and customers both, and as cross to his wife as he dared be to the heiress of all the Stuyvesants direct and collateral; but neither they nor she knew what underlay his ill-humor, or guessed that the fair, wistful face of a girl came between his eyes and his ledgers far too often for his peace or comfort.

It was far into May, and Parson Dyer was long settled in the Hillside farmhouse, before Philip Kent thought it wise or safe to go to Trumbull. Then some one who came from that way told him that the old house needed some repairs outwardly, so he had a fair pretext for his journey. The roads were well settled along the coast, and the frail blossoms of a New England spring starred the wood-edges and roadsides, as Philip Kent rode swiftly on his way; his horse was fine and fast; he was perfectly at home in the saddle: the weather was mild and dim; the south wind blew softly; and he was about to see Esther again. He never considered for a moment the change in her position; with the calm arrogance of his nature, he felt sure that when she once saw his face, her old love would re-enter her heart, and with the credulous faith of passion she would believe what he said instead of what Parson Dyer might have told her.

She had been married now nearly a year; he argued that long before now she must have become tired of "that preaching prig" as he chose to style Parson Hall; and he imagined as he ambled along the sandy road the sort of welcome she would give him; forgetting that a woman however good, gentle, or devoted, will always resent neglect; and he had absolutely ignored Esther for the last two years.

Wise in his own conceit, he cantered gayly into the little village so familiar to his earlier life, and drawing rein at Deacon Swaddle's tavern ordered a good supper and their best bed, for he was both hungry and tired after his long journey.

The parsonage of Trumbull stood within sight of the tavern, and, after breakfast next morning, Philip Kent watched behind the dimity curtains of his window till he saw Philemon Hall enter his chaise, alone, and drive off; it was not Mr. Kent's intent to see Esther's husband, if he could help it; out of the gate he strolled in leisurely fashion, plucking the first bud of the cinnamon rose-bush by the door that had yet shown a line of red along its taper verdure, and twirling it betwixt thumb and finger as he went his way.

The old red house at which he halted was still and peaceful in the hush of the spring morning, but he broke the silence with a loud sharp peal on the knocker, heard hurried steps approach, and at once the upper half of the wide hutch door flew open and in that quaint frame, showing like an old picture against the dark background of the inner house, stood Esther.

CHAPTER XXXIII.

NO!

Late, late, too late! Ye cannot enter now.

ESTHER looked at Philip Kent in pale silence; he doffed his hat to her with a strange thrill of emotion. by no means all pleasure.

It seemed an hour, it was not half a minute, when she opened her rigid lips, and unbolting the lower half of the door, said, —

"Will you enter?"

Philip Kent walked in, and placed himself on the chintz sofa in the parlor, he hardly knew why; but Esther, instead of sitting down beside him, took a tall chair opposite, evidently a chair of state in her eyes.

She did not say a word; she sat like the legendary ghost, waiting to be accosted.

"I am pleased to see you looking so well, Madam Hall," said Philip, at last, with courteous conventionality.

"I thank you. I am well," was the cold reply; yet Esther's heart beat fast and loud under her bodice. She had tried day after day not to dream of this meeting, not to think what joy it would be to see Philip again, for she, like Guinevere, believed

— "What is true repentance, but in thought, —
Not even in inmost thought to think again
The sins that made the past so pleasant to us."

And lo! there was no joy. She was not glad, but troubled.

Some strange terror of loss and want filled her soul; she did not comprehend that she had lived for a year in an atmosphere as alien to a character like Philip Kent's as possible; while he had been steadily deteriorating, she had all unconsciously been lifted to a higher plane of thought and life.

This man's face showed the result of self-indulgence and dissipation; marriage had not refined but hardened and degraded it; for while Philip gave way to Annetje's will and way, for the sake of keeping in her good graces in order to profit by her money, he had yet enough pride left to despise himself for his abject compliance, and his cowardly terror of her hot temper.

His eyes had lost the clearness of youth; they looked tired and dim; his face was sodden with wine-bibbing and late hours; his hair prematurely threaded with gray; and his loose under-lip hung more heavily downward. He had fretted and rebelled at first against the thorns in the lot he had chosen; and finding this in vain, had drawn his native selfishness about him like a heavy mantle, and choked out under that close ꝏvering every aspiration toward good. He needed only added years to become that burden to humanity doleful, whining, complaining, self-centred hypochondriac; at once a tyrant and a scorn to all about ; a man slowly drawing nigh to the grave, down with the contempt and dislike of his fellows, for men never die young.

Even his appearance at her door after his long neglect of her, added to Esther's swift disillusion; she divined instinctively that it was not sentiment which had brought him, but some scheme.

She had lived long enough side by side with Philemon Hall now to understand, partially, the beauty and strength of his character. She perceived in her husband, a man whose religious principle was the power and governance of his daily life, the spring of all his actions; there was no Sunday religion about Philemon Hall. She began, too, to see how perfect was his truth, how manful his courage; while he appeared to the mass of men to be mild and tender, a man full of sympathy and generosity, she knew what depths of steadfast valor and righteous indignation underlay that saintly aspect. Even as with the Apostle John, his loveliness to all about him made men forget that he was "a son of thunder"; though the Newport County Consociation began to think that meekness was not Brother Hall's strong characteristic.

While these thoughts crossed Esther's mind, Philip Kent had also some revelations of a change in her. Strangely enough there was nothing of the matron about her; none of that *status* which even a few months of marriage often gives a woman; the result of feeling that she has a place and is a power in the world. Esther had a certain girlish dignity about her, but it was yet girlish; her face wore the vague bloom of a girl when its first paleness has vanished, and her slight figure kept the uncertain, swaying

grace of immaturity that lingers so long with even
"old maids" as an unfriendly tongue calls the
eleven thousand virgins of St. Ursula. But the
change to Philip was in her face; the large, tender
eyes were icy and proud now; the mouth set in firm,
if sad curves; the whole aspect of her countenance
was different, it expressed neither regret, nor love;
its weakness was gone; evidently she had no tenderness for him left, — had she for any one?

He inquired politely for Mr. Hall; Esther answered with the same politeness; he felt like a man
with the nightmare; invisible forces seemed to quell
his energy and stifle his speech. He had thought to
find the loving, complying, self-lost creature who had
risked so much for him; whom he had made utterly
happy with kisses, and rewarded with sweet words;
whose heart he had well-nigh broken, but who had
yet again been his tender and faithful comforter.

Here was an ice maiden; chilly, proper, separated
from him by a wall, which he could never break
through. He grew confused, disturbed, and incoherent. He forgot that he came to tell her a plausible
story about the will, and to confute whatever Parson
Dyer had said or might say. He sat a moment longer,
fumbled for his hat under the sofa where he had
unintentionally kicked it as it fell from his hands,
rose to his feet and saying "Good-day, madam,"
strode out of the door, cursing under his breath at
everything and nothing.

It was as well for them both that he did not see

Esther, as soon as his steps died away in the distance, rush up the stairs to her chamber, and flinging herself on her knees, bury her face in the cover of her bed and burst into a flood of passionate tears. Poor girl! she had lost what is worse than losing a lover, she had lost love.

It is a terrible pang to know that the one absorbing, entrancing passion of life has vanished forever; no death of mortal creature is like unto it; for a dead love there is no resurrection, not even a future hell; it has gone into utter nothingness and left a void that is fast filled with self-contempt, disbelief, scorn of man, and bitter, biting prudence. Where that love has indeed been the ardent and solitary child of a matured soul, a soul that can love but once, it is a death by murder if ever it does die. Cruelty, treachery, neglect, may stab it to the heart, and the whole life of the hapless lover becomes sunless and desperate.

But it was not so with Esther; like many another girl she had made unto herself the image she adored and fastened it on to the real Philip, who was truly most unlike the fair mask. It was the loss of her ideal she deplored; she was too young at heart to have felt the consuming fire that burns on of its inherent vitality, and, dazzled by its own supernal glory, cares nothing for the altar on which it burns, or the faults and follies of the god at whose shrine its sacrificial flames are offered.

Yet for days and months Esther went about

haunted by a vague sense of loss; it woke with her in the morning and reposed with her at night; but her interview with Philip Kent was after all a relief to her, she had no longer any temptation to think of him or of her past infatuation; it was no longer pleasant to her to remember her folly; she shuddered to think of what might have been. And she was becoming more and more interested in her husband's struggle with the bigotry and tyranny of the Consociation.

On receiving his reply to their admonition, they had resolved, and sent him their resolution, which ran, —

Resolved that the Rev'd Mr. Hall soe preachynge was Disorderlie. That Mr. Hall should not Sett as a member of this Counsil for his disorderlie Preachynge.

Upon this Mr. Hall returned to Trumbull, having waited upon the act of the Consociation at Newport town, expecting no more trouble.

He laid the whole matter before a special meeting of his church, and was heartily sustained by them in the course he had followed.

A year passed in comparative quiet. Now and then, by their request and urgency, he preached to the Watertown Baptists; but he supposed he should hear no more of the matter, when very unexpectedly, at the Consociation held the next May, in Chester, a fresh complaint was exhibited against him. He heard of it accidentally, but could not learn the names or the number of the complainants, nor what were the articles of their complaint. The next association meeting at North Newport drew up a confession which they sent to him, requesting that he would sign it. It ran as follows, —

> Whereas I, Philemon Hall, was condemned by the Consosiation of Newport County for disorderlie Preachynge in the first society of Watertown: I do now Aknowledge that my preachynge there was Disorderlie; and I Purpose to preach disorderlie no more, and desire the Reverend Association of Newport County to over-look it; I purposing and resolving, if Opportunitie favor, to go to said Consosiation, and acknowledge the said disorderlie preachynge before them, in Order to be restored to their Favor.

Esther was indignant to her heart when Mr. Hall, in pursuance of his intention that she should not be kept ignorant of his course, laid this document before her. He smiled to see the hot color rise up in her face as she read it, and her eyes flash as she looked up at him when she finished.

"Sure, never was there such tyranny abroad in this land before!" she cried, in an eager, angry voice. "Was it for this our parents left their own people and their father's house to have freedom of soul in these howling wildernesses? Shall we have to move on amid wild countries and red Indians once more?"

"Restrain your anger, Esther. Hath not the Lord said that he will make the wrath of man to praise him? I believe that all this seething and noise of men's passions shall in the end purify and establish the Church of God."

His face glowed with lofty feeling as he spoke. Esther looked at him with a sort of awe.

"And what will you do in this strait?" she asked.

"I am well convinced that I have done nothing contrary either to the word of God, or the Saybrook Platform, unto which our churches conform in their belief and government; and my conscience being void of offence in this matter, I cannot set my hand to the confession they have sent me; but I am willing for the sake of that peace which should reign among brethren to write a confession of mine own, and offer it to the Consociation."

Esther looked up at him, astonished.

"I see not what you have to confess?" she said.

"It may be that I have troubled the minds of the brethren and given offence to them that are weak, by adhering to my own belief, and practising upon it. 'Wo unto him by whom the offence cometh!' Yea, Esther; though my own conscience be clear before God, and stayed with much prayer and strong crying, yet were it better for me that a millstone were made fast about my neck and I cast into the depths of the sea than that I should offend the least of these, if by making such confession as I can truly make, I may appease their indignation."

Esther said no more. What was she, weak, sinful creature!—who had already by her idle self-love wrecked this man's life,—that she should put forth her voice or her hand to meddle with his saintly career?

She went about her work, humbled, yet warm with righteous anger. She felt unfit to abide in the house with the saint she called her husband, yet she could have risen up in wrath and scattered the men who maligned and grieved him, if she had only the power to do so.

But what could a woman do against a Consociation in those days? — or, indeed, in these?

Philemon Hall, shortly after, did send to this ecclesiastic tribunal, a confession of his own, which they curtly refused to accept. His people being of the average sort to whom a following of the multitude is far easier than making a stand for right with the few, began to grow uneasy under this persistent disapproval of the powers of the church. They loved Mr. Hall, and believed him to be an apostle of truth; but still it was very uncomfortable to be in the right, when it separated their individual church from all the others in the Conference; and yielding as far as his conscience would allow, for the sake of peace, and the wish of his own people, he went the next year, when the Consociation met in Stamford Centre, and offered three confessions, drawn up by himself, to that august body. The first ran thus, —

> I, the subscriber, do acknowledge that I preached in Watertown, within the bounds of the first Society, and without ye Consente of Rev^d Mr. Wappinger: Pastor of ye first Society on Jan'y ye 10th, three years ago. And now I do Acknolege that my preachynge there was a Breach of the order that the Ecclesiastick Authorities of Newport county have come into by

Agrement and Vote in sayde Year, and so disorderlie preachynge in that Respect, as it was contrary to sayde Vote.

And now I declare that it is My full Purpose, at present, not to preach contrarie to sayde vote of sayde Authorities Ecclesiastick for time to come, nor contrarie to the Act of ye General Assemblie in May the last.

And furthermore, I humblie ask that the Association of Newporte county would Overlooke what is past, and receive me to Sit with them, &c., as formerlie, and recommend me to be Received by ye Consociation, upon my making this Acknolegement before them, whh I stand Reddy to do when Opportunitie presents.

PHILEMON HALL.

"Do not, do not send it!" urged Esther, when Parson Hall read to her this document.

"I think it best, Esther. I have not herein avowed that I did wrong in the sight of God, or set at naught the general ordinances of the church. But inasmuch as the church hath made unto itself new rules since I disturbed them, I cannot but, for the truth's sake, acknowledge that I did transgress those rules, though, indeed, before they existed. This much have I need to admit. I cannot strain my conscience to say more or less."

Esther remonstrated no more; but her heart cried out against the injustice and bigotry of the Consociation, and she burned with a sense of the great wrong done to such a man as her husband.

Yet what was it to her?

CHAPTER XXXIV.

PATIENCE

> Patience! why 'tis the soul of peace.
> Of all the virtues nearest kin to heaven,
> It makes men look like Gods.
> The best of men
> That e'er wore earth about him was a sufferer;
> A soft, meek, patient, humble, tranquil spirit,
> The first true gentleman that ever breathed.

WHEN this confession was presented to the council, there was much debate as to whether it should be received. It was impossible to accept it without tacitly acknowledging that Parson Hall had not been arraigned for any real offence either against the Word of God or the Saybrook Platform, and such acknowledgment proved the Consociation to have blamed him not only wrongfully but illegally, inasmuch as the law under which he was condemned was not made at the time he was declared to have transgressed it. Could it be expected that a body of such men, "grave and reverend seigniors," would publicly admit they were or had been in the wrong, even if it were true?

A few honest and godly souls were willing, nevertheless, to accept this confession, but they were in the minority, as honest and godly souls always are; so this confession was rejected by the majority.

Desirous, above all things, to do his whole duty, Parson Hall offered them another, differently worded, but to the same effect; but equally unsatisfactory to these lords spiritual. Not once, it is to be noted, in all this struggle, did Philemon Hall lose his self-control, reproach his brethren for their despotism, or fall into any contention with them; he opened not his mouth in wrath, nor did he set before the Consociation what an uncharitable and persecuting spirit possessed them, nor what discredit and shame they thereby brought upon the church of Christ, not alone at that time but so long as its records should last. With an almost divine patience he set aside his own opinions and emotions, striving humbly, yet firmly, to be at peace with his brethren: yet steadfast in his resolution to keep to the exact truth, he could not say that he had sinned in the matter when he was devoutly assured he had not; but he was willing to concede all other points, so to "seek peace, and ensue it." Therefore he prepared a third confession, which he offered to the Consociation, but they refused to hear it. One of the minority, however, desired to see it, and borrowed it of Mr. Hall, on the assurance that it should be returned to him; and in the parson's own mind, as well as the minds of many of his own church, there was no doubt that the council heard this document in private session.

It was, and is, a remarkable instance of honest endeavor to placate ecclesiastical displeasure, combined with sturdy resolve not to tamper with the writer's steadfast spiritual convictions, and ran thus : —

> I, the subscriber, do humbly aknolege that I preached at Watertown within ye Bounds of ye first Society, to the people Called the baptists, upon January ye 10th 1742, for which ye Reverend Consociation have Secluded me from ye Priviledge of sitting with them, and people at Home and abroad have been Uneasie. I do therefore declare, that, though if I was Instrumental of any spiritual Good to any souls there, I must soe far Rejoice; yet upon every other Accounte, I am sorry that I went; and desire the Association and Consociation of said County to overlook it, and receive me to Sit with them, &c., as formerlie.
> PHILEMON HALL.

But the Consociation made no sign of having heard this remarkable address to them, and convinced that they did not intend to forgive and receive him, Parson Hall went home and told his wife how things had gone with him. If he was hurt and grieved Esther saw no sign of it; his face and his voice were alike calm, his eyes clear if unsmiling; had his home been that blessed shelter and consolation that a home should be, had tender arms clung about him, and loving hands and lips caressed him, no doubt the pent-up flood of feeling within his weary and disheartened nature would have found wholesome outlet and comfort; as it was, he could only pray for strength to possess his soul in patience, and go about his parish work with his usual devotion.

Esther's heart ached within her; it was not in her nature to live in the society of any one and not become attached to them; she had loved Delia and

Tempy, and loved them still; and now she added to this habitual affection for Mr. Hall both deep reverence and almost painful pity. She delighted in serving him silently, in a thousand ways that he never knew, absorbed as he was in this conflict with the church; she watched his tastes and prepared for him the dishes he liked; she kept the whole house in exquisite neatness; his clothes were brushed and mended dutifully; she was a model wife — if only she could have loved him; yet Parson Hall like many another man, from Merlin down, would have mightily preferred

"The charm
Of woven paces and of waving hands."

the devotion of a sweet, demonstrative, submissive woman, though she might be slatternly, careless, or deceptive. Still Mr. Hall respected Esther for her honesty. it was a trait that always appealed to him; and out of his great heart he pitied her for her false position and her unmurmuring endurance.

The news of the Consociation's pitiless rejection of Parson Hall's confessions soon spread abroad. Parson Dyer drove over from his home at Hillside to express his sympathy and indignation, and in the course of his conversation related to Mr. Hall his interview with Philip Kent at the time he bought the farm of him. Mr. Hall listened intently; he had long been convinced that Esther had been cruelly wronged in the matter of her Uncle Dyer's inheritance, and this story of Parson Dyer's only strengthened his conviction that Philip Kent was to blame. Some time he meant to enlighten Esther a little, or at least give her a chance to enlighten herself; but where there is no love there can be no confidence, and while he was willing to tell her all his troubles she had never yet breathed a word to him that the whole parish might not have heard.

Close on Parson Dyer's heels came Tempy Hopkins ablaze with righteous wrath.

"Why, Esther Hall! I never was so took aback in my mortal life as I was when the deacon come in a Monday, and told how that plaguey old Consociation had treated Mr. Hall. I never heerd nothing like it. How darst they call 'emselves Christian critters and go on that way? I s'pose they wouldn't let a man preach to th' Indians because they ain't orthodox! *I* don't see nothin' into *my* Bible 'bout orthodoxy nor no other doxy. Says 'believe on the Lord Jesus Christ, and thou shalt be saved,' and Parson Hall hasn't never preached anything *but* that since I've knowed him. And he's a master hand to preach, as well I know. That's at the bottom on't, Easter; that's the conclusion of the hull matter; the' ain't one of them parsons can hold a taller candle to him, and they're jest crawlin' with envy an' jealousy, wrath, malice, and all oncharitableness, as Scriptur' remarks. He ha'n't done a thing that's wrong: not a thing! He's a saint upon 'arth, and that isn't no place for saints; folks here below don't know how to treat 'em!"

Esther could say amen to this last statement; little had she, who entertained an angel unawares, known how to treat Parson Hall herself! But Tempy only took breath and went on.

"It's a nawful privilege for you, Easter, to be married to sech a man. I tell ye when you're tied up to a man for better or worse, it's a sight more easy to get along when it's for better. You're a fort'nate woman to have sech a man for your husband. I did look for'rard to tendin' your little ones on my lap sometime or 'nother, but it don't seem so to be. I s'pose the Lord don't give folks everything to once."

The hot color flashed over Esther's cheek; she felt its glow and turned her face away; here was her life lie again confronting her! and oh! had she not dragged her husband down to touch her level in that? Saint and sinner stood together on the one slippery point of a continuous deception; and it was her fault.

"Mr. Hall is indeed too good!" she answered, tremulously; for she knew Tempy's keen eyes were fastened on her, and she was glad to hear Aunt Ruthy's slow, heavy steps in the kitchen, and to see her enter; she, too, had come on Tempy's errand, and that perceptive female divined it at once.

"Why, Miss Ruthy!" she exclaimed. "I'm proper glad to set eyes on you; it's been a month of Sundays sence I see your face. I come over to tell Miss Hall, here, how worked up I be about the way that old Consociation has acted tow'rdst the parson. Ain't it amazin'?"

"It certinly is," said Aunt Ruthy, the benign face clouding over. "It certinly is; and I feel real put about because of it. I set athinking about his first wife yesterday, and I did feel so thankful that she was took away from the evil to come. She was a'most perfect, but 'twas through suffering; and she was a woman after all. She worshipped the ground he trod on, as well she might; for he giv' up his life for her, and more'n his life, you may say. She had to take everything, and give nothing; and it hurt her to the quick. Many and many a time I've see the tears come into her eyes and trickle down, real big and slow, and I'd say, 'Why, my dear, don't cry, it isn't good for you;' and she'd whisper, 'Oh, Aunt Ruthy, what a useless, miser'ble creature I am. Philemon is like a saint on earth to me, and I never can do a thing for him.' I used to sort of comfort her up, and tell her 'twas worth everything to have her love him so; but my! she knew jest how things was. But I b'lieve, to my soul, she'd have died right off if he'd had these trials come onto him whilst she was livin'. It's a mercy, Mis' Hall, that he's got you to turn to. If ever a man needs a strong, bright, lovin' wife, it's when that he is in trouble; and it's a privilege to be able to help such a man as Mr. Hall."

"Jest what I was a sayin'!" triumphantly chimed in Tempy. "I've always said that 'twas queer to call menfolks the strongest sect, when they're forever an' always holdin' on to some woman the fust minute trouble teches 'em. I make no doubt but what when Scriptur talks about Aaron and Hur holdin' up Moses's hands, 'twas a mistake in the printin' that Hur wasn't spelt with an e. Why, there's Deacon Hopkins, take him days when everything goes right, and he's as pompious, and capable, and self-sufficient as an old turkey gobbler; he's the top o' the heap, and crowin' on it too. But let him get a touch o' rheumatiz, say, or a crick in the back. Or come a spell o' rain in hayin', or a dry time for growin' corn, and, mercy me! he ketches holt of my apern-string, so to speak, jist as though I was Goliath o' Gath. It's the way they're made from the beginnin'; but most of 'em acts as though the Lord had said, "I will make a hindrance for him," instead of a helpmeet for him. After all, when you sift it down, the Lord's ways most gene'lly come to pass, spite o' man."

Aunt Ruthy's words had probed Esther's hidden wound so deeply that her face had lost its color, and her forehead had drawn into lines of pain; but nobody could help smiling at Tempy's oddities, and they saved Esther from any need of replying to Aunt Ruthy. Yet the latter good woman had meant to touch Mrs. Hall's heart, if she could, and find what hidden trouble lay in the quiet parsonage; for well she knew there was not the peace within its walls that she earnestly desired her beloved pastor should enjoy, but Tempy's appearance and talk had prevented her from trying to win Esther's confidence, so she went home with as heavy a heart as she brought. Tempy skipped bravely up into the old chaise, and drove off to Pickering Centre, with the cheerful consciousness that she had not only freed her mind with regard to Parson Hall's affairs and the conduct of the Consociation, but had also vindicated her own importance as the wife of Ammi Hopkins, if she had thereby delineated the deacon when he was abased from his pedestal.

Esther was left alone with her thoughts, and sad enough they were. Hopeless enough the outlook. Never, since that fatal wedding, — or, rather, the day after it, — had Parson Hall spoken or looked as if he wished or thought that their mutual compact could be broken.

He had made no advances toward a better and more natural condition of life. Never had his eye softened as he looked at her, or his voice taken on a gentle tone; in fact, he rarely did look at her, and his tones, always calm and cool to every one, were even more so to her.

Esther's heart was undergoing a radical change, though she was not as yet aware of it. Her vanity was a little piqued, that she could not charm Mr. Hall; but, far deeper than her vanity, lay an inscrutable feeling, that grew more and more assertive.

"The soul has inalienable rights, and the first of these is love," says Emerson; and though the poet-philosopher's utterance lay far in the future, and Esther could not have phrased her own state in fit words, it was really a want of love that made her so restless, so bitter, so discontented as she was now.

She could not understand that Philemon Hall all this time was on the defensive against himself; that his averted eyes, his cool tones, his hours of solitude, even his strict courteousness, were all barriers of his own building, which he dared not pass.

How he had longed for that comfort and peace which Aunt Ruthy had congratulated Esther on affording him, words could not tell.

Even Ammi Hopkins had his poor share of help and consolation from Tempy, but this saint walked on his straight way, alone with God. No human hand clasped his. No human love shone, starlike, on the dim horizon. The light that guided him was all supernal; the heart that comforted him, all divine.

CHAPTER XXXV.

A CONFIDENCE.

Forgetting the things which are behind.

For a time the subject of Parson Hall's contumacy was either laid aside by the Consociation or talked of privately among its members.

It was evident that no pressure of theirs, so far, had bent what they were pleased to call his stubborn will, or brought them one step nearer to their end, which was manifestly now to abase him in the sight of men, and force him to confess that he was, and had been, altogether in the wrong. They thought that time would work for them, forgetting that Parson Hall's position related to eternity; a rock on which their noisy surf should break — and break in vain!

But in these years of armed neutrality, Mr. Hall's congregation grew uneasy; they did not altogether like the fact that their minister was under a cloud; that none of the neighboring parsons, except Mr. Dyer, would preach for him, though he no longer preached for the Baptists who had now a church, if a feeble one, of their own, as well as a settled pastor.

The disaffection of his church in Trumbull showed itself to Mr. Hall in various ways; his salary became hard to collect, Esther was forced to strict economy;

her wedding dresses were of the good material and enduring fashion of those days, or they would have been well worn by now; but, as she still persisted in doing without a servant, her working gown had to be patched, and turned, and re-turned, because she would not buy new ones; she preferred to set aside her own needs rather than her husband's.

With the ordinary blindness of a man to a woman's requirements, so long as his own are attended to, — for, saint as he was, he was also strongly human, — Philemon Hall never noticed how shabby Esther's garments grew, but he was much concerned at the wearing off of the paint on his church; the broken panes of glass in its windows, proofs that hail as well as rain falls on all places and persons alike; and the rusty stove-pipes, from whose crevices smoke was too apt to steal out and choke the congregation. In fact Parson Hall feared that the roof itself would some day break from the weight of wintry snows, its ancient timbers sagged so, and its shingles were so worn that rain dripped through and was slowly rotting the beams.

He sat one day musing by the keeping-room fire, after dinner; a most unusual proceeding for him, but the day was cold and cheerless, a wild November storm swept across the coast, darkened the air, lashed the streaming panes of the windows, shrieked and wailed in the eave-spout, roared down the chimney, and seemed to blot out the exterior world with a mist of gloom.

The parson's mind was on his poor old meeting-house, which stood on a little rise of ground in such a position that this northeast tempest dashed full against its side; he remembered the windows on that side were more warped as to their sashes and dilapidated as to their glass every year; and he could almost see the water pouring in on the worn hymn-books, paintless floors, and uncushioned seats of the square pews; he knew that the shingles must some of them be torn off by the force of the storm, and the quaint little bell-shed, — no stretch of civility could call it a tower! — must be rocking fearfully; it seemed to him as if he could hear the cracked tinkle of that bell across the howling wind and hissing rain which had really kept him from resorting to his study, since that occupied the darkest corner of the house, and had a chimney that would smoke in a great stress of wind and rain together. Esther sat by the window knitting; she had her own thoughts, but she did not speak until the silence became oppressive, and a great gust of wind drove against the house and made it tremble.

"Oh!" she said, involuntarily, "what a dreadful storm!"

"It is dreadful," said Mr. Hall, lifting his eyes to the outlook. "I have so felt it, though sitting up here, because my mind hath dwelt upon our meeting-house; it is so worn and out of repair, I fear the tempest will well-nigh beat it down."

"It is indeed well-worn!" said Esther, turning very pale.

But Philemon Hall did not see her, his gaze was fixed upon the slant streams of rain that beat down on the earth so heavily that human sight could not pierce their veils of water more than a few rods from the window.

"It is herein that I feel most the thwart action of the Consociation," he said, slowly and half unwillingly. "I had hoped so long as I have been here, that before this time my people should have been willing and able to build a new place of worship; and had all things gone well and peacefully with us I think it would full surely have been done. I cannot but see a lack of unity and zeal amongst them, and there are those who bring to me hard sayings that come from my own membership, concerning our solitude amid the other flocks of the Lord round about us, and the coldness of my brethren, who deprive me of their help and companionship. So I cannot ask for a new house of prayer, yet; though I would gladly labor with mine own hands in the building thereof." He ended the sentence with a deep sigh.

Esther could bear no more; she dropped her knitting to the floor and came across to the fireplace. Her eyes were wide with anxious distress, her face pale.

"I must tell you!" she said, in a voice that made Mr. Hall start and look up at her. "I must! I can hear it no longer; it is my fault that the meeting-house is not rebuilt."

"Esther, what do you say?" cried Mr. Hall. "Child! are you mad?"

"Ah, no; if I were — but no, I am in my sober senses. But for me the church would have long ago been built anew; it was in Uncle Dyer's will, the one they could not find, and I — I"—

An agony of tears choked her speech. She could not with that convulsed throat, those dry lips, utter another word. The parson rose and went to her, gravely laying his hand upon her shoulder.

"Esther!" he said, with a sudden, strong quiet in his voice; "say no more; you are over-worn. You know not what you say."

She looked at him with her beautiful, agonized eyes, like a dumb creature that pleads for life. She could not know how he longed to put his arms about her and let her sob out her passion of remorse on his breast. Nor could he know how she longed to have him! His very self-control hardened his face. She made a desperate effort for control herself, and recovered her speech.

"Yes, I know well what I am saying. I heard — I thought — yes I knew he had left his money to the church for the rebuilding of it, and it seemed to my folly that it was unjust. I — ah! God forgive me! *I burnt that will!*"

She hid her face in her hands and leant her head on the mantelpiece. The parson's hand dropped from her shoulder. She felt it with a shudder, she was too wicked to be touched by her saint; a sinner fallen too far! There was a long pause, for Mr. Hall was trying to command his own voice, and the thoughts that rushed over him shook his very soul. She had not mentioned Philip Kent's name; she had not hinted how she knew the contents of Uncle Dyer's will, — or thought she knew them. She had left the matter so merely hinted at, that another man might have thought she expected to be Uncle Dyer's heir herself.

Parson Hall could not speak. She found words before he did.

"I have repented. Oh, sir! I have repented in the dust, of my great sin. I have had it ever before mine eyes. All this time it hath been an anguish unto me. I would have made confession before, had it been of any use; had it not" —

Mr. Hall knew well why she paused here. "Had it not involved another" she would have said, but she stopped just in time: she would not put her sin upon Philip Kent's shoulders, though there it belonged, even more than to her.

"Esther," said the parson, "believe your repentance is accepted of heaven; and comfort your heart, for you have not done the evil you thought. I know of a certainty, from one who had it from your uncle's lips, that his last will mentioned nothing of rebuilding the church. He left his estate to you, saving a small legacy to his nephew. You robbed yourself, my dear, not God."

"What?" she answered, as one who hears what they dare not believe.

Parson Hall repeated his words slowly. Esther's

arms fell to her side; she drew a long, gasping breath, and then the New England conscience, with pitiless strength and stinging thong, recalled her from the momentary relief.

"But it was an equal sin, an equal sin! I stole that which was not mine; I destroyed the thing that was another's: 'I have sinned; what shall I do unto Thee, O thou Preserver of Men?' If it were to mine own loss, still it was sin!"

If Parson Hall agreed with Esther theologically, nevertheless his heart was wrung with pity.

"Esther, Esther, remember who hath said that there is joy in heaven over one sinner that repenteth; recall the word of the Lord, my friend: 'the blood of Christ cleanseth from all sin.' Come into the light, Esther, for in Him is no darkness at all!"

Esther bent her head lower. Alas! well she knew that this was not the only sin she repented of, daily and hourly; and she knew also that however healing to the worst terror of the soul was the forgiveness of sin against God, yet the consequences of sin, the results that follow one wrong done, are never to be washed away; never to be averted; sin has its own punishment this side of the grave even for the most earnest penitent, the most faithful believer. The true purgatory lies in the memory of the repenting sinner; the real purifying fire is a remorse that never ends while life endures, however sure and certain may be the everlasting peace and purity beyond.

"Can *you* forgive me?" said Esther, in a half

whisper; and in the wistful tone that said more than the low words.

"I have nothing to forgive, Esther," said the parson, looking at her with an almost divine expression; but her drooped eyes did not see it.

"My poor child; how you have suffered! I would you had told me before."

"I could not!" she said; sobs forbade her to explain, but the parson knew what that morbid, timid soul, that sensitive conscience must have undergone. He asked no question; he never alluded to any motive, or any encouragement she might have had for an act so foreign to her direct and innocent character as the destroying of that will; but in his secret heart he had not a doubt who tempted her to do it.

Who beside Philip Kent had any interest in the older will? who but he had enough influence over Esther to induce her to do such a deed? The parson's heart sank as he began to comprehend how she must have loved the worthless man; it was worse to know how worthless he was; more degrading to her who loved him. But of all this he said nothing; he was a thorough Christian gentleman, and he would not only keep his lips closed, but he resolved, then and there, that never would he allow Esther to tell him any further details of this matter. It should be buried forever; and if he could not hope that flowers would grow over its grave, it should at least be sealed with a great stone.

With the gentlest care he persuaded Esther to lie

down, wheeled the sofa up to the fire, and covered her carefully; but still her face was unquiet, her lips quivering; with an instinctive knowledge that she had best be alone, he said, — "And now that the storm hath lulled somewhat, I will go out and see what it hath wrought; perhaps you may fall into sleep, Esther. I think that would be your best elixir!"

When he shut the door behind him, however, her forced composure gave way, and she cried long and bitterly; she saw now what Philip Kent had been; how deliberately he had deceived her; it was true she had discovered this partially before, but that he should have left her all these years under the strong delusion that she had really robbed the church she had so learned to love, seemed the overflowing drop of bitterness in her cup.

And oh! how lonely she was, lying there in that silent room, the only sounds that fell upon her ear the slow purr and occasional snap or crackle of the wood fire, for the wind had gone down and the rain fell no longer from the low, leaden sky.

But her husband was more lonely; once out of the house he sought his usual relief in grief or excitement, a long walk. The sea itself seemed to be sympathetic with his mood, for its fury had not ceased; in the wildest commotion it roared and raved against the rocky shore, and reared its crested billows high against the cliff, only to fall back into futile milky foam, to toss and murmur in vain.

It was strangely soothing to Parson Hall's troubled soul, this elemental war; his thoughts quieted as he watched the wrathful water; and He who once said to the furious waves, "Be still" spoke the word again to Philemon Hall, but added, "and know that I am God!"

CHAPTER XXXVI.

THE WORLD.

*Heaven save me from my friends!
I can take care of my enemies myself.*

For nearly two years, Mr. Hall had a sort of respite from the persecution of the Consociation.

He felt however, all the time, that his struggle with the powers that be was not over. Nor was he at rest in his own house; it hurt him cruelly to see how Esther's confession affected her; he had thought it would be a relief to her vexed soul, but it proved also to be a distress and a humiliation. She went about with so sad a countenance, so humble a demeanor, that her husband's heart ached for her; he longed to comfort her with the strength of his affection, and so repair her broken self-respect, but he dared not intrude on her such a form of consolation; for now more than ever he was convinced she had loved Philip Kent deeply. He could not imagine that any transience could be possible to an affection that could beguile such a woman to commit a great sin; he had never understood Esther's deep capacity of self-sacrifice, for he had given her no chance to exercise it; but rather had sacrificed himself for her instead.

It was a silent and melancholy dwelling, that Trumbull parsonage; and Esther felt in her mistaken heart that every hope for the future had drifted quite away from her, now that her secret was known to Mr. Hall. And she felt also that she had cared for him far more deeply than she knew, measuring her hitherto unacknowledged feeling by her great sense of loss and pain. And to this she added another distress; it had been little comfort to her to know that Uncle Dyer had meant to leave his property to her, for she knew that if it was hers now, she should gladly expend a great share of it on the old meeting-house, or build a new one. It never occurred to her that if she had been the independent woman that legacy would have made her, she never would have married Mr. Hall, but probably gone away from Trumbull and its associations forever.

Now, she thought, all her illusions and hopes were dead. Philip Kent she never wanted to think of again; she despised herself to think her love for him had been so long-lived, so tenacious; her husband's love was gone from her; a loss she appreciated keenly, for with her as with most women, and Esther was a veritable woman, the thing she had not was far more valuable in its loss than in its possession. No wonder she was sad! But there was a repetition of the old trouble in the church coming fast upon them now, and there is something weighty in "the expulsive power" of a new trouble, as well as that of a "new affection."

In May of the second year after Mr. Hall's third and latest confession had been refused even a hearing by the Consociation, a new complaint against him was privately drawn up and submitted to that conclave, sitting at Chester; and another paper was presented at the same time, signed by fifteen members of his own society, urgently requesting the Consociation to consider the difficulties and grievances under which they labored owing to the displeasure of that body with their pastor.

Though the complaint was drawn up secretly, it soon became known through those who, though few, were still faithful to Parson Hall, and who attended the meeting at Chester; the names, also, of the fifteen petitioners were soon equally well known through the same means, and all the parish of Trumbull was agog and set by the ears; some for and some against the minister.

Parson Dyer drove over from Hillside to remonstrate with his dear friend.

"Brother Hall," he said, solemnly, as soon as the study door shut behind him, "I have come to counsel with you concerning this matter of your refusal to submit yourself to the Consociation. I have known you too long, brother, to doubt your honesty of purpose, but may it not be that Satan hath laid a snare for you herein, and clouded your better judgment with his crafts and assaults?"

"Brother Dyer," answered Mr. Hall with an odd little smile in the corners of his mouth, "Satan is not wont to array himself on the losing side."

"Pshaw, pshaw! Will you answer me with a quip,

Philemon Hall, when I come to plead with you for your own good and the peace of your flock?"

"Nay, brother! I meant not to anger you; but there be straits wherein a word of cheer doeth the soul good, and a quip is but the sparkle of a light that is nigh to go out."

Parson Dyer's face softened "My friend," he said, "is there no way open unto you wherein you and your brethren may walk together in concord?"

"How can two walk together except they be agreed?" answered Mr. Hall, sadly.

"But I would fain have you agree, my brother, and I think you do in vital matters; what availeth it to disturb the concord of brethren and the peace of the church of God with a differing in non-essentials? You see how your own people are at variance one with another; how your brethren in the ministry stand aloof from you; how the very walls of Zion crumble because of the disaffection amongst the flock thereof. Why is it that you cannot bow your stiff neck to the furtherance of the Lord's work and obedience unto the laws of the church?"

"Brother Dyer, I know that I have done all that a true man can to seek peace and ensue it. I have thrice, nay, more than thrice, laid before the Consociation mine apology for transgressing their laws, but no man, no men, shall force me to consent unto a lie. I believe that in dispensing the Word unto that people who were hungering and thirsting for it, I obeyed the will of Him who said 'Feed my sheep,' nor did

I find anything in the platform of doctrine accepted in our churches contrary to my so doing; thus far am I justified. In that I pursued my course after the new laws were made by the council of churches, I have already acknowledged that I erred, although in ignorance. I meant, and I mean to obey those laws, though I approve not of them. If I am forbid to preach unto these Baptists because they are not orthodox believers, I am also forbid to lay the Gospel before Papists and Prelatists; yea, if I hold to the logic of this matter I must even frown upon that apostle John Eliot, who hath given his life over to carry the Gospel unto the Indian savages, a race well behind so much as the understanding of the word orthodox."

"I intend not to chop logic with you, Brother Hall," replied Parson Dyer, sternly. "It appeareth to me that you have in view rather the fulfilling of your own will and purpose, than any other thing. 'Seest thou a man wise in his own conceit? there is more hope of a fool than of him!'"

Parson Hall flushed up to the roots of his hair; he had a naturally hot temper that had taken him half a lifetime to control, and its merely physical expressions he had not yet conquered; but his voice was quiet and cool, as he said, —

"I am grieved, my friend, that you should think so evilly of me; but I must even bear it. I have prayed with strong crying and tears that the Lord would guide me in this matter, and I have assurance within myself that he hath done so. I have made humble submission unto the Consociation, so far as my conscience allowed; it lieth with them to accept the olive branch or cast it back unto me. But no earthly power shall make me lie before God or man. I am well assured that I did well to preach unto the Baptists the eternal Gospel of God. I took no part in their peculiar belief, either to further or to hinder it. Forms and ceremonies seem to me slight things; it is the spirit that giveth life; and the Spirit of the Lord followed upon my words in the conversion of souls. Shall I draw back after that seal?"

His face glowed with fervor and truth. Parson Dyer's keen eye softened as he looked at his friend, and it may be that his speech too would have been kindly, but at that moment a sharp rap at the door heralded the entrance of Deacon Ammi Hopkins, who bustled in, mopping his round face and stubbly gray head with a big yellow silk handkerchief, for the day was warm, even for July, and the young colt he drove down from Pickering Centre had been unusually hard on the bits.

"Good-day, Parson Hall," he began, tipping about on his toes like an excited bantam cock.

"Good-day, sir; hope I see you well. Why! Jeeruslem! if it ain't Priest Dyer. Well, well! and how do *you* do, sir? I ha'n't set eyes on you for quite a spell; seems folksy to see you round, reelly it doos."

"And how is all at Pickering Centre?" asked Mr.

Dyer, smiling, for Ammi's entrance just at that juncture seemed providential to him. He knew not how either to condemn or sympathize with his erring brother, and was glad to give place to another train of thought.

"Reasonable well; yes, reasonable well. I don't think that the state of religion is over 'n above flourishin'. We've got a good man into the pulpit, a likely man; but ruther worldly, ruther giv' to lookin' arter the loaves and fishes, as you may say; wants his sellery paid up prompt, and his wood drawed *as* prompt. He'd ought to pay more attention to speritooal things our folks think, than to the meat that perisheth."

"Hm," grunted Parson Dyer; "got ten children, hasn't he?"

"Yes; oh, yes! the minister's blessin', ye know. Quiver full, and smart, likely young ones too; the heft of 'em boys!"

"Pretty prompt to their dinner, probably!"

"I expect they be. I think likely they be; but ye know Scriptur' says we mustn't be a-thinkin' what we eat and what we shall drink the hull time."

"And it says too that 'the laborer is worthy of his hire,' friend Hopkins."

Parson Hall saw his clerical brother's face darken, and interposed a question.

"How is Mrs. Hopkins, deacon?"

"She's well, middlin' well. She come over with me; she's in the keepin' room, 'long o' Mis' Hall."

"I think I will go in and visit her there," said Parson Dyer, and disappeared accordingly.

Deacon Hopkins cleared his throat with a long "A — hem," put the tips of the fingers of both hands together, and rising on the toes of his squeaky boots, as he was wont to do when he prayed or exhorted in conference meeting, began, —

"I came over to-day, Parson Hall to hev a leetle talk with you. You know I've always been friendly in my feelin' tow'rdst you, and Mis' Hopkins bein' so attached to Mis' Hall, why, I feel as though that was a bond as you may say.

'Blest be the tie that binds,'

ye know. I am aware that is a weddin' hymn, but its referable to friendliness too, I expect, and seen' I have the peace of Is'rel to heart as well as your'n; and bein' along in years, and a man of exper'ence, as you may say, hevin' been married four times and b'en deacon five-and-forty year, for I'm eighty-two to-morrer; why, I said to Mis' Hopkins, ses I, when we heered of the trouble Trumbull folks was a gettin' into about the Consos'ation, and the hard place you have sot down in; yes, I said, 'Let us go over to Trumbull and have a dish of talk with the parson and Mis' Hall. Mebbe, he'll hark to me a mite, and you can comfort her up. Now, parson, don't you feel as though you could *comply* with that meetin' an' say what would soot 'em?'"

Parson Hall was naturally a little indignant at the

intrusive Ammi, whose reputation was that of a conceited and meddlesome old fellow wherever he was known; but he did not indulge his wrath any further than a cold and courteous manner and restrained speech expressed it.

"Mr. Hopkins," he said, "there are times in life when a man must consider higher things than mere tranquillity of existence. 'First pure; then peaceable,' is the order of Holy Writ; and be assured there is no abiding peace except in purity of conscience. What I have done, is, I am confident, right and just in the Lord's sight. The consequences I must abide; they are in His hand."

"Well, well, that sounds hullsome, but do ye now, honest, think it al'ays answers to live right up to the letter o' Scriptur'? A'n't it better not to give occasion to th' enemy to revile?"

"I shall be glad, alway, to have the enemy revile me," said the parson, sturdy as Luther.

"Well, — why, — you don't seem to sense it; I mean an't it better to kind of com—promise so to speak; give up a few o' your idees here and there, for peace's sake. Why, land's sake! do see what you are a comin' to. Here's your sellery ain't half-paid, at least, that's the tell; and you can't get folks to take no int'rest in fixin' up the meetin'-house; and the hull of the s'ciety is buzzin' like swarmin' bees, and ye know when bees doos swarm 'tis to fly out o' the old hive; what's a goin' to become of you and Mis' Hall ef they deepose ye from the ministry?

and I have heered there is some talk on't. Ain't it a sight better to bend than to break? Is't worth all you'll lose to be so sot in your way? Think on't! you've got a good home, and a reasonable good sellery, and nice folks in the church, an' good neighbors; a'n't it the best way to give in a mite whilst that you can?"

"'All these things will I give thee, if thou wilt fall down and worship me,'" answered Parson Hall, in a tone deep and solemn, as if he were in his pulpit.

Deacon Hopkins stood aghast; then his face grew red; even under the thin, stiff crop of hair his head flamed.

"Well said! well said! when you undertake to even a deacon, forty-five year in good and reg'lar standin' to the evil one, I guess it's time to go, and shake the dust off my feet a-goin'!" squeaked the irate Ammi.

Mr. Hall stretched out his hand, —

"Brother," he said, "I thought not of you when I spoke; but of the times upon times when I have pondered on this matter in the silence of my study, and all these reasons of yours, yea, far more cogent ones of their sort have confronted me, as if there stood at my side one who pleaded with me; but I thank God I have kept the faith. No, brother! though I and mine be sent out into the brook Cherith, there to be fed by ravens in a homeless solitude, I will fear no evil; the Lord will provide; but neither man nor devils shall make me lie. I did that which the Word of God, my conscience, and my vows at the altar called upon me to do; and I will neither repent of so doing or admit that it was wrong."

Ammi looked at him in amazement.

"Well," he said, placated but yet doubtful. "If you wa'n't a parson I *should* say you was the pigheadedest feller I ever come acrost. But I s'pose you think you've got Scripter for 't, and I must shut up."

"'Be thou steadfast, immovable, always abounding in the work of the Lord,'" said the parson, with a sad smile.

"Well, I guess I'll say amen," responded Ammi.

CHAPTER XXXVII.

MORE.

> Who ne'er his bread in sorrow ate,
> Who never through the mournful night
> Upon his couch hath weeping sate.
> He knows you not, O Powers of Light!

ALL this time Esther had her own trouble in the keeping-room. Madam Stanley had but just returned from England, where she had been almost ever since Esther's marriage; the governor having gone thither on business concerning Sybil's property, as well as a certain legacy left him, of real estate.

Of course the whole matter of Parson Hall's contumacy, and the holy wrath of the Consociation, came to their ears as soon as possible after they were again settled in their house at Trumbull, and with her usual domineering spirit, Madam Stanley proceeded to the parsonage to deal with the parson and his wife both; but when she reached the house, finding that Mr. Hall was closeted with Parson Dyer, she turned upon Esther.

"Well, Dame Hall! I hear there is a pretty to-do in your church, and indeed in the town itself, about your husband's obstinate resistance to the power ecclesiastic. 'Tis mighty odd, methinks, for one man to set up his will against the whole body of the church. This comes of schismatics. Were he a member of that sound and wholesome body the English Church, he would not think of such rebellion. Good lack! I would he were under the thumb of a lord bishop! 'Twere well for his soul, and for his matters temporal, too."

"Madam Stanley," answered Esther, with serene dignity, "Mr. Hall hath obeyed God rather than man in this matter. He hath a clean conscience within, concerning it."

"Fiddle-faddle! so says every man-jack of the dissenters. To hear the fellows among whom Sybil hath settled herself talk of their consciences, one would think conscience were the pope himself. Hath your good man no common-sense, so to quarrel with his bread and butter?"

"I think he hath not only sense, but religion to back it, withal, Madam Stanley. And well I believe, that there lives not any lord bishop, nor any pope, who could beguile Mr. Hall into doing the thing that unto him seemed sin."

Esther's eyes shone, and the color rose in her expressive countenance, as she looked straight into Madam Stanley's haughty visage.

"Tut, tut, Dame Hall! why will you encourage him to cut his own throat, as well is to be seen you do? I hear it said that already his salary is delayed, that the meeting-house is dilapidated more than is seemly or decent, and even that the Consociation hold talk of deposing him from the ministry for contumacious conduct and contempt of ecclesiastic authority.

If these things are so, and you have any such influence with your husband as a good wife should have, it behooves you to plead with him for his own good, in season and out of season, that he will submit himself unto the powers that be, which are ordained of God, as Holy Scripture saith."

"I think, Madam Stanley, you misapprehend the situation," said Esther, calmly. "Mr. Hall hath not, knowledgably, disobeyed the laws of the Consociation. Since the new law, concerning preaching to schismatics, hath been passed, he has not once ministered to the Baptist congregation; indeed, that people have disbanded, and ceased to be an ecclesiastic body for more than a year. These few sheep in the wilderness have perished of spiritual starvation, and I believe the Consociation have their blood upon their hands to answer for. But that is with God. Mr. Hall's offence was, that he would not so perjure himself before man as to say that he had done wrong in preaching the gospel to them who were hungering and thirsting therefor. He was convinced in his own mind, that neither the law of God nor the Saybrook Platform — which seems unto me to be held in equal respect with scripture in these churches — were transgressed by his so doing, and I am well assured that neither men nor devils will force him to lie unto God and man by such acknowledgment."

"Pshaw! I like this prate of 'schismatics'! What are ye all but followers of heresy and schism, in departing from the faith of your fathers and the mother country? What does the dictum of a little body of country dissenters import, that a man should cast away his living rather than temporize with, and appease them? I lay this at your door in great measure, Dame Esther. I see where his contumacy is cherished with sympathy and respect. Moreover, were this house filled, as it should be, with a flock of children, clamoring for daily bread, he would not be so stiff-necked!"

Esther's face was scarlet with anger and shame; she spoke hotly in reply. The rather abstruse reading, for that time, with which she had solaced her loneliness, came to her aid now.

"Madam Stanley, I think the Church of England is itself a dissenting body from the beginning. Sure Martin Luther dissented from Rome, and, denying papacy, brought the reformed religion into its place. If since this hath degenerated into prelacy, it is none the less a dissenting body from its birth; and well I know that neither papacy nor prelacy, nor the tyranny of this schism, as it pleaseth you to call it, will shake my husband from the rock whereon he standeth. For poverty, if it cometh upon us for this cause, let it come! I thank God there are but two of us to strengthen each other and to suffer, if more would make Mr. Hall's soul falter in the path of duty. But I cannot think that any such consideration would daunt him. I am proud and joyful to believe that he loveth God more than His gifts, granted or denied; and for me, I am willing to labor with mine own hands for my daily bread — and his — rather than have him abate one jot or tittle of his righteous obedience to the Word. I care not so much for the Saybrook Platform!"

"Well said, young woman! well said! I love a spirity dame who will do battle for her good man, even though I be a little worsted in the fray; but yet I am not shaken in my " —

The door from the kitchen opened with a rush and Tempy Hopkins burst into the room, flung her taffety mantle and her calash down on the nearest chair, and flying up to Esther, embraced her with both arms.

"Oh, my dear soul! my dear soul!" she exclaimed, panting with heat and haste; "I have heered about thy troubles so much I could hear it no longer without a sight of thee. What will become of this world I don't know no more than nothing when sech a pious, meek-sperited man as Parson Hall is set upon by his brethering, and parsecuted!"

"Fie upon you, Goody Hopkins!" interrupted Madam Stanley; "do you call a man pious and meek who setteth himself up against constituted authority as Parson Hall hath done?"

"I don't care a copper about constitooted 'thorities ma'am, not when they try to stomp on a good man; pious he is, for I've knowed him many a year; and meek he is too, for I've seen him when

Afflictions sore
Long time he bore.

as my grandsir's gravestone says; but the worm will turn, ye know; and he's got more grit 'n a fennel-worm even, and they're consider'ble spunky. Deacon says, ses he, 'I ain't reelly made up my mind what *to* think 'bout this business,' when in come Eben Salt and tells that how there was talk of deeposin' Mr. Hall, and leavin' of him to starve, mabbe. Then I riz up, and ses I, 'He won't starve, not a mite; the Lord 'll send ravens for to feed him fust. And I'll be one of 'em.' 'Oh! ho! ho!' says deacon; 'don't ye be so forehanded, Temp'rance. We a'n't got no great o' means ourselves, and don't ye make no rash promises!' 'I don't care nothin' for that,' ses I. 'Whilst that I've got a crust o' bread, Easter Hall shall have half on 't, and parson t'other half!' 'Law, now!' ses deacon, 'don't ye take on so! the Lord 'll pervide.' 'Yes!' says I. 'I've heerd that before! It's mighty easy to shove your feller-creeters over on to the Lord; you don't noway consider how that he pervides for 'em by the means of man. We don't have meracles now-a-days, though I must say 'twould be nigh about to a meracle if you done anything for anybody 't you wa'n't obleeged to by law!' Then he got wrathy; and we had quite a little season, nyther short nor sweet; and the eend on't was that he 'greed to tackle up the colt and come down here to deal with the parson, and see if he couldn't noway help tow'rdst straightenin' on him out, as he called it. Deacon thinks 'twould have improved the airth ef the Lord had asked his idees about makin' on 't. Some pork will bile so; ye know. So I clapped on my calash and come too; I'm 'fraider o' that colt than I be of the Evil One a'most; he don' know what his front legs is good for, yet, he's so giv' to standin' up on his hinder ones. I was scar't out o' my life comin' but I would ha' come ef it had a' be'n a fiery flyin' dragon instead of a black hoss, I wanted to see you so, Easter; and to tell ye to take heart, child. You stan' by the parson and spunk him up, dear; I dono as he needs it, but you can make the trouble a sight easier for him."

"Goody Hopkins," spoke out Madam Stanley, who was drawing on her gloves to go. "It seemeth that you scarce know your place here. Doth it become you to aid and counsel Dame Hall in this matter? To encourage this obdurate parson with your comfortable words? You are of another parish to begin with, and another station in life; it passeth a jest that you should put yourself up in a godly minister's household with your advice on spiritual matters. Go your ways to your pots and pans and your frugal deacon, Goody; intermeddle not here!"

"Goody me none of your goodys, my fine madam!" shrieked Tempy, with her arms akimbo and her little puckered face red with anger. "And for my station in life, 'tis respectabler than a cumberer of the ground who nyther toils nor spins! Look to the pit whence you was digged yourself, madam, before you Goody me! What have all the Stonebridges been unto this colony? What evil savors follow after them as though they was pole-cats? Is not John Stonebridge's bastard abiding at Hillside Farm to-day? You'd better look back to them that went before ye, and not sass honest women that has come of godly payrents. I come here out of love for my dear friends, to help 'em and comfort 'em. What'd you come for? Why to bring a railin' accusation ag'inst 'em as Scriptur' ses. What" —

The door opened again, and Parson Dyer came in. Madam Stanley swept past him without a word, and entering her chariot with the air of an offended peacock, drove off, and was seen no more.

Tempy's reference to the Stonebridge family had wounded her to the quick, for well she knew what their past record had been; and for her own ancestry she had not much more to say on the side that had intermarried with John Stonebridge's ancestors. Even the memory of the few brilliant exceptions to that record had not been able to leaven the whole lump in the eyes of their fellow colonists.

As soon as Parson Dyer closed the door behind Madam Stanley, Tempy sat down in the nearest chair, in haste, unfortunately, it was that which held her calash and mantle, and burst into a flood of angry tears.

Esther withdrew her hand from the parson's and hurried to her friend.

"Dear Tempy!" she said, "don't cry; don't! Madam Stanley hath gone; she will vex you no further."

"Indeed, I think she swept out with the air of one

something vexed herself!" said the parson, with a quiet smile.

"W-w-we-el!" sobbed Tempy, "I dono but she was. I aimed to give her as good as she give me. Oh! o-oh! I never *was* so sassed before in all my born days! never! 'Goody,' indeed! Wa'n't her pa Stonebridge Edwards, I'd like to know? As big a raskill as ever driv' his coach-an-four through Har'ford town; an' to hear her talk as though she was king, lord, an' devil!"

"My friend! my friend! remonstrated Parson Dyer, "Doth not Scripture tell us in those days they shall say no more, 'the fathers have eaten a sour grape, and the children's teeth shall be set on edge?'"

"Well, if it doos, I can't gainsay it; but there's a sight in the breed after all; didn't you go an' buy a Narraganset pacer now, Parson Dyer? and did it come of cart-hosses, or Arabs like the governor's? Not a mite! and I tell ye Stonebridge blood is bad blood. Here I be, come to comfort up Mis' Hall, friendly like; hearin' she and he is like to be driv' out of house and home, and want for bread, jest because he's steadfast to his conscience; and find here my madam a tryin' to make him give in, or a persuadin' Easter to try and make him, and I hadn't said ten words before down she comes, a-pounce, like cat to mouse and bids me not meddle with my betters. Lawks! as if she was anybody's betters!"

"Softly, softly, Mistress Hopkins; answer not a

fool according to his folly; be not hasty in thy spirit, if Madam Stanley is. Let her pass; a proud, loveless, childless woman hath her own sorrows; and for our friends here, know that so long as Billions Dyer hath a home, they shall share it in their extremity, and should I be called to cross over Jordan before such crisis comes, the home shall be all theirs."

Tempy wiped her eyes with her flowered apron.

"I always said you was as good as the Lord ever made, Parson Dyer!" she said.

Esther grasped his hand, her lips trembled, but her beautiful eyes spoke for her; they shone with affection and gratitude that he felt to the depth of his heart.

"Well! here's the fust raven!" Tempy said to herself.

CHAPTER XXXVIII.

AT LAST.

> The flower of the hour may have vanished
>   In tempest and night;
> Its bloom and perfume may be banished,
>   From sense and from sight;
> And desolate all the fair garden
>   Of color and glow:
> But that God is its master and warden,
>   The fruit-time shall show.

WITH the self-distrust of a conscientious man, Philemon Hall began to consider after these visitations whether he had done all that Christian charity demanded of him to make peace with his brethren. Nothing could shake him from the standpoint of right and duty as to what he had done in preaching to the Baptists; but in view of the disturbances among his own people it occurred to him that he might once more try to conciliate the angry Consociation. It was now five years since this melancholy controversy began, and the confession, or rather the appeal he offered them opened by saying that for more than three years he had given himself to prayer and meditation concerning this matter, and likewise studied upon it; but he could not be convinced in conscience that his preaching to the Baptists was contrary to the Holy Scripture or to the mind of God; but he was willing to humble himself so far as in honesty he could, and the document concluded thus, —

And now, Gentlemen, I humblie crave Forgiveness; let my Ignorance of It's being a Crime apologize for me that I may Be Restored. And I would humblie offer one Motive to engage your Compassion, viz. a prospect of Peace among my People who have been uneasy, for I think that in other Respecks they are Friendly and kind; but this case has been an Uneasiness with them, and a Prinsipal uneasiness, if I may Judge by their Complayntes, or what I heare from their own Mouthes. And therefor Gentlemen as you Are professed Lovers of Peace, you will undoubtedlie Promote it by restoring your unworthy Serv't.
PHILEMON HALL.

Stung perhaps by the implied or suspected sarcasm of calling this belligerent and implacable body "professed lovers of peace"; angered no doubt by the persistent refusal of Parson Hall, to say he had done wrong in consenting to preach the Gospel to schismatics; well-nigh as wrathful as if he had said that he was not sure that God would damn the heathen tribes who had never heard of Him, without giving them another chance in another world, — the Consociation showed themselves to be men of like passions as we are by refusing to accept this confession, or even grant it a second reading. They did not, however, let Parson Hall alone; with a perseverance too tedious to detail they discussed his case at every meeting; wrote him letters officially and personally; visited him for reproof and remonstrance; exhorted at him and prayed for him in the pulpit, till he might have said in the spirit of the unrighteous judge that he would grant their request because by their continual coming they wearied him. But no such truckling to ease and sloth was possible to Philemon Hall; not a step would he take to reverse his position; he was like Luther on the road to the Diet of Wurms, though he saw hundreds of devils skipping upon the housetops by the way, they should not hinder him.

Yet being merely a mortal man this continual dropping did wear upon him; he grew thin, pale, and listless; he lost his appetite and consequently his strength, and was ill-prepared to meet the crisis when it came.

For, one year after they had refused to accept his humble yet manful confession the last confession he made, there was another meeting of the Consociation, at which they unanimously passed this edict.

> This Consociation do now and upon the Whole judge and determine ye sayde Hall, unworthie the Ministereal character and Christian communion; and Accordinglie do, in the name of the Lord Jesus Christ, accordinge to Ye Worde of God, and the Powers innvested in this Consociation by ye Ecclesiastical constitution of the Government, Depose the saide Hall from his Ministereal Office and ministereal and Pastoral relation to ye First Church in sayde Trumbull and doe Debarr and Suspende him from Communion in any of the Churches of our Lord Jesus Christ.

Duly engrossed by the scribe of the meeting, signed by its members, and sealed with a great seal, the foregoing document was left at Mr. Hall's door by Deacon Stearns of Chester, deputed for that errand;

he was a kindly man, and thankful enough to find that the parson was out for the morning, so he only asked Mrs. Hall to lay it on the minister's study table, and rode away through the pink-blossoming orchards, by the new-leaved forests, and sparkling streams of June, with a heavy heart, for he had once been of the minority who favored Mr. Hall, and was still uncertain in his own mind about the rights of the matter; though, like all the Laodicean tribe, he had now voted with the majority because they were the majority.

Philemon Hall came in an hour before dinner-time and went as usual directly to his study; he looked at the ominous document and shivered a little, though the day was summer-warm; but he was no coward; he took up the paper with a steady hand, opened, and read it.

For a moment his brain reeled as if from a blow, then he sat down, and flinging his arms across the table, laid his head upon them, and the force of the situation came full upon him. Outcast! Forbidden to preach! Debarred from the table of his Lord! What worse penalty could have been dealt out to him if he were the vilest sinner on the face of the earth? All the long train of consequences made a sort of funereal procession through his mind; he saw himself and Esther ostracized from social life, which in those days was inextricably mixed with religious affairs; he saw his means of living vanishing from his grasp, for he had no handicraft to fall back on;

his life, his soul, were all fitted for and given over to preaching the Gospel; he saw his isolation from his brethren, his people, almost from his kind, lowering over him like a cloud of blackness; he seemed to himself to be exiled from God and man both, and then came the thought of deepest anguish, the thought of our Lord upon the Cross when the death throe of His humanity darkened even His Godhead, and he uttered the desperate cry of despairing man, the words that broke now from Philemon Hall's tortured spirit.

"'My God! my God! why hast Thou forsaken me?'"

Had he not been faithful to God in all this weary past? Had he not glorified Him in the fires? What but loyalty to his Master's will and word had brought him to this pass?

Involuntarily he broke out in the familiar words of the Psalmist. "Thou hast known my reproach, and my shame and my dishonor; mine adversaries are all before thee! Reproach hath broken my heart; and I am full of heaviness; and I looked for some to take pity, but there was none; and for comforters, but I found none!" His whole nature cried aloud for some companionship in this dreadful solitude of grief. "Oh! had Rachel but lived!" was his first thought; yet even as the thought framed itself, he recalled the fact that he had never carried his serious troubles, or what had seemed serious then, to her. She had been sheltered by his care from every bitter wind that chanced to blow, morally or physically. Now!—if Esther could but have loved him!

At that moment Esther came in. She had come to say that dinner was ready. Dinner will no doubt be boiling in the pot at the crack of doom! our daily necessities go on through all tribulation or despair; the protest of the poor feeble body, against the pangs it suffers from the strong and agonizing soul.

She saw at once that something had come to Mr. Hall; not only did his posture tell the story, but one hard dry sob, the awful sob of a man in deep mental suffering, shook his whole frame as she entered; she sprang forward and laid her hand on his shoulder.

"Philemon! what is it?" she asked, in a voice no man could mistake; for in that instant love, true wife-love was born in her bosom, full-fashioned and strong, no puny or untimely child, but the growth of silent years, ready to see the light.

He lifted his head a little and with one hand pushed the decree of the consociation toward her; she took it up and read the brief anathema. She did not pause to consider, her soul was in a tumult of wrath, and protest, and indignant love; she fell on her knees at her husband's side, clasped both arms about his neck, laid her head on his shoulder and cried out, "My dear, dear husband! My dear! don't! The cruel men!"

Philemon Hall raised his head and looked into her face; he could not believe he had heard her aright.

"Esther!" he asked hoarsely. "Do you know

what you say? Can it be? Oh, woman! speak, speak! lest it be as a dream when one awaketh!"

Esther lifted her head too, and returned his gaze; her face was one roseate blush, her red lips parted eagerly, her eyes lambent as planets, with love and pity, there was neither doubt, dread, nor coldness in that lovely countenance.

"My dear, dear husband!" she said, in a passionate whisper.

The parson's face lit up like a sun-burst through a cloud; he gathered Esther close in his arms and kissed her as solemnly as if that kiss had been their last; then he lifted his face heavenward and said, as if he saw into those celestial regions.

"Lord in wrath thou hast remembered mercy. I will sing praises unto thee while I have my being!"

It did indeed seem to him as if a miracle had been wrought in his behalf, but he was too humble and too little introverted to question Esther or himself how this wondrous blessing had been brought about. It was enough for him that it had come in his hour of direst need, when not a ray of light seemed either near or possible.

Dinner stood in its dishes long into the afternoon that day, while Parson Hall and his wife held counsel together concerning this last blow.

"It seemeth little to me now, Esther," he said, with a radiant smile, "the flesh was weak before, and the spirit failed; verily, I thought that God had forsaken me as well as man; I was impatient when I should have trusted, I was so solitary that I became unduly cast down."

"Do not say so, Philemon! You have endured even as a martyr of old; and but that I was fearful lest you could not abide it, I should have tried to comfort you before."

"Fearful, Esther! of me?"

"Even so. Does it become a sinner like me to love a saint like you? Much less to think my affection could be endurable to you who know of mine own confession what I had done!"

"Hush! hush! my wife!" and Philemon Hall laid his hand lightly on her lips. "Speak no more of the past; let us forget the things that are behind, and lay our sins before Him only who hath loved us and washed us in His blood. Nor call me a saint, Esther. Who is clean in His sight? I am a man, with a man's sins and follies struggling within me; and I may not find peace except in the sacrifice of Christ for sinners. We are saved by grace, both of us; let us hereafter walk together, being agreed. And for me, since I heard your words of cheer, and saw your beloved face upon my bosom, with shining eyes looking into mine as never did they look before. I feel like the youth unto whom the prophet of old spake, saying, 'Fear not! for they that be with us are more than they that be with them.' I trust I should have had strength to be steadfast unto the end; but lo now, 'out of strength cometh forth sweetness,' and manna from above into this wilderness of Sin."

It made even Esther's happy heart quiver with late remorse to see how the light returned in a calm shining to her husband's eyes, and peace to his worn face ; their unnatural position toward each other had been irksome to her, tormenting to him ; but now the real life of a home sheltered them; they were no longer young lovers, but Esther's love was young, and Philemon's as tried and faithful as his truth.

Aunt Ruthy was the first person to hear of the action which deposed Mr. Hall from the ministry, and that very evening she went over after sundown to the parsonage to give her hearty and affectionate sympathy to Mr. Hall; but when her slight knock at the side door was answered and she went in, she found no downcast, or unhappy, or wrathful man there.

Mr. Hall sat on the chintz sofa beside Esther, holding one of her hands like a lover, — as he was. Esther started and blushed, but the parson tightened his grasp. " Sit here, Miss Ruthy," he said, making a place for the good woman at his other side. " You came, I know, to condole with me ; and indeed I think I have been dealt with sharply, but I have good courage ; my dear wife and I have talked the matter over, and by God's grace I will not cease to preach ; what can man do unto me ? And the Lord hath given me a home wherein to rest and be comforted in the pauses of the battle."

Aunt Ruthy's sweet old eyes grew dim; she did not understand all that she saw, but she knew that her saint had found a shrine, and that was enough for her tender and unselfish heart; she looked round into Esther's face, blooming as she had never seen it, and said half under her breath,—

"Thank God, and take courage!"

"I will," answered the parson, reverently.

CHAPTER XXXIX.

NOT DESTROYED.

> Stern lawgiver! yet thou dost wear
> The Godhead's most benignant grace;
> Nor know I anything so fair
> As is the light upon thy face.

It seemed indeed to Philemon Hall that the world wore a new face for him now; he was not a man whom joy could enervate or absorb; his duty reigned over all other inducements, and was respected as the ruler of his life; but it gave duty a new aspect, and his loyalty thereto a fresh impetus to know that at last Esther loved him. He went out into the fray once more determined to resist the tyranny and injustice of the Consociation as long as life should last, if it became necessary.

Some time before, in the thick of his troubles, while yet all his flock were with one accord on his side of the dispute, his church had by its own voluntary action voted to renounce the jurisdiction of the Consociation, and become an independent body; now, this was a point of support to Parson Hall, for, shortly after his deposement, a petition was preferred before the General Court that they would eject Mr. Hall from his meeting-house, that a regular minister might be settled in his place. This could not be done, since the church in Trumbull belonged to no ecclesiastical jurisdiction, and, accordingly, the first Sunday after Mr. Hall had not only been turned out of the ministry but practically ex-communicated from the church because he would not deny and repudiate his conscientious convictions, he had the church bell rung at the proper hour, and having as usual made a short prayer of invocation went on with the services.

The church was well filled, though some of the congregation went with fear and trembling, uncertain whether Mr. Hall would preach, or, if he did, whether they would stay and hear him.

He began his second prayer, however, before any man or woman left the house; his face uplifted, his hands clasped, his voice full of deep emotion. "Oh, Lord, Thou art our Father," he said, "though Abraham be ignorant of us, and Israel acknowledge us not; Thou art our Father; our Redeemer; Thy name is from everlasting. And because we are Thy dear children whom Thou hast loved with an everlasting love and saved with an eternal salvation, we bring to Thee our wants and our needs, knowing that Thou wilt not give us stones for bread, but will grant our prayers as seemeth good unto Thee. Lord, give us strength to do that which is right and true; endue us with Thine own power, that our duty may lie plain before us and we may be able to do it to the last jot and tittle. Give us that peace in believing which is in itself courage; help us to 'put on the whole armor of God, to fight the good fight, to lay hold on eternal life.' Yea, Lord, though we lay down our lives for Thee, let us be Thy faithful servants and soldiers, and endure the shame that cometh upon us, the estrangement of friends, the censure of brethren, the loss of all earthly things, rather than deny Thee or betray Thee. Life is Thy gift; all we have and are cometh from Thee; let us with joy and gratitude glorify Thee even in the fires, and offer up to Thee our souls and bodies to serve Thee as living sacrifices, holy and acceptable unto God.

"And oh! Lord, let us not be cast down, neither destroyed. If Thou art with us can any be against us? Remember this Thy temple, where our fathers worshipped Thee before we were; build it up, O Lord! Let Thy truth keep its walls, and Thy salvation be its bulwarks. Restore unto it the joy of them that shout in harvest, and be the gathering in of souls here, like unto the crowding of doves that fly to their windows. For if Thou dwellest here, who shall turn the head to mock as they pass by? or say 'Aha! how is Jerusalem fallen!' Come down from Thy dwelling-place unto our altar, and touch it with fire from heaven; then shall all men know that the sceptre hath not departed from Zion, but that the Lord is there.

"And oh, dear Father! if there be those who seem to be our enemies, who thrust out their tongues against us and turn their faces from us, do Thou shine into their hearts with all the splendor and sweetness of Thy great love to man. With the flame of Thy divine goodness melt their souls, and separate the pure gold within them from the dross of mortal passion and prejudice, that they may shine with Thy light, and be Thy treasured vessels. Be Thou with them and bless them in their going out and their coming in; bless their basket and their store; give them peace on earth, and goodwill toward man. And finally, minister unto them an abundant entrance into the kingdom of heaven. And Thine shall be the glory forever: Amen."

There was something in this fervent, tender prayer, so different from the usual formal petitions presented to God, as one might lay an engrossed plea, drawn up by a lawyer, before an earthly monarch, that the congregation were taken by surprise.

Parson Hall had not prayed for his enemies as if they were men of evil disposition and causeless anger, but merely as if they were mistaken brethren, to be pitied and loved for that reason. It is the way of the world unto this day to be merciless to mistakes. The closest ties of kindred are rent apart because one or another does that which in itself is no moral evil or apparent wrong, but merely unadvisable in the eyes of self-elected judges. Alienations that make life a long regret, and add an enduring sting to death, assail us, for the shadowy reason that we have mistaken our proper path in life, in the estimation of those who should have shielded, supported, even loved us more, because we needed such charity more than ever.

But this was not Philemon Hall's charity. He was too like his Master not to love the sheep that went astray upon the dark mountains better than the ninety and nine who needed less his affection and his care.

Therefore that prayer seemed to his audience something almost above their comprehension,—a matter of wonder and awe. In the language of the record, "They judged that such a prayer had never been made in that house. They all tarried to hear what he would preach."

Tears rolled down many a sober visage as that prayer ended. Esther's face glowed with love and pride. Never before had she known the depths of Philemon Hall's heart; even now she knew not — nor did he — how his satisfied human heart had given fervor and strength to his spiritual affections. Never could he have uttered that outpouring of brotherly love with such ardent honesty, if he had not inwardly felt the blissful consciousness that his wife at last loved him. We are so "bound up in bundles," so interwoven of body, soul, and spirit, that when one string of the harp is sounded, the others vibrate in unison, and it is our dim consciousness of this that makes us rejoice in the prospect of a new body as well as a redeemed soul when the "day of the Lord" shall arise.

Then, after singing a psalm of the Sternhold and Hopkins version, a general stir and hush pervaded the congregation, as they settled themselves to hear the sermon. No one thought of leaving the church. Parson Dyer, who was there, in the front pew, took a sonorous pinch of snuff, to last him through the discourse, and many another elderly man followed his example, and each folded his red and yellow handkerchief and laid it over his crossed knees, to be ready for an emergency. The old women rubbed their spectacles, and tucked them away carefully in the hymnbooks. Mothers of young families distributed fragrant bunches of dried "meetin' seed" among their flocks, and settled the little ones further on to the high seats, lest they should fall asleep and meet the fate of Eutychus, wearied with their dangling feet, idle hands, and the "blessed hum" of the preacher. But all was quiet as Philemon Hall arose in his tall pulpit, and, opening the Bible before him, gave out as his text, "For necessity is laid upon me; yea, woe is unto me, if I preach not the gospel."

The sermon, like most of that day, was long; but it did not seem tedious to his hearers. It had no reference to his personal trials nor to his future intentions; he only dwelt upon the importance of the Christian ministry to the salvation of the world, and the stringent obligation that was laid upon every man who made that ministry his profession to preach wherever and whenever the Lord gave him opportunity and strength, to the end that no living human soul should be lost through ignorance of the way of salvation.

He spoke of the ministry as a work almost too awful and responsible for man to undertake; one that no man could carry on without the instant and continual help of God; of the need that the preacher should live so uprightly as to illustrate the Gospel he made known to man, in his own life, as far as humanity could portray the lineaments of the Master; and then in the most earnest and fervent manner he described the joy of the holy calling; the sweetness of making God's love and mercy and fatherhood known to those who were ignorant of him; the peace that came to the preacher's own heart in offering hope to the desperate, and consolation to the afflicted; in casting the glow of heavenly day down into the earthly darkness of the grave; and most did he enlarge on the rapture of the shepherd, who persuades wandering flocks to enter the fold and be at home, and safe for time and eternity.

All these considerations, he said, made it the more imperative a necessity that a man entering the ministry should be utterly faithful to his vows in so doing; if he neglected or degraded his office in the eyes of God or man, there awaited him only the woes denounced on the unfaithful servant, who should be cast into outer darkness where there was wailing and weeping and gnashing of teeth.

This is but a skeleton of the discourse which, clothed upon with the earnest purpose, the deep feeling, the steadfast faith, and eloquent words of Parson Hall, entranced and electrified his people. As one man, they felt an inward conviction that no human authority could depose from the ministry of God, a man so fitted by grace and experience for that holy calling.

After the last hymn and the benediction, a crowd waited at the door to shake hands with the parson.

In the rigid Sabbatarianism of New England they held it no day to have any conversation on secular matters; but the most punctilious among them could see no harm in a friendly hand-clasp, or a look that warmed Mr. Hall's heart like a gleam of sunshine.

Parson Dyer walked home with Mr. Hall and Esther, but he said nothing till he was alone in the study with his friend, waiting for Esther to prepare their simple "nooning." Then he turned to Philemon Hall.

"My brother!" he said, with a deeply moved voice and expression, "I rejoice with you to-day. Verily the Lord is with thee, and I take shame to myself that ever I exhorted you to follow the wisdom of this world and deny Him who was in you, both to will and to do. Brother, I ask your forgiveness with the Lord's. I touched the Ark, and it is of His mercies that I am not consumed!"

Philemon Hall grasped his friend's hand with a clasp of warm strength.

"Brother Dyer," he answered, "I have naught to forgive; you spake unto me as a friend, and after the light that was granted to you then; I rejoice and am glad that you are come to see that I was not willingly obstinate, or opionated, but only desirous with all my heart to do the will of the Lord. I do not say it hath been easy or pleasant alway to follow that will; but He helped me, having set my hand to the plough, not to look back. Yea, though a host should rise against me, in this one thing to be confident, that I was about my Lord's business, and the issues of life were with Him."

"I fear there are yet trials before you, brother Hall," answered Mr. Dyer; "but you know in whom you have believed, and there can no worse thing happen to you in church matters, than hath already befallen. Therefore, in His name I say unto thee, 'Go forward!' 'The Lord bless thee and keep thee! The Lord make his face to shine upon thee, and be gracious unto thee! The Lord lift up his countenance upon thee, and give thee peace.'"

And Esther, who had half-opened the door, whispered to herself, "Amen."

CHAPTER XL.

LIFE.

> How fresh, O Lord, how sweet and clean
> Are thy returns! e'en as the flowers in Spring,
> To which, beside their own demean
> The late past frosts tributes of pleasure bring.
> Grief melts away,
> Like snow in May,
> As if there were no such cold thing.

"Our life," says a modern philosopher, "is like March weather, savage and serene in one hour."

So it certainly seemed to Philemon Hall; the services of that Sunday when in meek defiance of the Consociation he preached in his own church, suddenly re-instated him, as it appeared, in the former love and respect of his people. Parson Dyer came down again from Hillside farm on the Monday, early in the morning, his creaky wagon loaded with offerings from Delia and Hiram.. A great basket of eggs, a wooden pail of June butter; a little roasting pig, "a weakling and a flower," embedded in young beet greens; and a bag of meal from Hiram's own corn, ground but Saturday at the Mountain Mill.

"I bring you some creature comforts, Madam Hall," said Parson Dyer, with an odd smile, as he unloaded his vehicle at the door. "My friend and housemates would have it, in their simple souls, that you and Brother Hall were like to starve for earthly food since the Consociation have debarred him from the table of the Lord. It was vain for me to remonstrate; their kind hearts must have outlet; and I trust you will take as kindly as they send."

"Indeed I will, Mr. Dyer," said Esther with a charming smile. "'Tis long since we had but treacle to our bread; butter will be indeed a lordly dish for us; and I have killed my fowls for our sustenance as need arose, though it was their laying time, so that eggs are also a rarity; and my meal bin is well-nigh bare at bottom!"

"Say you so! Why, I do not take it friendly that you did not come to me, my friend! Had I not abundance, that you should want?"

"Nay, sir; we had enough for our need, we did not go hungry; the word that 'thy bread shall be given thee and thy water shall be sure' was fulfilled unto us, day by day; we were not afraid."

Parson Dyer looked at the calm beauty of Esther's face, as she spoke, and thought a man might well be gifted with endurance when such a comforter stood by his side. It is true indeed that we "walk as strangers"; never would he or any other know the bitter and secret grief of Philemon Hall's wedded life up to the hour when his open and public troubles culminated.

"Is Brother Hall at home?" asked the parson.

"No; he hath gone to a dying woman out beyond Dog's Misery quite a way. I think he will be back to dinner, but I know not; for there is to be a meeting of the church this afternoon for business matters, and he said he would rather be away than here; he wishes not to make nor meddle more with the church affairs; he thinks it best to leave all to them."

"He is a wise man, madam, but since I also belong in the parish I will even ask a bit of dinner from you and remain."

Esther was heartily glad to entertain her old friend, and in talking of past days the hours flew by, till she was surprised to see how near noon-mark it was, and left him to prepare her frugal dinner.

Soon after the meal was over, the clank of the little bell called the church and congregation to the lecture room which was in the basement.

The meeting was well attended by the men of the parish; in those days it was not thought seemly or decent that women should have their say on such occasions; their talking was done by their own firesides, their influence exerted in their own homes; perhaps both were as weighty and powerful as if they had appeared on platforms or in pulpits, or poured out incoherent and meandering prayers in the church or the conference room. Certain it is that the men of those days held Scripture in reverence, and suffered not a woman to teach or to preach in the churches.

It was well done that this meeting had been called while the enthusiasm aroused by Parson Hall's prayer and sermon was yet fresh and active in the minds of his hearers, and there had been no time for the timid and the cautious to consider the *pros* and *cons,* or be moved by an afterthought of the constituted authorities, and what should or would befall the luckless wight who defied them. Everybody there was full of zeal and admiration for Mr. Hall; little was said, but much done; it was resolved and unanimously carried, that his arrears of salary should be promptly paid; that his salary itself should be increased, and that they would stand by him resolutely if he would go on and preach to them as before, and administer the sacraments. "For it doth not appear to this meeting," rang out the sonorous voice of Parson Dyer, "that our minister, Mr. Hall, hath merited the action of the Consociation in any manner. Had he been an open and headlong sinner, breaking the laws of God and man without stint or repentance, he could not have been more than deposed and excommunicated as he hath been merely for preaching the Gospel to a few harmless schismatics. Therefore, brethren, let our scribe draw out two copies of these our resolutions and send one of them to Mr. Hall and another unto the Consociation of this County at its next annual meeting."

No doubt the Consociation received the document as a bundle of bitter herbs, but they made no sign.

Parson Hall went on his way as though their thunder had never been sounded in his ears, or their bolts levelled at his head, in vain endeavor to lay it in the dust. What had he now to ask for? His people were united, and his home blessed with all that makes a home happy.

It could not be that in this reversed condition of affairs, Ammi Hopkins and Tempy would refrain from testifying their emotions; this time they found Mr. Hall and Esther together. Tempy, bristling and blooming with delight entered, however, before the deacon, who had his horse to tie, his reins to fasten, and a measure of oats to pour into the nosebag which he had provided to keep his restive young colt quiet.

"I did tell Ammi 'twas kind of forrard to come down, right off, and wish ye joy," she began. "But he's as oneasy as a fly on a winder-pane, when he can't get his spoon into other folkses messes and help to stir 'em. I mean to take an int'rest in my feller-critters; some on 'em, that is; but I don't want to poke my nose through the crack of a door before 'tis opened. However, I don't b'lieve you will begrutch seein' of me, Easter, for you know past doubtin', that I've always set by you a sight; and a gladder cretur than I was when I heered about that meetin' never was. I hope them folks to Consociation will hev to eat an amazin' big cut of humble-pie now, and see how they like it."

"Sister Hopkins, it is not seemly to revile dignities," put in Mr. Hall, with a smile that meant more than his words.

"I know *that*, Parson Hall, but I don't call 'em dignities, them folks. Why they haven't got dignity enough amongst 'em to salt a hummin' bird's egg! Ef they don't want to be reviled they've got to mend their manners, and not make folks that's as fur above 'em as a bean-pole's above cowcumber vines their music."

"Dear Tempy! let them go," said Esther, putting her arm about Tempy's shoulders. "They cannot trouble Mr. Hall further; nor me, so long as they leave him in peace. It is good to have friends, you dear woman; and it is good to forget your enemies."

"Can't always be did, though; not as long as natur' is natur'," obstinately retorted Tempy.

"Then we must fall back on grace," said the parson.

"Grace 'tis a charmin' sound!" squeaked Ammi, who had heard only the last word as he opened the door. "Yes, yes, we need grace, lots on't; or we sha'n't never get to glory! I come over, Parson Hall, to sort o' hold out th' olive-branch so to speak, to ye. I dono as you call to mind that you was some flustered last time I see ye. I s'pose 'tis ag'inst natur' to enjoy counsel that goes contrairy to our own idees. Well, faithful is the wownds of a friend, parson. I felt to tell ye my honest mind about what you done, accordin' as brethring should do one to another."

"I wonder how you'd swaller it, Ammi Hopkins, if some brethring of your'n should up an' tell you their 'pinions about ye!" interrupted Tempy, with a snap.

"Mis' Hopkins, I b'lieve I'm a talkin' now; women had ought to keep silent and learn, the 'Postle Poll ses."

"Depends some on who's talkin'" muttered Tempy. The deacon looked at her with an irate and matrimonial eye, but he went on.

"Well, parson, I'm glad to see ye kep' up your grit; and I'm proper glad to see your folks has come round to ye, and paid up your sellery; the laborer's worthy of his hire."

"When you hain't got to pay it," put in the irrepressible Tempy.

"And I come down from Pickerin' Centre to offer ye the right hand o' fellership and say I should be pleased to see you in our pulpit—that is, if the Conso-shashun lets up on ye, as I expect it will. You've stuck to your text like a good feller. Mabbe you rek'lect I said amen to ye after all, last time."

The parson laughed.

"Shake hands now, Deacon Hopkins. I do remember that you bestowed on me that crumb of comfort when I was in sore need."

"You come 'long now, Ammi; 'tis as good to let folks alone a spell as 'tis to cackle to 'em. You've done enough crowin' for to-day. Easter, you blessed cretur', good-by; the same to you, parson. Come, Ammi!"

The deacon glared at his peremptory wife, but followed her with repressed wrath.

Esther turned to her husband.

"Philemon, you surely have the grace of patience unto perfection."

"I learned it waiting for my wife," he answered, with a glint of mischief in his tender smile.

There was no more trouble now lying in wait for Esther and her saint. It would have been more accordant with poetic justice had Philip Kent been seized with remorse and restored to Esther the property that Uncle Dyer intended she should inherit, but he did not seem to imagine such a course possible; indeed he grew, like all dissipated men, so reckless of his money that but for his wife's inheritance, which was carefully secured to her, he would have fallen into poverty in his latter years. Esther he saw no more; neither of them wished it; she was happy beyond her dreams in her husband's love; and the comparative poverty of a country parson's wife she had long been used to; riches she never sighed for; being content and dwelling among her own like the Shunamite matron of old.

Mr. Hall went on his way steadily and serenely; in a few years all the opposition to his course died of its own futility, and he was formally invited to attend the Consociations again. Like a candid and humble Christian he took his place once more among his brethren, gratefully and thankfully; but as long as he lived, his church showed their still-smouldering resentment by never sending a delegate with him to any of these meetings.

But long before this desirable end of contention came to pass, another and almost as great a blessing entered the quaint old parsonage of Trumbull. The year following after his excommunication, and the general uprising of his people to support and re-instate him, one soft June evening just as the sun threw its last rays into the keeping-room, Parson Hall stood beside an old-fashioned wooden cradle with a deep light in his eyes and a wonderful smile on his worn countenance, as he looked down at the fair child that lay there sleeping with the calm and regal innocence of infancy, a white drop of milk yet resting on his puckered pink mouth, and his dimpled hands clenched as if he would still hold fast to his mother's breast, though sleep prevented; the parson looked across to his wife, pale but serene in her lovely motherhood, as she sat with one hand on the cradle and her eyes, too, fixed on her child.

"Esther," he said; "it is well-nigh time the child was presented for baptism; what shall be his name?"

"There can be but one Philemon Hall for me, my husband; yet I would have him called after his father. Let his name be Steadfast."

ROSE TERRY COOKE'S WORKS.

SOMEBODY'S NEIGHBORS.

The titles of the stories are as follows:

Eben Jackson.
Miss Lucinda.
Dely's Cow.
Squire Paine's Conversion.
Miss Beulah's Bonnet.
Cal. Culver and the Devil.
Mrs. Flint's Married Experience.
Amandar.
Polly Mariner, Tailoress.
Uncle Josh.
Poll Jennings's Heir.
Freedom Wheeler's Controversy with Providence.

"A bouquet of native New-England flowers — and the flowers have a peculiar beauty and fragrance, too."—*Hartford Courant.*

"The dialect is most deliciously correct — a collection of thoroughly delightful tales — an acuteness and comprehension which is simply inimitable."—*Boston Courier.*

"More than 400 pages, covering twelve charming idyllic stories of New-England life and manners, showing that profound insight into Puritan character, and that remarkable command of Yankee dialect, in which Mrs. Cooke has but one equal, and no superior. These exquisite chronicles of the hill-country are full of high local color, pathos and piquancy, and their perusal is attended with alternate tears and smiles. Their narration is vigorous and spirited, sparkling in all points, and outlined with rare dramatic skill.

"Certainly no ordinary novel illustrates a greater variety of types, or illustrates them better, than this single group of short stories — less than half the number in the book — and in no recent novel of New-England life are individuals more graphically portrayed. . . . Truly a work of rare literary excellence. It offers even to novel readers a larger return of interest than most novels do."—*New York Evening Post.*

Sold by all booksellers; sent, postpaid, on receipt of price, $1.50, by the publishers,

TICKNOR & CO., BOSTON.

ROSE TERRY COOKE'S WORKS.

THE SPHINX'S CHILDREN
AND OTHER PEOPLES'.

1 vol., 12mo . . . . $1.50.

The titles of the stories are as follows:

The Sphinx's Children.	Too Late.
The Deacon's Week.	My Thanksgiving.
A Black Silk.	How She Found Out.
Jericho Jim.	Ann Potter's Lesson.
Lost on a Railway.	Aceldama Sparks.
Doctor Parker's Patty.	Salathiel Bump's Stocking.
Doom and Dan.	Sally Parsons's Duty.
Some Account of Thomas Tucker.	A Hard Lesson.
	Liab's First Christmas.
The Forger's Bride.	

"The short stories in this volume are of the very essence of New England. A somewhat fanciful revery lends its peculiar title to the book; but the 'Other Peoples'' offspring are the individual product of the soil, full of the grit, the doggedness, and the grim humor that came over with our grandparents' furniture in the Mayflower. These stories are the fruit and blossom of all that is noblest and best in the qualities of the Puritan, and it may be that their appreciation — though not their beauty or their power — will be restricted by reason of what is distinctive and individual about them. Surely no short story of recent years has surpassed 'The Deacon's Week' in pathos, in artistic truth, in the inspiration of a sublime and noble purpose. It would seem that no one could rise from its perusal without an impulse toward kindness and charity and a sense of benefit received. Without a word of moralizing or tawdry reflection, it gives the same lesson that is practised out by true and manly conduct and unselfishness. And all the time the perfection of the picture as a work of art, as a truthful portrait set out with exquisite literary finish, captures the mind and entrances the imagination."—GEORGE CARY EGGLESTON, in the New-York *Commercial Advertiser.*

For sale by booksellers, or will be sent, postpaid, on receipt of price, by the publishers,

TICKNOR & CO., BOSTON.

www.ingramcontent.com/pod-product-compliance
Lightning Source LLC
Chambersburg PA
CBHW030549300426
44111CB00009B/909